# MEDICALIZED

# MASCULINITIES

# MEDICALIZED MASCULINITIES

EDITED BY
## Dana Rosenfeld and Christopher A. Faircloth

 Temple University Press

**PHILADELPHIA**

**Temple University Press**
1601 North Broad Street
Philadelphia PA 19122
*www.temple.edu/tempress*

∞ The paper used in this publication meets the requirements of
the American National Standard for Information Sciences—Permanence of Paper
for Printed Library Materials, ANSI Z39.48-1992

Library of Congress Cataloging-in-Publication Data

Medicalized masculinities / edited by Dana Rosenfeld and Christopher A. Faircloth.
p. cm.
Includes bibliographical references and index.
ISBN 1-59213-097-6 (cloth : alk. paper) — ISBN 1-59213-098-4
1. Men—Health and hygiene—Social aspects.   2. Masculinity—Social aspects.
3. Body, Human—Social aspects.   4. Social medicine.   5. Men's studies.
I. Rosenfeld, Dana, 1958–   II. Faircloth, Christopher A., 1966–

RA564.83.M43 2006
613'.04234–dc22

2005050664

2 4 6 8 9 7 5 3 1

# Contents

# Acknowledgments

The editors would like to thank the contributors to this volume for agreeing to participate in this project and for their patience, enthusiasm and insights. They also thank Micah Kleit, their editor at Temple University Press, for his encouragement and his editorial and practical assistance, Kim Hoag of Bytheway Publishing Services for her impeccable production services, and anonymous reviewers of the manuscript for their suggestions. Thanks are also due to the American Sociological Association, whose support for the editors' special session, "Medicalized Masculinities: History and Culture," which took place at the 2004 American Sociological Association Annual Meeting in San Francisco, provided valuable feedback from other sociologists to the editors and individual authors alike. Dana Rosenfeld is grateful for the partial funding she received from Colorado College and from a Louis M. Benezet Summer Research Grant to research and write the introductory chapter to this volume. Christopher Faircloth thanks the Rehabilitation Outcomes Research Center at the North Florida/South Georgia Veterans Health System for its ongoing support and the Veterans Affairs Rehabilitation Research and Development Disability Supplement that made this project possible.

# Introduction

## Medicalized Masculinities: The Missing Link?

Dana Rosenfeld and
Christopher A. Faircloth

A funny thing happened on the way to theorizing medicalization: men's bodies were ignored. This seems a startling statement, given the sheer number of articles and books written on the medicalization of—well, everything, it would appear. But with the exception of a few scattered but important pieces (see Ehrenreich 1983; Tiefer 1994; Potts 2000; Riska 2002, 2004; Mumford 1997), most of which are very recent, medicalization research has focused on genderless or female bodies. In medicalization research, as in most social-scientific research, gender seems to mean womanhood.

This is not to say that the male body is absent in social scientific research. It is clearly present in work on the body and in masculinity studies, both relatively recent strains of research, but neither of which considers male bodies as having been medicalized. It is also present in work on men and health, which often actively applies medical reasoning to male health, pathologizing masculinity as a health risk rather than commenting on its medicalization. Are we to assume that, of all the things that have been medicalized (from sexuality to reproduction to emotions to deviance to the family and caregiving to aging to race to femininity), masculinity has somehow managed to elude medical definition and regulation? And if it hasn't, how do we account for this gap in

2 Dana Rosenfeld and Christopher A. Faircloth

the literature? The substantive chapters in this volume will address the first question; the second we try to answer here. In this chapter, we trace the history of work on medicalization (which failed to consider masculinity as an object of medical definition and regulation) on the one hand and of several other substantive social-scientific traditions (which considered masculinity but not its medicalization) on the other to consider why they functioned in practical isolation from each other. This will be a somewhat tricky business—it is, of course, far easier to explain why something did happen than it is to explain why it did not. But we suggest several causal factors here. First, the answer lies in habits established during the 1970s and 1980s, when (a) feminist work on the medicalization of femininity was taken to represent a one-to-one correlation between the two as regards gender, (b) the heavy focus on the medical control of underrepresented groups effectively excluded men from the picture, and (c) the masculinities literature's pathologizing of masculinity as a health risk limited its ability to recognize that medicine might be pathologizing men. Second, over the last twenty years, the sociology of the body's Foucauldian emphasis on the surveillance and discipline of bodies failed to intersect with an emergent focus on the embodiment of everyday life.

## Medicalization: A Brief History

Medicalization emerged as both a concept and a theoretical tradition in the 1970s. The power of medicine to define and regulate social action was introduced by Talcott Parsons, who, in 1951, wrote about medicine's role in controlling deviance and, in the process (in true functionalist fashion), reproducing and strengthening the social order by holding the sick accountable to dominant social norms of productivity—a function that was beneficial to all. In 1970, Elliot Freidson provided an alternative to the functionalist view of medicine as a beneficent and politically neutral institution by depicting it as composed of actors devoted to monopolizing the production of health knowledge to achieve professional autonomy.

The medicalization thesis introduced by Irving Zola in 1972 accepted this vision of medicine as an agency of social control motivated by a quest for professional power, but deepened extant understandings of medicine's power by establishing that this was beginning to expand beyond its original goals by defining and controlling an increasingly wide array of human troubles—in short, by expanding its practices and authority into areas of life previously outside its purview. Medical agents did this by redefining social problems as medical ones and claiming that their own expertise was the most appropriate one to cure them. While Freidson situated medicine's growing power in its own professional agenda, Zola pointed to the increasingly technical and bureaucratic nature of Western society as the engine behind the "medicalization of society"—the exponential labeling of aspects of everyday life as medical in nature by medical agents. According to Zola, processes external to medicine potentiated its galloping control over everyday life—while medicine certainly benefited from medicalization, its desire for power would not have resulted in medicalization had not the larger social context's desire for technical solutions to social troubles accommodated medicine's tactics and tendencies.

Thus, areas that had previously been seen as social problems, usually centered in or involving human bodies (i.e., homosexuality and alcoholism), and exclusively handled by the church and the state, were now seen as medical ones. Following on the heels of sociological critiques of psychiatry and working within a social constructionist perspective, Zola (1972) and Freidson (1970) depicted medicine as an agency of social control whose authority was partially due to its expanding power to define and regulate deviant behavior. Viewed within this frame, diagnoses (and diagnostic categories) are not neutral "discoveries" so much as highly subjective interpretations, and a number of studies published in the 1970s and 1980s (see, e.g., Schneider 1978; Conrad 1975; Conrad and Schneider 1980) traced the shift in interpretation of deviant behavior from moral to medical deficit, or "badness to sickness" (nested in the secularization and rationalization of Western society—see Turner 1984; Conrad and Schneider 1980. For more current work in this vein, see Rimke and Hunt 2002.) Indeed, that medicalization is primarily a matter of defining already-problematic behaviors in medical terms is central to this tradition: according to Peter Conrad (2000, 322), medicalization "consists of defining a problem in medical terms, using medical language to describe a problem, adopting a medical framework to understand a problem, or using a medical intervention to 'treat' it. Medicalization occurs when a medical frame or definition has been applied in an attempt to understand or manage a problem." As we'll see, this has led to an antagonistic relationship between medicalization scholars and Foucauldian ones.

These early (and subsequent) studies uncovered the explicitly political nature of medicalization—and, by extension, of science itself (see Knorr-Cetina and Mulkay 1983; Lynch 1997; Latour 1999 and 2000; Clarke and Fujimura 1992). Medicine is not above politics but deeply embedded in them, as can be seen in its control and regulation of politically disenfranchised populations such as women, children, the poor, sexual nonconformists, members of racial minorities, and the aged. Through the medicalization of abortion,[1] reproduction (see below), menstruation (see Pugliesi 1992), childbirth,[2] childhood (see Halpern 1990; Pawluch 1983, 2003) and childhood behavior such as attention deficit disorder and juvenile delinquency,[3] welfare seeking (Schram 2000; Blackwell 1999), homosexuality,[4] race[5] and racism (Wellman 2000), aging[6] and the life course (Rosenfeld and Gallagher 2002), medicine not only expands its own powers, but limits the political power of already subject populations while claiming to protect them.

Thus, as an institution with increasing power to define deviance in medical terms (see Melick, Steadman, and Cocozza 1979; Robbins and Anthony 1982; Rosencrance 1985; Morrow 1982), medicine's self-styled and popular status as a scientifically neutral, even beneficent, institution was challenged by those who saw it as engaging in the social construction of medical "conditions" and "problems"—and, of course, in the production of medically suspect populations, albeit ones that participated, often eagerly, in their own medicalized identities (see, e.g., Schneider 1978; Markens 1996). The expanding market of services and treatments made medicine a profitable industry and bolstered its new status as a source of social control, as medicine was depicted as strengthening both the mechanism and the ideology of capitalism (see Waitzkin 1991). Moreover, medicalization was depicted as inherently political in that it helped to regulate populations, defined acceptable behavior, and individualized and decontextualized political issues.

While rooted in a concern with the medicalization of deviance, this body of work also examined the medicalization of areas of life that had not originally been seen as deviant, primarily life processes. The shift in focus from the medicalization of deviance to the medicalization of everyday life produced an explosion of studies on the medical definition and control of female reproduction (see Leavitt 1989; Becker and Nachtigall 1992; Sievert 2003; Barker 1998), death (see Kozak 1994), menopause (see Bell 1987 and 1990; Lock 1988; Worcester and Whatley 1992; Friedan 1993; Oudshoorn 1994; McCrae 1983), the family (see Donzelot 1979; Finkler 2000, 2001; Finkler, Skrzynia, and Evans 2003; Wolf 2002) and caregiving (see Lock 1984; Chappell 1999; Abel 2000; Binney, Estes, and Ingman 1990), and emotions (see Lock 1987; Pugliesi 1992)—and indeed, it was evident that these studies were not merely the product of an analytical shift, but the product of a growing recognition that medicalization was proceeding, apparently unchecked, to gain control over everyday lives, including healthy ones. These did not represent a shift from the state as an agency of social control to medicine as its central agent; rather, they signaled a more complex shift toward a risk and surveillance society.

## Biomedicalization and the Risk Society

According to Adele Clarke and colleagues (2003, 1), medicalization (again, the control by medicine over the definition and regulation of social problems) transformed into the more micropolitical biomedicalization: the definition and regulation of bodily processes themselves, mainly through "such technoscientific innovations as molecular biology, biotechnologies, genomization, transplant medicine, and new medical technologies." The seeds of biomedicalization were sown in the 1970s, when aspects of life that had not been seen as social problems (e.g., PTSD, PMS, and physical stigmas) began to be framed in medical terms. In 1985 this process accelerated, riding the shift from modernity (which focused on controlling external nature) to postmodernity (which focused on transforming the internal nature of humans and other creatures through, for example, the genome project). Computer and information technologies are central to this process, which occurred through the emergence of what the authors call "the Biomedical TechnoService Complex, Inc."—a fast-growing biomedical sector that is at once socio-political, cultural, and increasingly technological.

Biomedicalization is more widely dispersed throughout society than is medicalization, expressing its power through technological innovations and the production of "risk groups" that are both self-governing and governed by medical agents and agencies. These "technologies of the self" (Foucault 1988) take up an increasing amount of time and energy in actors' everyday lives and help to shape new identities and experiences.

Key to biomedicalization is the commodification of health itself. As Robert Crawford noted in 1985, social actors are becoming morally obligated to be healthy, just as Parsons's social actors are obliged to strive to overcome sickness. Health thus becomes a project rather than a taken-for-granted state; people are exhorted to adopt healthy "lifestyles" and to be open to health "promotion" messages. These messages and directives inhere in innumerable sites outside of the traditional clinical setting—indeed, they have become part of our culture and are embedded in key institutions such as school and the workplace.[7] Depicting health as constantly endangered by a myriad of decisions and contexts renders all actors medically problematic. Because "they create standard models against which objects and actions are judged," risk technologies are normalizing and give rise to distinctive types of surveillance. These use the results of risk assessments "that take epidemiological risk statistics, ostensibly meaningful only at the population level, and transform them into risk factors that are deemed meaningful at the individual level" (Clarke et al. 2003, 8–9). That social actors embrace this discourse themselves makes health both more biomedicalized (by virtue of self-surveillance techniques applied at home) and less medicalized (by virtue of the social actor's increasing responsibility for her own health and a lessening of the power the doctor holds over it).

Thus, biomedicalization expands the range of medicine in everyday life from merely controlling bodies to actually changing them to conform to new health standards and identities (see Haraway 1991 on cyborgian bodies). Through preventive health messages that entail "lifestyle" changes, biomedicalization produces new identities, anxieties, and mundane practices. This clearly resonates with the recent risk society thesis that was itself inspired by the Foucauldian tradition.

According to Lupton (1999), the theoretical perspectives on risk that have emerged since the 1980s (the cultural anthropological approach, the work of Ulrich Beck and Anthony Giddens, and Foucauldian work on governmentality that explores how governmental structures "manage and regulate populations via risk discourses and strategies"—Lupton 1999: 1) all see risk as those working in the area of the social construction of social problems view social problems: as the product of claims makers rather than as objective phenomena and as serving social and political purposes. Clearly, then, research on risk shares much with research on medicalization. Of these three strains of research, however, the Foucaldian governmentality perspective is the most mindful of the social construction of risk, focusing not on the "nature of risk itself, but rather the forms of knowledge, the dominant discourses and expert techniques and institutions that serve to render risk calculable and knowable, bringing it into being" (Lupton 1999, 6).

Foucault held that over the past four centuries, "the modern system of liberal government, with its emphasis on rule and the maintenance of order through voluntary self-discipline rather than via coercive or violent means" (Lupton 1999, 4) fashioned an increasingly wide array of interlocking bodies of expertise and a plethora of institutions and mechanisms for their production, distribution, and use. To those working within the Foucauldian tradition, risk is just one of a number of disciplinary techniques that the government uses to survey and control populations. Epidemiological knowledge is used to construct a standard of health and health practices, against which individuals are judged, and those who deviate from this norm are categorized as at risk of any number of health dangers. "To be designated as 'at risk,' therefore, is to be positioned within a network of factors drawn from the observation of others" (Lupton 1999, 4–5).

Despite the resonance of the risk society approach with work on medicalization and social control, however, tensions exist between the two. As Lupton (1997, 94) states,

> the writings of Foucault and his followers, while not necessarily using the term 'medicalisation' or adhering to the versions of power relations usually presented by proponents of the orthodox medicalisation critique, tend to present a consonant vision of a world in which individuals' lives are profoundly experienced and understood through the discourses and practices of medicine and the allied professions.

Lupton writes that supporters of the medicalization thesis (those who adopt a feminist, Marxist, or consumerist approach to medicine) see medicalization in wholly negative terms and thus as something that should be resisted or escaped. To these supporters, medicalization "deflect[s] questions of social inequality into the realm of illness and disease, there to be treated inappropriately by drugs and other medical therapies" (1997, 96). This is particularly damaging to powerless groups, who are both more medicated than the powerful and the most likely to suffer the effects of inequality in the first place. The solution, say these scholars, is, again, escape or resistance through "demedicalization." According to Foucauldians, however, this is both oversimplistic and naive: the first because it elides the potentially beneficial aspects of medicalization, and the second because it assumes that medical power can be undermined through a process of redefinition alone.

The key difference between these two approaches centers on their different definitions of power itself. To Foucault, medical (and all other forms of) power exists not only in local sites and in the definition and control of a particular trouble (these are expressions of power) but in overarching disciplinary discourses and practices. Because power informs all social relations, it cannot be considered the possession of particular power groups, nor can power be transferred from one group to another. Medical agents are actors in a web of power relations and of discourses that exist independent of their situated deployment. For proponents of the medicalization thesis, however, power *is* the possession of powerful groups (here, medical agents) who actively and motivatedly work to secure power over populations (here, patients). In Conrad's (1992, 216) words,

> the social control that medicine gains through expanding its domain comes from its power to define that domain by defining human behavior and characteristics as medical in nature. Implemented by medical agents and strengthened by medical technology, it is nonetheless the definitional power that medicine holds that legitimates its control and

that allows for medical agents to apply medical technologies in the first place.

For Foucauldian scholars, however, thinking of medical power as located in the hands of particular agents and agencies rather than in "a series of loosely linked assemblages, each with different rationalities" (Lupton 1997, 100) is misguided. Moreover, medicine is not omnipotent, clashing as it does with state and other agencies. This, then, is the third Foucauldian critique: medicalization scholars oversimplify the terrain in which the medical gaze works and assume that medicine's political and financial ambitions drive its expanding powers.

## Gender and Medicalization

Riska (2003) identifies three phases that the medicalization thesis underwent in its consideration of gender. (The third, which she calls a "return to reductionism," is essentially a new wave in the medicalization of masculinity). The first, fashioned by Zola and Freidson, disregarded gender entirely, although research on the medicalization of deviance tended to concentrate on troubles that were assumed to exclusively affect males (e.g., hyperactivity and alcoholism). The second wave began in the mid-1970s, when feminists identified modern medicine's control of women as part of its central logic, pointing to the replacement of traditional women healers by male doctors in the nineteenth century and portraying women as the victims of medicine (see Ehrenreich and English 1973, 1974). Scientific medicine was depicted as an imposition of "abstract male knowledge" on women's previously reflexive awareness of the workings of their own bodies:

> There was a common assumption shared by various branches of the women's movement that women's health had been medicalized in the past, and that gender-biased medical knowledge and diagnoses and treatments decided by biased male physicians had resulted in the over treatment of women documented in high surgery rates for hysterectomies and mastectomies, and overuse of drugs, especially psychotropics. (Riska 2003: 66–67)

Feminists called for a reevaluation of women's bodies as healthy rather than as unhealthy when compared to the dominant male standard of health and for the demystification of women's bodies to be achieved by women learning about their own bodies.[8]

Thus, although the concept of medicalization was not inherently linked to gender, this era—and strain of research—inspired a deluge of pieces on, *inter alia*, the medicalization of the life course and all aspects of women's reproductive lives (cited above). In concert with the burgeoning feminist writing on women's bodies and their regulation (see Boston Women's Health Collective 1973), women's bodies took center stage in much medicalization research. Indeed, many scholars asserted that women are more vulnerable to medicalization than are men. Reissman (2003 [1983] 58), for example, cited the greater external visibility of women's bodily processes in relation to men's (i.e., pregnancy, menstruation, and birth), the fact that women's social roles (i.e., as caregivers) bring them in more contact with medical agents than do men's, women's tendency to devote more time and energy to self-care than do men, and "women's structural subordination to men" as reasons for women's status as "especially appropriate markets for the expansion of medicine." While occupational medicine and stress management programs have tended to examine men's bodies rather than women's, and while "medicine has focused on childhood hyperactivity and the adult addictions—problems more common in males than females" (Reissman 2003 [1983], 57), Reissman argues, it is women's *ordinary* physical and psychological functions that have been medicalized, as opposed to men's exclusively *deviant* ones. (The exception Reissman notes is male impotence, which had begun to be medically scrutinized in the 1980s, but she states that male hormones and the male climacteric had not—a claim that no one would make today.)

Riska notes correctly that this exclusion of men's bodies and behaviors from the medicalization thesis is only beginning to be critiqued by scholars who write that the medical assumption that men's bodies properly function as the "prototype" for all human bodies ignores the gendered nature of men's bodies and health; again, while women's natural functions are pathologized by medicine, men's are not. Indeed, Judith Lorber (1997) and Vicki Meyer (2001) uncover just one of many contradictions in medical approaches to health. As Riska (2003, 71) writes, "chronic diseases in women are attributed to 'failed ovaries' and 'hormone deficiency,' which put women at risk, while lifestyle and physiological processes associated with aging are presented as primary risks for men." These and other insights into the hitherto ignored medicalization of men have just begun to be voiced in the last four years. Examples are work on the medicalization of masculinity in the context of coronary heart disease (Riska 2002—although Ehrenreich raised this as early as 1983) and recent work on the medicalization of male sexual "fitness" (Bordo 2000, Potts 2000, Marshall and Katz 2002)—according to Hartley (2003), an interesting, and rare, case of men's sexual problems having been medicalized before women's (but see Maines 1998). But the sense that women are more prone to medicalization than are men endures; despite medicine's recent focus on men's bodies, Conrad (2000, 221–222) agreed with Reissman that "it is abundantly clear that women's natural life processes (especially concerning reproduction) are much more likely to be medicalized than men's" and cited Zola's claim that, since most elders are female, "it is likely aging and gender issues will continue to converge."

Until the twenty-first century, then, despite the significant concern with gender in much medicalization research, this was exclusively explored in the context of women's lives. While men were included (indeed, took center stage) in historical studies about the medicalization of homosexuality, it was their sexuality rather than their sex that was examined as the object of medicalization. (The same applies to studies about the medicalization of AIDS—see, e.g., Epstein 1988; for an exception, see Etzioni 2000.) While gender emerges as an object of medicalization in the context of the medicalization of the family, it is the medical definition and constraint of mothers, not fathers, that is documented (see Litt 2000; Donzelot 1979—but see Williams and Umberson 1997). Many studies of the medicalization of aging treat elders as though they were sexless, and while there is abundant work on the medicalization of female menopause, there is little on the medicalization of male aging *per se* (but see Marshall and Katz 2002; Hepworth and Featherstone 1998). Men's voices appear in work on chronic illness (see Charmaz 1995), but as objects of physical suffering rather than of medicalization. The sociology of mental illness considers the medicalization of female emotions into hysteria (see King 1989; Orr 2000; Zavirsek 2000; Briggs 2000),[9] but while there is certainly work on men's emotions and emotion work (see Umberson et. al. 2003; Gaia 2002; Scheff 2001; Katz 1988), there is little on the medicalization of male emotions (but see Cancian 1986 on the feminization of love). Work on the medicalization of race and ethnicity has concentrated on entire racial and ethnic groups and on minority women (see Roberts 1997; Kaw 2003) rather than on the medicalization of, say, African American masculinity (see Saint-Aubin 2002 for a strong exception). Thus, at the intersection of gender and medicalization, femininity has prevailed. Nascent in the research into medicalization are the seeds for considering the medicalization of masculinity (e.g., male menopause, criminality, homosexuality, the feminization of emotions and therapy), but with few exceptions already described here, these have been neither nurtured nor harvested. Indeed, with the exception of Riska's (2002) analysis, the few works on the medicalization of masculinity that have appeared over the past several years have concentrated on its most obvious instances—the medicalization of male aging and sexuality—rather than on the myriad other aspects of masculinity cited above. This is due to the equation of gender with femininity in the context of medicalization, which is itself rooted in the assumption, brought about by the discovery of medicine as an agency of social control, that only underrepresented groups are medicalized.

## Masculinities

The masculinity studies of the last three decades were inspired by the insight that while men had previously been studied as social actors of historical, political, cultural, and scientific significance, they had not been considered as gendered beings in the same way that women had—as actors whose gender mattered in the course of their daily lives and actions. Grounded in and ideologically affiliated with the second-wave feminism of the early 1970s, most of these studies have been explicitly feminist (or, in these studies' local argot, profeminist, given its claim that only women can be feminists). As had women, men involved in the Men's Liberation movement who were positively influenced by feminism began to question and politically contextualize their lives. Writing on masculinity in this era was both popular (e.g., the 1977 anthology *A Book of Writings for Men against Sexism*) and academic, with sociology, psychology, and social psychology showing the most interest in the area. Moreover, issues surrounding male homosexuality arose almost immediately, given the number of gay and bisexual men involved in Men's Liberation, some of whom drew connections between homophobia and sexism.

Early masculinity studies (e.g., Fasteau 1974 and Farrell 1975) challenged functionalist approaches to sex role theory, still dominant in the 1960s and present in the 1970s, which normalized the existing gender order. They stated that masculine roles, while assuring men political and economic power over women, were nonetheless damaging to men's physical and emotional health as well as to their social relationships. Thus, from the outset, this research tradition not only sought to problematize masculinity, but to pathologize and frame it in medical terms as well. The 1970s saw the release of a number of feminist books on masculinity that listed both the benefits of male power and privilege and the physical and emotional costs associated with traditional masculinity (see David and Brannon 1976; Pleck and Sawyer 1974; Pleck and Pleck 1980). While some of these feminist publications were written by women who critiqued masculinity as an essential aspect of patriarchy, others were written by men who used men's liberation to escape restrictive sex roles, and academic studies, mostly produced by men, approached masculinity as a problematic amalgam of sex roles that were damaging to both sexes. A key example of the latter is Pleck's *The Myth of Masculinity* (1981), which argued that the male sex role model failed to capture the actual experiences of men and proposed a "male sex-role strain" model that sought to capture the costs of conforming to traditional masculine expectations. This book was a pivotal one, shifting the focus from sex roles to power and oppression (which in turn led to an emphasis on the multiplicity of masculinities and the importance of socialization in their development—masculinity studies' third wave). Clearly situated in the larger critique of functionalism, these early works critiqued sex-role theory for eliding the role of power in male-female relations, drew on conflict theory to call for masculinity studies' consideration of men's patriarchal roles, and demanded a systematic and structural approach to the topic.

The central challenge became to understand men's lives as embedded in systems of power and control while appreciating the fact that men may also be victims of those very systems. In the writings of the late 1980s and early 1990s, the answer lay in masculinity's own precarious status: men may be disempowered relative to other male groups, and men of all socioeconomic-political statuses rely on others to validate their masculinity (see Pleck 1992 and Kaufman 1987). Masculinity, with all its benefits, is thus socially constructed and fragile, requiring interactional reproduction and reassurance. This new focus on masculine practices and its interpersonal accomplishment led to a concern with how boys are socialized into masculinity (e.g., Kivel 1999), claiming that masculinity was a limiting (and, as we'll see below, unhealthy) set of practices. Masculine socialization limited the parameters of acceptable gendered behavior and severely punished deviations from them. While this research focused on the classroom, the gendered use of space, the role of parents, and cultural assumptions (e.g., McGuffey and Rich 1999; Connell 1996; Kenway 1996) as forces of social control, however, it failed to consider the role of medicine in defining and regulating masculinity. Rather than intersect with other work on social control (i.e., medicalization), the masculinities literature of the 1990s veered toward an engagement with issues of diversity within masculine culture and lives, as profeminist scholars studying men argued against accepting one type of masculinity as normative while labeling others deviant. Following the multiracial focus of feminism, the differences between men that received the most attention were identical to those that differentiate women: race, class, sexuality, age, and disability (see Gerschick 2000 and Gerschick and Miller 2004 on disabled men; Majors and Gordon 1994 on black men; Chen 1999 on Asian American men; Fine et al. 1997 and

Karen Pyke 1996 on working-class men and class more generally; and Connell 1992 and Levine 1998 on gay men).

The dual foci on diversity among men on the one hand and on the power that men hold on the other converged in Connell's well-known theoretical work, which sought to balance an understanding of masculinity as part of a tool kit subordinating women (and, in his later writings—see Carrigan, Connell, and Lee 1985—subordinated men such as homosexuals and marginalized men such as the poor and men of color) with an appreciation for the different ways that men actually define and enact it. In 1995, Connell defined masculinity as "simultaneously a place in gender relations, the practices through which men and women engage that place in gender, and the effects of these practices in bodily experience, personality and structure,"[10] and defined hegemonic masculinity as "the configuration of gender practice which embodies the currently accepted answer to the problem of the legitimacy of patriarchy" (Connell 1995, 77). These definitions allow for the agentic male practice of distancing the self from a dominant (and historically variable) traditional masculinity while retaining the latter's centrality to the gendered social order under patriarchy. Despite some criticism,[11] the concept of hegemonic masculinity is widely used in current work.

Thus, the relatively new area of masculinity studies that emerged in the 1970s and picked up steam in the 1980s and 1990s bypassed issues of medicalization for issues of socialization, gender roles, and the role of masculinities in pitting men against each other as men are pitted against women. This tradition's explicitly feminist agenda[12] led it to follow the same theoretical trajectory as had feminism and to echo feminism's condemnation of masculinity as a source of power and of damage to men and women alike.[13] These scholars depicted the reproduction of hegemonic masculine gender roles and men's use of their superior political and economic locations as the central means of subjugation by men. This encouraged a structural focus that nonetheless ignored the existence of medicine as an institution that controlled men, and the pathologizing of masculinity as damaging to health meshed with medicine's tendencies to normatively rank certain behaviors through the lens of health. Despite Whitehead and Barrett's (2001, 1) claim that "today there are no areas of men's activities that have not been subject to some research and debate by both men and women," the result of these emphases was a body of work that, while useful in certain ways, fails to recognize the significance of medicine for the production and control of masculinity, despite its feminist allies having documented the medicalization of femininity throughout the years that masculinity studies developed.

## Masculinity and Men's Health

With few exceptions, both masculinities and epidemiological studies pathologize masculinity as a health risk and thus take an active role in the construction of the risk society rather than adopt a critical stance towards it. The central argument is that traditional masculinity—comprised of sexual difference from women, superiority (and superior power over others), independence, aggressiveness, competition, and physical strength—leads men to (1) engage in risk-taking behavior such as excessive drinking, fast and risky driving, risky physical endeavors, and violence, all of which allegedly account for higher accidental or homicidal deaths, (2) suppress their emotions to act overambitiously in the pursuit of power (which, in the unimaginative epidemiological logic embraced by this strain of work, leads to coronary heart disease [CHD]), and (3) deny their pain and its significance, which leads to a failure to seek medical treatment. As we've seen, the men's movement of the 1970s depicted men as victims of the same gender order that victimized women, although not in the same way and not to the same degree. Current men's studies scholars continue to assert that "health seems to be one of the most clear-cut areas in which the damaging aspects of traditional masculinity are evident" (Sabo and Gordon 1995, 17), although they locate these behaviors in the gender order rather than in any innate male tendencies. Indeed, Harrison, Chin, and Ficarrotto (1992: 282) wrote that

> it is time that men especially begin to comprehend that the price paid for belief in the male role is shorter life expectancy. The male sex-role will become less hazardous to our health only insofar as it ceases to be defined as opposite to the female role, and comes to be defined as a genuinely human way to live.

(Given many men's studies scholars' assertion that masculinity is, by definition, a rejection of the feminine, this would be a neat trick indeed.)

The product of this reasoning was a causal link between masculinity, specifically "traditional white middle-class male sex-role characteristics" (Riska 2003, 74), and ill health. These were constructed as health risks because they cast men in the role of the primary breadwinner of the family—a major health burden. Men became an endangered species, threatened "by the operative effects of the male mystique: men's own self-destructive and risky behavior to prove their heterosexual male identity" (Riska 2003, 74–75).

A similar discursive process has occurred in regards to men's limited health-seeking behaviors and use of medical resources relative to women's, which have been cited as causal factors in men's higher mortality rates and lower life expectancies. Just as women have traditionally been held up to the standard of men's bodies, men are now being held up to the standard of women's health behaviors; in short, men's health behaviors are now depicted as deficient by using women's health behaviors as the gold standard for health practices (Riska 2003, 77). Given that men's relatively light use of medical resources has been attributed to their masculinity, this results in once again positing masculinity itself as a cause of ill health: a discursively medicalizing move (in Foucauldian terms, becoming one of the assemblages of governmentality).

Embedded in the construction of masculinity as a health risk is a wholesale adoption of the medical model's dogma that CHD is caused by poor diet and emotional inadequacies and that early medical surveillance and intervention prevents and/or cures disease. In short, it reproduces and elaborates the risk behaviors argument that dominates medical, epidemiological and popular thinking. (The clearest example of this is the construction of the type A man whose stereotypically masculine commitment to success is a risk factor for CHD—see Ehrenreich 1983, Riska 2002.[14]) That constructing a set of behaviors as risk factors "detracts from the possibility that we will recognize and rectify social circumstances that impact people's health" (Segal, Demos, and Kronenfeld 2003) makes this construction eerily reminiscent of medicalization, which individualizes and decontexualizes political issues. Gendering these alleged risks has placed men in a subservient role with respect to health, as men's higher mortality rates and lower life expectancies in the West are attributed to their own behaviors, albeit behaviors that originate in the larger socioeconomic, political, and gender systems. Thus, rather than critically uncover the medicalization of masculinity that, as this volume's chapters demonstrate, is occurring, epidemiology and men's studies are seemingly unaware of it, albeit for different reasons: epidemiology because of its essentially medical vision of human health, and men's studies because of its tendency to pathologize masculinity as damaging to men and women.

## The Sociology of the Body

While the last fifteen years have seen an explosion of sociological and historical studies of the body, this focus has a long, if only recently recognized, history in the social sciences. Indeed, a concern with the body as a social rather than merely biological entity is deeply embedded in classical theory. Karl Marx ([1867] 1954), for example, wrote that capitalism's survival depended upon the continual reproduction of human bodies, and Friedrich Engels (1987 [1854]) documented capitalism's disastrous impact on the working-class body. As Williams and Bendelow (1998) show, Emile Durkheim (1960 [1912]) established the body-soul relationship as central to the distinction between the sacred and profane, and the ascetic body is key to Max Weber's (1958) argument in *The Protestant Ethic and the Spirit of Capitalism*. Norbert Elias's work on the civilizing process (1978 [1939] and 1982 [1939]) traced the historical shaping of the human body from an impulsive and unrestrained vehicle of a volatile medieval personality to a calculating, rationalized, pacified, and repressed entity—a process characterized by the replacement of external restraints on the body to internal ones (an insight that resonates with Foucault's work on repression) and which he considered ongoing and perhaps endless.

This sociological concern with the body remained dormant until it was awakened by the work of Michel Foucault and, to a lesser degree, Erving Goffman, who is ironically considered more of a symbolic interactionist than a sociologist of the body. Foucault's work (1973, 1977, 1978) uncovered a new form of bodily discipline, beginning with the production of the clinical body that was reduced to its anatomical parts and processes and regulated through the medical gaze and practices and made compliant through such other key institutions of social control as the school and the prison. Foucault's work documented the body as an entity under increased surveillance and regulation designed to monitor it and fashion it into a productive tool, and spawned a new sociological and historical perspective on the body as a socially and politically constructed and, as we've seen, increasingly self-regulating entity—a theme taken up by Bryan Turner in later years (see Turner 1984). Goffman's work on stigma (1963a), impression management (1959, 1967), and relations in public (1963b) highlighted the body as a vehicle for social identity and interaction and, indeed, for the "interaction order" itself.

There things rested until 1984, when Turner's (1984) seminal work, *The Body and Society*, reminded scholars that the body is, in sociological terms, an "unfinished entity" bound within institutional discourses that constantly form and reform it as an experiential one (Gubrium and Holstein 2003; Shilling 1993). Turner's text led to further breakthrough works on the body from Pasi Falk (1994), Chris Shilling (1993), Emily Martin (1987), and the 1995 debut of the journal *Body & Society*. In a few short years, the sociology of the body had emerged as a topic of great debate and discussion—a state in which it remains today, as this substantive focus engages new areas of discussion, from somnolence (Taylor 1993; Hislop and Arber 2003) to the body postmortem (Freiden 2003). Indeed, having critiqued the Foucaldian approach for its ironically disembodied approach to the human body wrought by its emphasis on discursive power, a new strain of work has called for an examination of the body as an everyday, active entity, not as simply the inarticulate construction of disciplinary forces, à la Foucault. To quote Loic Wauquant (1995, 3), "One of the paradoxical features of recent social studies of the body is how rarely one encounters in them actual living bodies of flesh and blood. The books that have appeared in recent years on the topic... typically offer precious few insights into the actual practices and representations that constitute the human body as an 'ongoing practical achievement'."

Three recent edited volumes alert us to this shift—Nettleton and Watson's (1998) *The Body in Everyday Life*, Williams and Bendelow's (1998) *The Lived Body*, and Faircloth's (2003) *Aging Bodies: Images and Everyday Experience*. As Nettleton and Watson (1998, 2) note, daily lives are embodied. We wake up, brush our teeth, drive to work, trip on the sidewalk, have sex, and so on. These are all *bodily* functions. To quote the authors, "Everyday life is therefore fundamentally about the production and reproduction of bodies." More and more research recognizes the body as a central entity in its own right that engages ordinary men and women as they make their daily rounds. The result is a growing appreciation for the body as a "thing" experienced in daily life (Nettleton and Watson 1998) as well as a passive, docile object (Foucault 1977), an entity subject to its own government (Turner 1984), a civilizing presence (Elias 1978 [1939]), and both consumer and consumed (Falk 1994; Featherstone 1991).

The body is also, of course, both gendered and sexualized in a range of discourses and encounters, as several scholars have shown (Butler 1993; Backett-Millburn and McKie 2001; Jackson and Scott 2001). In addition to the feminist work on female bodies that began in the 1970s (see above), a new wave of feminist work has considered the construction and depiction of the female body. Judith Butler (1993), for example, provides us with an intriguing example of how the body has been gendered in Western society. Following Turner (1995), Butler suggests that the body is represented in terms of a patriarchal definition that explicitly constructs the body in terms of gender and sexuality, departing from a philosophical concern with the "Other." Faircloth (2003, 6) summarizes Simon Williams and Gillian Bendelow's argument, appearing in their book *The Lived Body: Sociological Themes, Embodied Issues* (1998), that dualisms that form the basis of our culture (mind/body, subject/object, nature/culture) are transferred to women in the forms of "reproduction/production, family/state, and individual/social." The result, Butler argues, is the female body's construction within ropes of hegemonic culture. While this sheds some insight into the female body's location between "natural entity" and cultural construct, Butler has been critiqued for having fallen victim to the Foucauldian tendency to focus on the cultural discipline of the body through interwoven tendrils of surveillance while ignoring everyday practice. Nonetheless, her work attests to the ongoing relevance of gender to the study of the body.

Despite the burgeoning work on the body, however, the medicalization of masculinity has gone unconsidered in this promising new tradition as well. Falling into two broad and seemingly mutually exclusive areas—the Foucauldian surveillance and disciplining of bodies on the one hand, and the embodiment of daily life on the other—the medicalization of the body itself has been omitted in the interests of capturing macro-level discursive impacts on the body and the embodiment of everyday life. Sociologists of gender who include embodiment in their fields of vision have focused on such matters as lived experience, gender, sports, and, of greatest significance to this volume, the impact of chronic illness on the body rather than its medicalization. If one reads what is perhaps the predominant journal in medical sociology, *Sociology of Health and Illness*, one is overwhelmed by articles on the everyday experience of illness, of birth, the impact of risk, and so on, but one searches in vain for an article that focuses on the actual medicalization of everyday life. By focusing on the experience of illness rather than its construction, medical sociology and the sociology of health and illness (the most obvious venues for the sociological consideration of the body) treat illness as a practical and moral exigency challenging the individual rather than as a social and cultural by-product of medicalization. Thus, while Williams and Bendelow (1998, 19) argue that "the male body has become increasingly prominent as an explicit topic of investigation for theorists and empirical researchers alike," this work has focused on discounting the traditional epistemological status of men's bodies as the standard against which women's bodies are measured, on calling for a theorizing of male embodiment, and on challenging the "tendency to see men and masculinity as separate, such as 'minds' using 'bodies,' " rather than on the intersection of male bodies and medical discourses and regimes.

The fact that the medicalization of masculinity has gone unrecognized (except as it is evident in Viagra and CHD) can be explained by reference to a number of factors. One of them may very well be that the masculinity aspect of medicalization is so subtle that it is almost imperceptible. After all, the prototypical examples of medicalization that tend to be cited are deviance and female reproduction, and since masculinity has not traditionally been seen as deviant and male reproduction has not been medicalized (although there is some anxiety about sperm count these days—see Halwell 1999), the medicalization of masculinity evaded the medical sociological imagination. Another factor is that once medicalization was discovered to be a source of social control, scholars focused on powerless groups (e.g., the poor, elders, women, racial minorities, and children) to the exclusion of other groups, such as men. Foucauldian scholars distanced themselves from the medicalization thesis, viewing its treatment of power and regulation as simplistic and naively reformist; why they failed to appreciate the increasing medical control of masculinity in particular, however, is particularly mysterious given their immunity from the medicalization critique's exclusive focus on allegedly "powerless groups" (a term hardly in keeping with Foucault's conception of power as a dynamic social resource shared by all). The early feminist argument that male medicine pathologized and medicalized women's bodies effectively precluded recognition of the medical control of men, and, for reasons cited above, the medicalization of masculinity has gone unnoticed by feminists and pro-feminists who pathologize masculinity themselves. Finally, the sociology of the body is split into two broad camps: the Foucauldian one that focuses on surveillance and discipline and the camp that has challenged it to consider everyday embodiment. Given the Foucauldian sense that the medicalization thesis is overly simplistic and the proponents of the latter's emphasis upon daily experience to the exclusion of the social and political construction of the fields in which embodiment unfolds, the medicalization of masculinity falls outside of either camp's purview. Despite this effective exclusion of men from research on medicalization, however, the social sciences have recently begun to recognize that male bodies may no longer be exempt from medical definition and regulation—if, indeed, they ever were. Partly inspired by the introduction of Viagra and other sexual technologies, by the reduction of male sexuality to hormonal imbalances (mirroring the discourse on female sexuality), and by the immense marketing possibilities this reductionistic interpretation offers, this work has yet to find either a focused voice or a publication venue.

  This book provides both, covering new sexual technologies and the medicalization of male aging, masculinity in the context of medical anatomy and therapy sessions, black masculinity, and underdeveloped male socialization. Given the vast array of areas of everyday life in which the medicalization of masculinity continues to unfold, however, a myriad of other case studies suggest themselves. These include the medicalization of masculinity through the construction and regulation of prostate and testicular cancer, sexual offenses (and offenders), homosexuality, female masculinity, and male aggression and criminality (through, for example, the "discovery" and attribution of causal significance to the XYY chromosome). We hope that the chapters contained in this volume will inspire others to expand the scope of current work on the medicalization of sexuality to include masculinity and thus to fashion a more sophisticated understanding of the intersections between medicine, gender, bodies, sexualities, and health.

# 1

## The Viagra Blues: Embracing or Resisting the Viagra Body

Meika Loe

n the months leading up to Super Bowl 2004, journalists[1] revisited a familiar theme, discussing which advertisements would air during the big game. That year more than ever, pharmaceutical advertising took center stage, particularly spots for new Viagra-like products Levitra and Cialis, claiming to treat "erectile dysfunction" (ED).[2] Such advertisements, like those for Viagra and Levitra, "official sponsors" of Major League Baseball and the National Football League (NFL) respectively, are known for using sports metaphors, such as "get in the game" and "step up to the plate," and professional athletes as spokesmen, including Mike Ditka, NFL coach and member of the NFL Hall of Fame, and Raphael Palmeiro, a professional baseball player known for his hitting consistency.[3]

We should not be surprised that sexual dysfunction is still at center stage. The Viagra phenomenon is still alive and well, and it doesn't appear to be going away. Six years after its debut, Viagra still appears regularly in popular discourse. Wall Street investors may describe a robust market as a "Viagra market." In the realm of mainstream reporting, *Newsweek* ran two cover stories in January and February 2004 discussing "Viagra babies" and Viagra's new competitors. My local newspaper, like most, runs ads for "masculinity clinics" located in major urban areas. In the realm of technology and ethics, Viagra is discussed as a possible harbinger of things to come—a not-so-far-in-the-future society in which sexual norms and standards are ratcheted up to the point where doctors and patients are creating and reinforcing orgasm quotas.

People are still talking about Viagra because it has proved successful, not only in terms of financial gain but also by appearing to reproduce and respond to existing sociocultural contexts. For example, the Viagra phenomenon successfully built upon cultural anxieties about aging, masculinity, and sexuality, to name a few, and demographic trends such as an aging populace and changing marriage and family structures. Viagra fits nicely with and reinforces cultural expectations about masculinity: male potency, for example. Other contexts aided Viagra's debut, including the recent growth and deregulation of the pharmaceutical industry, increasing scientific attention to sexuality, and expanding medicalization and technological innovation. All of these changes created fertile ground for a product like Viagra, which then altered how we conduct business in boardrooms and bedrooms. With the Viagra phenomenon institutionalized, we are faced with new ways to "do" medicine, health care and coverage, pharmaceutical research and marketing, sexuality, aging, and even marriage.[4]

All of this leads me to one conclusion: America is, as Bob Dylan once said, "tangled up in blue." Many of us find ourselves embedded in a web of products, services, institutions, people, and cultural scripts that reflect the Viagra era and an investment in the Viagra phenomenon. More specifically, we exist at a particular historical moment in a society that promotes at least two versions of "the blues," discontent and pills, specifically those pills modeled after the original "little blue pill," Viagra. On one level, these two ingredients result in medicalized discontent—a social reality that is highly pronounced in the Viagra era and thus difficult to avoid. At the most basic physical level, "the blues" are manifest in the Viagra body.

In the Foucauldian sense, Viagra and related institutions (including erectile dysfunction discourse) have become so ubiquitous that we are becoming accustomed to a certain level of surveillance and biotechnological control over men and their "docile" or fixable bodies. At the same time, the Viagra phenomenon has incited and empowered masculine heterosexual potency, reinforcing the legitimacy and centrality of the male sexual subject in the twenty-first century. Viagra, an erectile dysfunction pill packaged as a male enhancement drug, represents medicalized and commodified masculinity, reinforcing "normal" masculinity on both individual and social levels. At the center of this feedback loop is the embodied man, who must come to terms with the "clinical gaze" that represents medical social control as well as the potential for empowerment and, by association, self-control that Viagra appears to symbolize in our postmodern age.

This chapter tracks Viagra consumers attempting to make sense of "the blues"—the little blue pill and related cultural messages around bodily dissatisfaction, and social scripts for how to "do" masculinity, aging, health, and sexuality in the Viagra era. While it is certainly the case that women, experts, marketers, and others are embedded in the Viagra phenomenon, this chapter is most interested in those directly grappling with Viagra bodies.[5] Specifically, I will chart the rise of a new postmodern subject—the technologically enhanced Viagra man—through a brief history of biotechnology and social movements, paying close attention to how gender intersects with them. Then I turn to male Viagra consumers themselves, who share stories of Viagra bodies and Viagra blues. As they negotiate their relationships to this product, mainstream ideas about sexuality, masculinity, and health are reinforced and redefined in important ways. They construct various forms of manhood, including what I call corporate corporealities—or bodies literally infused with branded commodities—against the backdrop of the medicalization of masculinity, and the expanding medicalization of everyday life (Conrad and Schneider 1992; Lorber and Moore 2002). Interestingly, they also reject the necessity of a Viagra body and what it represents.

## Methods

In stark contrast to ubiquitous Viagra humor and advertising, the silence and relative invisibility surrounding actual Viagra users has proven difficult for a sociologist wanting to talk with Viagra consumers. Many times I asked myself, where do those seeking to recover their potency "hang out," besides in doctors' offices? This question was difficult to answer and left me sympathetic to the men who wanted an answer to the same question. Where did men who wanted to talk with other men about their experiences with ED or Viagra turn? In the end, the communities I found that are built around the experience of erectile dysfunction and recovery were support groups and Internet chat rooms.

The twenty-seven male consumers I spoke with are a snowball sample of men who responded to my requests for interviews through Internet postings, newspaper advertisements, practitioner referrals, senior citizens' organizations, personal contacts, and prostate cancer support group meeting announcements in the Southern California region. All names have been changed to ensure confidentiality. Semistructured conversational interviews were conducted between June and October 2000, either by phone, by e-mail, or in person. More than half of the men interviewed preferred phone or e-mail interviews for privacy and sensitivity reasons. For example, one man said to me, "I'm more secure on the phone, you can't see me blushing over the lines." All interviews were recorded, transcribed, and then coded using FolioView analytic software. A grounded theory approach was used to find emergent themes in the data (Glaser and Strauss 1967).

Those consumers who volunteered for an interview generally had experience with Viagra or a similar product and an interest in sharing it because it had affected their lives positively or negatively. For example, eight men from a post–prostate surgery support group agreed to speak with me over the phone under conditions of anonymity and confidentiality about their experiences dealing with surgery-induced ED. It is interesting that the fact that all had tried Viagra and none had had any "success" with it turned several of the interviews into "ranting" sessions, rendering visible how emotionally invested they were in Viagra's promise. Of the twenty-seven total male consumers I spoke with, all but two had tried Viagra, and half of these stopped using it after the initial trial because of unsatisfactory responses or preferences for a different product. This "take rate" is representative of the larger population of Viagra users nationally; Pfizer's research has shown that over half of those who receive a prescription for Viagra do not request a refill (Heaton 2003).

Differing markedly in age (17–86 years), health, and reasons for using Viagra (and less markedly in terms of race, occupation, socioeconomic status, and sexual orientation), my sample is representative of a diversity of Viagra users. While Pfizer does not release demographic information on Viagra users, in early marketing efforts, Pfizer identified its largest market as "men over forty years of age." It is no surprise then that twenty-one of my interview subjects are over forty years of age. But as revealed by more recent Pfizer advertising depicting professional athletes, office workers in their thirties, and leaping mailmen, the age, race, and class demographics for Viagra have expanded since the Bob Dole endorsement era. This is corroborated by the fact that I found teenaged boys and men in their twenties and thirties also wanting to talk about their own experiences with Viagra.

Diseases, medications, and surgeries were the most cited reasons for trying Viagra in my sample of male consumers. Nine of the twenty-seven male consumers I interviewed experienced erectile difficulties after undergoing prostate surgery. Others blamed erectile dysfunction on age (four consumers) diabetes (one), heart problems (one), and medications (two). Three consumers cited psychological (self-esteem) factors as the main cause of their erectile difficulties. Perhaps of most interest is the significant number of interviewees who denied they had ED (seven) and instead explained their use of Viagra as an assurance or enhancement drug. Pfizer does not officially acknowledge or discuss this population of Viagra users in its promotional or training information, although these users may fall into Pfizer's "mild ED" and "psychological and other factors" categories.

## A Brief History of the Medically Enhanced Body

Therapeutic, technological, and medical efforts to define, construct, inhibit, and enhance sexual bodies have a long history (Jones 1993). Such efforts, which evolved from the nineteenth century into the late twentieth century, represented a major mobilization of empirical, medical, and technological tools to treat sexual problems, usually thought to be synonymous with social problems (Foucault 1978; Irvine 1990, 189). In *The History of Sexuality: An Introduction,* Foucault used the term *technologies of sex* to refer to institutions of the nineteenth century that medicalized and controlled deviant sexualities. For example, the medicine of perversions and the programs of eugenics were two great innovations of the technology of sex of the second half of the nineteenth century (Foucault 1978, 118). These institutions and "apparatuses of control" are constituent of modern "scientific biopower," an era during which there was an explosion of numerous and diverse techniques for achieving the subjugation of bodies and the control of populations (1978, 140).[6]

By the twentieth century, medicine, with its models, metaphors, institutions, and distinctive ways of thinking, had come to exercise authority over areas of life not previously considered medical (Conrad and Potter 2000; Ehrenreich and English 1973; Figert 1996; Martin 1994). In the age of medical "progress," scientific knowledge and medical answers to problems are generally unquestioned as the best, most efficient, most legitimate solutions. Technology, as an applied science, is similarly constructed and championed. Thus, the history of science, medicine, and technology is also a history of attempting to solve social problems and control populations (Davis 1981; Ehrenreich and English 1973, 1979; Foucault 1973, 1978; Jacobson 2000; Maines 1999; Terry 1995). In twentieth-century America, biotechnology, or the merging of science, medicine, and technology, is deployed to solve social problems (deemed large-scale sexual problems) such as poverty, fertility, adolescent sexuality, teenage pregnancy, venereal disease, and AIDS.[7]

It is in this context of biotechnological hegemony, along with U.S. government deregulation of the pharmaceutical industry, that late-twentieth-century American society witnessed the rapid expansion of pharmaceutical power and the rise of the pharmacology of sex.[8] The development of reproductive technologies in the mid-twentieth century was a clear precursor to the pharmacology of sex. The oral contraceptive pill was an early success in medical, technological, and social worlds. Elizabeth Watkins (1998, 8) tracks how the combination of media, medical researchers, physicians, and manufacturers seduced the public into seeing "the pill" as the ideal "techno-fix" to solve individual and social problems related to fertility control without knowing the hazards of the drug until the late 1960s. The new oral contraceptive also served as a barometer of changes in social attitudes about science, technology, and medicine as well as illuminated conceptions about sexuality, women's health and medicine, and science and technology as applied to women's lives (D'Emilio and Freedman 1998, 339). Most importantly, Watkins (1998, 132) suggests that "although Americans expressed skepticism toward medical science and its products, for example, the pill, they continued to embrace the culture of 'modern' medicine and technology after the 1960s"—a "culture" that was rapidly expanding and changing.

In the past twenty years, there has been an increase in scholarship focused on the merging of technology and medical science to construct "postmodern" or cyborgian bodies, including the construction of sexual or gendered bodies through surgeries, implants, hormones, drugs, appliances, and reproductive technologies in the twentieth century (Basalmo 1996; Conrad and Potter 2000; Franklin and Ragone 1998; Haraway 1991, 1999; Hausman 1995; Irvine 1990; Raymond 1994). This growing field of research on biotechnology and sex explores the myriad ways in which gender, sexuality, and reproduction are naturalized, reinforced, inhibited, inscribed, surveyed, and controlled through technology in the twentieth century. Postmodern technoscience scholarship suggests that transsexual, reconstructive, and cosmetic surgeries as well as reproductive technologies provide a window onto both social constructions and medicotechnological interventions into gendered and sexualized personhood. In late capitalism, Americans have a newly transformed relationship with biotechnology, one that goes beyond "healing" to now "transforming" bodies (Basalmo 1996, Hausman 1995 Jacobson 2000; Raymond 1994). In the last twenty years, historians have outlined the convergence of markets and science in the new, "totally replaceable body" (Irvine 1990, 259). Thus, in a postmodern world where bodies are a collection of various parts and sexuality is fractured and dispersed in and around the body, the surgeon's knife and hormonal treatments become tools for sexual enabling, reinvention, and goal attainment.

Despite its insights, however, twentieth-century scholarship on biotechnology tends to overemphasize medical hegemony and domination and to underemphasize the role of human agency and resistance.[9]

Donna Haraway (1999) calls the convergence of sociohistorical forces and science and technology the "informatics of domination" (a concept similar to Foucault's "biopower"), referring to how bodies are produced, inscribed, replicated, and disciplined in postmodernity. Technology promises to be enhancing and lifesaving, while obscuring the fact that it also acts as disciplinarian and surveillant (Basalmo 1996, 5). The individual is taught to "know her body" to the point of self-conscious self-surveillance (Basalmo 1996, 6; Foucault 1977) and to view it as fractured, with constantly improvable, fixable parts (Jacobson 2000; Martin 1994; Mead in Basalmo 1996).[10]

Within cultural studies, sociology, sexology, queer studies, and feminist studies, the question of agency as it relates to biotechnological products and apparatuses remains urgent. Scholars have warned about the general overemphasis on the biotechnological "impact" in such writings on sexuality and technology, to the point of losing sight of human agency (Haraway 1999; Sawicki 1991). Jana Sawicki suggests using a Foucauldian analysis to view technology and medical science within a context of multiple sites of power and resistance operating within a social field of struggle (Sawicki 1991, 87).[11] Technological developments are many-edged, Sawicki (1991, 89) reminds us, for who today would deny women the contraceptive technologies developed in this century? This chapter balances agency and "impact" in considering consumers as subjects constructing and shaping medical and biotechnological realities, bodies, and masculinities. Nonetheless, these agents clearly operate within and against constraining social contexts.

## The Rise of the Viagra Man

The quest for manhood, to achieve, demonstrate, and prove masculinity, is rooted deep in American history, starting at least with the nineteenth century's self-made man (Kimmel 1996). But in the early twenty-first century, when gender equity is believed to be increasingly achievable and men are no longer the sole family breadwinners, male power and control is no longer assured. Scholars specializing in "masculinity studies" have had much to say about male confusion in the roughly thirty years preceding Viagra. Attempts to understand and locate "masculinity in crisis," while varied and incomplete, are crucial to understanding the success of the Viagra phenomenon.

In the 1970s and 1980s, gender scholars began to complicate and problematize normative (and thus prescriptive) white, heterosexual "hegemonic masculinity" (Connell 1995). Michael Messner (1997) is one of many to argue that a singular, reductionist, unified masculinity does not reflect a society in which at any given moment there are various and competing masculinities. Responding to feminist scholarship, early masculinities scholars argued that patriarchy forces men to oppress themselves and other men, inspiring many inquiries into male competition, power struggles, and self-objectification. Joseph Pleck's *The Myth of Masculinity* (1981) suggested that hegemonic masculinity and the promotion of unattainable ideals caused men to experience "sex role strain" in trying to attain the unattainable, sparking an interest in male confusion and "crisis" related to out-of-date, inflexible, contradictory, turn-of-the-century sex roles. Similarly, Lynne Segal, in *Slow Motion: Changing Masculinities* (1990) warned that lived masculinity is never the seamless, undivided construction it becomes in its symbolic manifestation. She argued that in the late twentieth century, masculinity was not in crisis per se, but was less hegemonic than before. While contemporary, increasingly visible and complicated masculinities can exist in tension with potentially outdated roles and expectations, this can also lead to confusion about manhood and how to "do" it.

Beginning in the 1970s, movements to liberate men and/or "recover" different forms of take-charge masculinity have resulted in numerous male rebellions (Kimmel and Messner 1989; Ehrenreich, Hess, and Jacobs 1986). Such recovery movements came in response to record numbers of women entering the workplace and rising to prominence in the public sphere. As a result, men's traditional sources of validation were newly challenged. With work, politics, and family no longer viable arenas for proving masculinity, new sites for recovering male power and control have emerged in the past several decades, including Christian revival meetings, the gym, exclusionary men's clubs, and wilderness retreats. Today much has been written on the Promise Keepers and Christian revival masculinity movements (Williams 2001). At these sites, various male liberation leaders have suggested that proving or recovering one's manhood could be achieved through self-control, exclusion, or escape (Kimmel 1996, 310). Masculinity movements have been mostly about reclaiming something that has been lost. The majority of these movements are profit based and predicated on a version of masculinity that, at the core, asserts and reclaims male dominance.

In the late twentieth century, masculinities scholars began to write about the connections between manhood and men's bodies. Australian social scientist R. W. Connell (1995 45) wrote, "True masculinity is almost always thought to proceed from men's bodies." Sander Gilman's (2001) work revealed how "aesthetic surgeries" such as penile implants can help in the achievement of masculinity. And sociologist Michael Kimmel joined sociologists of the body in suggesting that the realms of health and fitness have replaced the workplace in the late twentieth century as the next major testing ground for masculinity, where body work inevitably becomes a "relentless test" (Kimmel 1996). But few masculinity scholars have taken a critical perspective on current theories of the body as a machine or as a surface imprinted with social symbolism. Connell proposes his own, the "body-reflexive" model, in which the social relations of gender are experienced in the body, and constituted through bodily action (Connell 1995). Likewise, limited scholarship on male sexual bodies suggests that sexuality, particularly heterosexuality, is a proving ground for masculinity (Bordo 2000; Fasteau 1975; Kimmel and Messner 1989; Kimmel 1996).

Only recently have researchers, particularly feminist social scientists, begun to expand their inquiries to include the medicalization of male bodies. Since Viagra's release, a small number of female social scientists have written about the ways in which this product promises to reinforce "phallocentrism," or in my words, "erect the patriarchy"[12] (Potts 2000; Tiefer 1994; Luciano 2001; Marshall 2002). In other words, such scholars are concerned that a product like Viagra may hinder ongoing efforts for gender equality by reinforcing male potency, power, and sexual subjecthood, without a concurrent commitment to women's empowerment and sexual health. Others are concerned about the new commodification of masculinity and the related proliferation of mass insecurity around manhood (Bordo 2000). Additionally, medical sociologists Laura Mamo and Jennifer Fishman (2001) have written about Viagra's potential for liberatory or disciplinary effects.

In contrast, most male scholars who study masculinity have yet to fully take up the question of the new medicalized male body, or more specifically, the Viagra body. A very limited group of scholars, primarily historians, have written about how white men's heterosexual bodies have been normalized and naturalized, and in rare cases, pathologized (Bordo 2000; Bullough 1987). For example, Kevin Mumford (1992) explores how male impotence was medicalized, constructed, and cured historically. Starting from advertisements promising male virility and vigor, Mumford traces the "crisis of masculinity" along with modernization and the changing American conceptions of male sexuality and masculinity from the 1830s to the 1920s.

Drawing on the early work of Foucault (1973, 1977) and Goffman (1959) in particular, some sociologists have turned their analytical focus on the body as a locus for social problems and an ideal site for understanding the cultural valuation of fluidity, flexibility, and plasticity in late modernity (Martin 1994; Shilling 1993; Turner 1996). Martin (1994) observes a new conception of "fitness" being forged, in which bodies will succeed or fail based on their flexibility and reflexivity. Sociologists of the body Williams and Bendelow (1998) and others reject the idea that men's bodies are inert *tabulae rasae*, and suggest that only by paying attention to the "lived" experience of bodies can we truly appreciate individual agency, social change, and a society, or social body, built by individual bodies.

In the Viagra era a new and profitable masculine recovery movement is underway with the aid of a pharmaceutical drug, and the male body is re-emerging as a site for confidence and control. We have seen a similar phenomenon with over-the-counter male steroid use popularized in the late twentieth century. Now, millions of men turn to Viagra to reclaim something they lost, a portion of their manhood. As opposed to the masculinities movements mentioned above, this one is a silent movement to doctors' offices, internet pharmacies, and men's clinics, made by individuals who may be vaguely aware of other men pursuing "recovery" of potency, confidence, and "life," at the same time. But for most of the participants, the recovery process is too personal and too stigmatizing to discuss.

How have men themselves responded to this newfound medical attention? In the following pages, consumers grapple with "deficient" body parts, the concept of manhood, and medical diagnoses. In the process, they expose as constructs that which we take for granted; they imagine their bodies as machines, and use Viagra as a tool for fixing their broken masculinity. Embracing or rejecting the Viagra body, or Pfizer-inspired corporeality, becomes one way to respond to social pressures. As some consumers discover, Viagra not only solves problems, but sometimes produces them as well.

## Masculinity in a Pill

Five years ago, pharmaceutical companies could not advertise directly to consumers, and men rarely spoke publicly about sexuality, much less erectile insecurity. Today, celebrity spokesmen like Mike Ditka (aka "Iron Mike"), former NFL player and coach, are paid by pharmaceutical companies to say, "I have a problem. I didn't want my life to come to an end." After hearing this, it becomes normal to associate living with sex, and concurrently, lack of sex with dying. In addition, these advertisements contain social scripts about what it takes to be healthy, sexual, and masculine in America. No longer promoting the message "not for 'normal' men," Pfizer has expanded its markets to include men of most ages, races, and backgrounds (excluding minors and gay males, although it is used by these groups as well), who see a need for erectile improvement and, perhaps, a masculinity boost.

For the men I spoke with who experienced erectile difficulties or insecurities, many wondered if they were "normal" but suffered in silence because of the shame they associated with their bodies, and because of the lack of close friendship networks to turn to for support.[13] For these men, admitting to such difficulties (even to themselves) was like conceding that one was no longer young or masculine in a culture that conflates these identities with sexuality and sexual health.[14] Thus, the project of restoring "normal functioning" cannot be divorced from achieving normal masculinity. In this way, both patients and doctors construct Viagra not only as a treatment for erectile dysfunction, but also as a pill that restores masculinity.

Medical definitions of erectile functioning suggest that "performance" or achievement of an erection with the potential to penetrate and ejaculate is central to the "accomplishment" of heterosexual masculinity. In this way, medicine is actively shaping what is permissible and ideal in terms of gender roles (Raymond 1994) by medicalizing men's roles. Male performance expectations are clearly laid out in Pfizer's 2000 definition of erectile dysfunction in a brochure designed for doctors: "the consistent inability of a man to achieve and/or maintain an erection sufficient for satisfactory sexual performance." We are left to assume that the successful masculine performance requires a specific and successful penile performance, involving consistency, achievement, and satisfaction. Is this really the case?

In my conversations with male consumers, I asked if Viagra could be seen as a masculinity pill of sorts. Most affirmed this idea, reiterating the link between erections, potency, and masculinity. Below, white heterosexual male consumers ranging from twenty-seven to seventy-five years of age have literally bought into the idea of a masculinity pill.

ML: Is Viagra a masculinity pill?

FRED (seventy-five, white, heterosexual, retired marine) (laughs):
I can't argue with that. Without it you aren't much of anything.

ML: What do you mean?

FRED: If you have an impotency problem to any degree, you look for something to help it with, or you abstain completely. If they feel like this is a masculinity problem, I guess they are right.

CHUCK (fifty-three, white, heterosexual, architect): Oh yes. [Viagra] appeals to the male ego. A drug for potency makes you bigger and longer lasting. And this is important to males. As far as the guys in the [post-prostate surgery] group, there are men in their seventies, maybe even eighties, who are still interested in performance and sex and having a normal lifestyle. I thought that after seventy, I might start to lose interest in sex. But maybe not. These men are genuinely concerned with getting back to normal sex lives.

SCOTT (thirty-seven, Welsh, heterosexual, manager): Viagra to me is a miracle pill! It does boost confidence as well as other things! I suppose it can be called a masculinity pill, for without an erection, I believe that my masculinity is somewhat diminished!

DAVE (twenty-seven, white, heterosexual, student): Well, yeah, it's a pill that may make a man closer to what the ideal man is supposed to be, young and virile.

According to these men, Viagra can be seen as a treatment for lost, "diminished," troubled, or incomplete masculinity. And masculinity, in their words, means youth, virility, confidence, size, substance, and general sense of worth. As Fred mentioned, impotence reveals that a man is "not much of anything." Over and over in my interviews, in the face of erectile difficulty or even deficiency, male consumers cast themselves as incomplete, or "half a man." Taking a dose of Viagra allows men to be "whole" again. Below, Phil and Don, who have recently undergone prostate surgery, lament how "incomplete" they feel.

PHIL (fifty-four, white, heterosexual, insurance broker): You just want to be whole. You just want to be like you were before. It's like when somebody has a leg amputated. They get a prosthesis. They can now walk. Then can't run, but now they can walk like they used to.

DON (sixty-seven, white, heterosexual, retired fire captain): Prostate cancer patients [like me] run the gamut of radiation, seed implants, [and] surgical removal, and the thought of becoming impotent is overwhelming. They say why me? I've been strong as a bull all my life, god's gift to women, now I'm made a eunuch.

Marvin, who attributes his erectile dysfunction to diabetes, echoes Phil and Don in feeling like "less than half a man":

MARVIN (sixty-four, white, heterosexual, unknown occupation): Are physical relations still important? Damn right they are. That is so firmly imprinted on the consciousness of males like me that one feels less than half a man without it. I cannot understand those men who show no interest. Very important!

Again, masculinity is constructed as necessarily connected to sexual desire and interest, thus conflating sexuality and male identity. It is worthwhile to note that Marvin's comments, just like Pfizer's Viagra campaign, assume that heterosexual activity is compulsory for men. "Men who show no interest [in sex]" are rendered invisible in light of Viagra. Men who show interest but can't engage in intercourse, those rendered "incomplete," such as Phil, Don, and Marvin, are the focus of the campaign.

Bob, a black heterosexual barber in his sixties, shared with me how the image of a "shrinking" man conveys how erectile dysfunction can visibly take its toll. Bordo (2000) argues that in a culture where "big and bulky" represent male ideals, "shrinkage" is feared, as evidenced in popular culture. (For example, in one episode of the television sitcom *Seinfeld*, Kramer discusses his embarrassment associated with experiencing "shrinkage" while swimming in cold water.) As I flipped through Bob's booklet "Keys to Great Sex for Men over 50," I showed him the first page, which reads in large letters, "YOUR PENIS SHRINKS 19.8% AS YOU GET OLDER," part of an ad for testosterone treatment. I asked if he believed this. Bob replied,

> Yes, that's what prompted me [to buy the treatment]. Oh yeah, you wake up in the morning and you know something is different. Reading this stuff makes you more aware of what is happening. After taking stuff, there is a difference, a change.

For many men, being big and bulky rather than shrinking and diminutive is essential to "normal" manhood. This theme of "loss" came up frequently in conversations with practitioners and consumers, although expressed and constructed in various ways. Many times loss of erectile function is seen as a death. Social scientist Annie Potts (2000, 96), in a critical commentary on "The Hard-On," reminds us that the experience of "the fallen flesh," or the limp penis, causing the body to appear desexed, soft (feminine), and powerless is a common male horror story because it feminizes the body, rendering the person unidentifiable as a man.[15] Below, Ricardo (sixty-one, Mexican American, heterosexual, painter) enacts this horror story as he worries about the seeming death of his sexual personhood and sexual life, as viewed by his relatives.

> I hate for people to think that I can't do this. They think about it. I talk to my aunt and she says, "Oh, you can't do that thing anymore." I thought, "I don't like that." And I hate for them to think it's over. Like we're married but it's over for us...I never realized how important it was till after I couldn't do it. You just take it for granted. It's fine, and then when you can't do it—I was very depressed. Not to the point of killing myself, but I thought it was all over.

Ricardo describes his feelings of desperation, loss, and depression associated with impotence. Ricardo repeats the phrase, "it was all over" several times, perhaps mourning the end of his masculinity, his virility, his sexuality, his marriage, his good reputation, or even his life. Later, he discusses his fear of his wife thinking he's "not 'the man' anymore." For Ricardo, the only way to envision new beginnings came from trying every new medical treatment on the market. In Ricardo's case, Viagra, constructed as the miracle treatment, did not work. This may have reinforced his insecurities and sense of loss even more.

Like Ricardo, other Viagra users described their sense of manhood as being bound up with not simply erectile rigidity but also the ability to play the appropriate role in the bedroom. This may mean the ability to penetrate, assert themselves sexually, and perhaps by association, to please their partners. For example, Stanford (sixty-five, white, heterosexual, counselor) said,

> To be a good lover a man has to be able to balance the ability to not take over but to be just enough . . . to be just enough the aggressor for a woman to feel . . . [my partner] said to me, and it is true, 'We do love to be penetrated.' I think that's true. [Also I cannot] think of myself as a man unless I can satisfy my partner any time, all the time. Unless I can make her come.

For some of the men I spoke with, if they do not wake up in the morning with an erection or satisfy their partner in bed more than once, denial and then depression may set in. Bob, aware of his erectile difficulties, says he's not "ready to retire," and looks to Viagra-like products to delay this process. But Joel and Marvin literally compare erectile dysfunction to death, and see Viagra as a tool for restoring not only masculinity, but also "life" itself.

> JOEL (fifty-five, white, heterosexual, unknown occupation): I'm fifty-five and for some reason I just didn't seem to feel like I was alive and well like I was when I was twenty years old. And you know, I thought that shouldn't be so because that's not the way it is. I've never talked to anybody about that situation, so I told my doctor. For some reason or other I said I'd like to try something to see if I'm still alive or not. And so anyway he says, "Do you want to try this Viagra?" I say I don't like drugs or anything artificial. Maybe my time is over and that should be the end of that. But then I tried [Viagra].

> MARVIN (sixty-four, white, heterosexual, unknown occupation): Often [after taking Viagra] I awaken with this wonderful feeling . . . not enough to put to use, but enough to let me know I am alive.

When Joel and Ricardo agree that "their time is over" when they can no longer achieve erections, they seem to imply their own deaths. For most of these consumers, an active, erect penis symbolizes normal health, masculinity, and sexuality. A limp penis or absence of virility appears to symbolize death of the body as well as of manhood. To capture this disinterest in life that comes with erectile failure, Pfizer has chosen the tagline "Love Life Again" to sell its product.

As we have seen, male consumers communicating about pain, loss, and concerns associated with sexual problems can be difficult, embarrassing, and heavily laden with metaphor, myth, and shame.[16] Phrases such as "it's over" and "I'm no longer alive," along with labels such as "shrinking," "eunuch," and "incomplete," reveal male discomfort discussing sexuality and convey the degree of importance erectile functioning plays in men's sense of self, masculinity, and health. These men visit doctors with the hope of investigating ways to fix their broken souls, their manhood, and their health. To be a man again may mean feeling young, virile, confident, and strong. Presumably, for these men and for Pfizer, the true mark of therapeutic success is restoration of "phallic manhood" (Potts 2000, 94).

## "Broken" Parts and Viagra Bodies

As Donna Haraway first argued in her groundbreaking essay, the "Cyborg Manifesto," we are all "cyborgs." A cyborg is a hybrid creature composed of both organism and machine that populates a world that is both natural and crafted (Haraway 1991, 149). Consider Arnold Schwarzenegger in *The Terminator,* for example. Today, most medical language about the body reflects the overlap between humans and machines. Medical texts regularly describe bodies using mechanical terminology such as "functioning" and "maintenance." Osherson and AmaraSingham (1981) review the history of the machine metaphor in medicine and the ways in which medicine cannot be separated from a historical context of social mechanization and industrialization. In her research into twentieth-century understandings of health and the body, anthropologist Emily Martin found that the human body continues to be compared to a disciplined machine in medical discourse. Like a machine, the body is made up of parts that can break down (Martin 1994). Similarly, Elizabeth Grosz (1995, 35) argued that in a postmodern world, the body is treated as a mechanical structure whose components can be adjusted, altered, removed, and replaced. In this way, illness refers to a broken body part. To fix this part ensures the functioning of the machine. The metaphor of the body as a smoothly functioning machine is central to how Viagra has been presented. In this section, doctors and patients use mechanical metaphors to make sense of body and gender trouble, or "broken" masculinity.

For Pfizer, the focus is on treating the dysfunctional penis. Emphasis is on "optimal" or "maximal" performance, rigidity, and sustainability of the penis, which means that anything less than this constitutes erectile dysfunction. We see this in Pfizer marketing when "Alfred," a Viagra consumer and member of the Pfizer speakers' bureau, shared how he promotes Viagra: "Men ask me, 'What's it like? What's it like?' These are men who are in their 50s and 60s and I always look at them and ask, 'Is your erection now as good as it was?' They look at me and say no. And I just smile at them" (www.pfizer.com, 2000).

Likewise, in the world of science, prominent sexual dysfunction researcher Irwin Goldstein has written that "submaximal rigidity or submaximal capability to sustain the erection" is another way of understanding erectile dysfunction.[17] In other words, "maximal" erectile rigidity and longevity are normal and expected. This understanding of the penis as dysfunctional and fixable (even perfectable) is exemplified in the following statements by Chuck, (fifty-three, white) a heterosexual architect.

> I'd say as far as functioning sexually, I'm probably at 70 percent. I just can't get hard enough to penetrate. Everything works but the erection. If I were to rate my erectile functioning prior to surgery with now, I'd say it's at 75 percent. It will never be back to 100 percent, I know that. So I'm somewhat satisfied. And the doctors always tell me that this is a long process, and that I need to be patient about getting back to functioning. So I'm in a wait and see mode.

Pfizer's "Sexual Health Inventory for Men," in which four out of five questions ask the patient to rate his erection, is distributed by Pfizer representatives to doctors nationwide and appears to be used commonly by urologists and less commonly by other practitioners. The medical professionals I spoke with were clear that if a patient experiences "deficiency" or complete lack of erectile function, Viagra might be helpful. But "dysfunction" may not be as black and white. As Pfizer Pharmaceuticals and its promotional information suggest, "erectile dysfunction" lies on a continuum from a complete inability to achieve erection to a consistent ability to achieve one. Many patients who are currently looking for treatment for erectile dysfunction inhabit the in-between, "mild ED" arena and appear to be concerned with restoring their "machine" to a "normal," level of functioning (e.g., a "10," as described in interviews by patients and practitioners.) Despite Chuck's focus on "getting back to functioning," sexual standards have changed, perhaps in part as a response to Viagra, and now "normal" is often not enough. In this way, Viagra is thought to assist in the creation of a hypermasculine ideal body while pathologizing a "normal" one.

It is important to point out that while many "erectile health" discussions are focused on the penis, they may also reflect expectations about normal manhood and aging. As we have learned, sexual normality is tied up with conceptions of masculinity. Also implicit in these pursuits of "normality" is a sense of denial and rejection of bodily change and perhaps aging. Thus, Chuck may be just as focused on "getting back to" manhood and youth as he is on returning to normal sexual functioning.

## New Improved, On-Call Bodies

As evidenced in my interviews, Viagra is used by heterosexual and homosexual men who feel that normal penile functioning is not good enough, and "extra-normal" functioning is now the goal. While these men claim they do not "need" Viagra, they are more satisfied with their performance when they do use it.[18] While some (including several of my gay interview subjects) have suggested that gay males are a ready market for the "enhancement" uses of Viagra, both gay and straight men in my interview pool expressed interest in the enhancement uses of Viagra.

In the quotes below, Viagra consumers Will and Stanford imply that the pre-Viagra penis is slow, unpredictable, and uncertain and thus problematic.

> WILL (fifty-three, white, homosexual, program coordinator): [I was] totally surprised in my ability to stay erect without effort and the ability to repeatedly snap to attention. Amazing effect. Sorta magical in a way.

> STANFORD (sixty-five, white, heterosexual, counselor): I noticed that if I get titillated [after using Viagra], then the penis springs to attention. Not atypically. But more facile. It's easier. I don't know if it takes less time. It's more convincing. It's not like maybe I'll get hard and maybe I won't. It's like "Okay, here I am!"

For Will and Stanford, the Viagra body may be preferable to the natural body because it is consistent and predictable. While rigidity is the goal, part of optimal penile performance is to appear responsive; thus, the Viagra body is, in part, a reliable body.[20] According to cultural anthropologist Emily Martin, responsiveness is a trait cherished and cultivated in all fields, including health. In *Flexible Bodies,* Martin (1994) shows how the healthiest bodies in the postmodern era are disciplined machines that also exhibit current cultural ideals such as flexibility, fitness, and elasticity. Viagra can be used as a tool to achieve this ideal elastic body—a body that is always "on call."

Interestingly, the Viagra body is both elastic and controlled, in  contrast to the common cultural expectation that men are virile and "out of control," particularly when it comes to sexuality. Such stereotypes appear regularly in sex education curricula, popular media, and advice manuals. Whereas girls and women have historically been called upon to regulate and control what is commonly thought to be male, mostly adolescent, testosterone-driven, hypersexuality (D'Emilio and Freedman 1988; Tolman 2002), men are now able to pharmaceutically regulate and empower their bodies. For Stu, (thirty-six, white, homosexual, student) the "on-call" Viagra penis will consistently respond when it is needed, whereas the "natural" body is unpredictable, and therefore unreliable.

> Erections are a lot more temperamental than people are willing to admit. But we have this image of masculinity and expectations of male sexuality as being virile and always ready to go and be the conqueror. And I think that this pill allows people to finally live out that myth (laughs). That was one of the things I had to learn early on is that I had irrational expectations of sexuality. And that men don't have big erections every time they want to, usually, and that to believe that one did was to set oneself up for disappointment.

As Stu points out, Viagra exposes the flawed "natural" body and enables a man to achieve mythic, powerful, and controlled masculinity. By appearing "natural," the Viagra body can easily replace the problematic body in order to avoid the inevitable disappointment. In this way, the Viagra story is one that slips between artificial and natural and even beyond to supernatural levels.

For many, the promise of Viagra is the fact that it can deliver "optimal" results, pushing the consumer beyond his own conceptions of "normal" functioning into the hypermasculine realm. In this way, Viagra comes to be seen as a miracle cure because it not only "fixes" the problem but also makes it "better."

In my research, I have found that doctors and patients tend to collaborate in imagining Viagra as a magic bullet that can "extend" the realm of "normal" and push people to the next level: extranormality, or superhumanness. By pushing the boundaries of erectile function, performance, and sexuality, Viagra sets new standards for men and in the process marks countless male bodies in need of medical repair. Consequently, millions of men are being convinced by pharmaceutical companies that their sexual and masculine performance can be improved with Viagra, evidence of a major move to medicalize masculinity. In an era of direct-to-consumer advertising, companies such as Pfizer make it their business to medicalize and sell masculinity to the masses, packaged with equally enticing messages about power, health, romance, and youthfulness. While Pfizer may be more subtle about marketing masculinity in a pill, marketing for the over-the-counter impotence product Enzyte, which debuted in 2002, gets right to the point. According to Lifekey Health print and television ads, Enzyte promises to increase penile size and confidence and to "enhance masculinity." Viagra, Enzyte, and others represent the potential for new, improved reliable and responsive masculine bodies. It is no wonder that the marketers for Levitra have chosen a tagline that reads, "Ready, set, go."

## Viagra Blues: Resisting Viagra and Its Demands

Despite the proliferation of pharmaceutical marketing, consumers are not dupes, swallowing whatever corporations try to sell them. Likewise, not all consumers buy into the techno-fix model. Some consumers comment that although Viagra may promise bodily repair or enhancement, it can actually cause more trouble than it is worth. In this section, consumers indicate that Viagra creates problems, not solutions. For Joel and Don, Viagra is constructed as techno-trouble, rendering the male body increasingly out of control.

> JOEL (fifty-five, white, heterosexual, unknown occupation): I don't ever want to try [Viagra] again. The thing about it is, the side effects could be very dangerous for someone a little older than I am. Because you do end up with palpitation. Your body is just not your body. So if [your functioning is] not normal, I think it's better to just let it go at that. Or make pills that are much, much weaker. But I wouldn't recommend it for anybody.

> DON (sixty-seven, white, heterosexual, retired fire captain): I have tried it. I went a long time and the bottom line is I don't like it. It hasn't done me any good and it had a harmful side effect—heartburn and indigestion. I'm a little fearful of it. I'm a healthy guy and I don't take any maintenance medicines of any kind. My system seems to be functioning nicely. I think I'll just leave it alone.

As we saw earlier, some men see Viagra as a tool to create the ideal on-call body. For other consumers, Viagra may produce a body that is "no longer his own," a body that ceases to be familiar. For Don and Joel, the Viagra body can be scary, producing only discomfort. For these men, the

Viagra-effect is "unnatural" and uncontrollable and consequently undesirable. This was also the case for Dusty and Stanford, who found Viagra bodies overly rigid and constraining.

> DUSTY (seventeen, white, homosexual, student): Well, I also didn't likeit because it was unnatural. Like you were hard and you stayed hard. And I also didn't like the fact that it guaranteed things would be sexual until you weren't hard. I didn't like the idea of being forced into being sexual. You can't do anything nonsexual when you are on it. So basically it guarantees that the entire period you are on it is going to be sexual.

> STANFORD (sixty-five, white, heterosexual, counselor): The idea that I thought was hilarious at first—that erection that won't go away—is not hilarious at all. In fact it happens and sometimes endangers one's life.

For Stanford and Dusty, Pfizer's Viagra tagline, "Love Life Again" is inappropriate. Instead of regaining an appreciation for life, these men see Viagra as constraining, dangerous, or even deadly. While priapism (a prolonged and painful erection that can last from several hours up to a few days) or death can occur in rare instances of Viagra use, and even Pfizer admits that Viagra is not for everyone, neither Stanford nor Dusty experienced real bodily danger while taking Viagra. Nonetheless, both take Viagra seriously, remaining cautious and seeming to prefer the nonmedical approach to the artificial alternative.

Rather than experience trouble through Viagra use, some men construct alternatives to the pharmaceutical quick-fix model, accepting their bodies as they are or just "leaving it alone." Despite overwhelming evidence that Viagra is associated with the production of normal and/or mythic masculinity, men like Phil, Ollie, and Joel work hard at reconstructing masculinity as separate from "erectile health." They insist that heterosexual masculinity can be achieved without the help of Viagra and even without a consideration of erectile potential.

> PHIL (fifty-four, white, heterosexual, insurance broker): I watch baseball games sometimes and I see Viagra on one of these big boards in the background. Ads behind home plate. It kind of blew me away. It's not like we're talking about going out and picking up six-packs of Budweiser. . . . Well, maybe some guys are taking it be super or something. But I'm taking it for other reasons.

> JOEL (fifty-five, white, heterosexual, unknown occupation): Oh no, if you don't feel like a man before you take the pill, you're not a man anyways. No, you have to know where you're at. If you have a little misfunction,

that's minor. But you have to be a man before you go through that. It's not a macho pill.

OLLIE (sixty-four, black, heterosexual, printer): I've talked to a lot of different men about this. Some cannot live without sex. They feel their sex makes them the man that they are. And I'm not sure how important that is to me. I'm a man anyways. It's about self-esteem. What do you think about yourself to begin with?

For Phil, Viagra is a serious product, not to be diminished or trivialized by marketing or associations with extranormal masculinity. For Joel and Ollie, masculinity is something that cannot be medicalized or purchased but is instead derived from self-esteem, reflectiveness, and perspective. Phil, Joel, and Ollie all seem to agree that Viagra fits perfectly in a society that is known for pushing the limits of normal. Along with Hancock and Miles, they are critical of American culture and of Viagra's role in perpetuating the endless pursuit of the quick fix. Hancock and Miles warn of a hedonistic, money-driven, artificial world where there is a pill for everything. For them, Viagra functions as a crutch or Band-Aid solution to social problems such as relationship tensions or male insecurity amidst increasing performance pressures and vast social change.

HANCOCK (sixty-nine, white, heterosexual, retired teacher): We are willing to take the latest thing that is fast and painless. Also, Americans seem to think happiness is their birthright. They take Viagra to become better, happier. And supermen. . . . And maybe those guys who think they need Viagra just need to chill out and reduce stress in their lives. It's about lifestyle modification more than anything, I think.

MILES (forty-five, white, heterosexual, paramedic): I think there is a gross overuse of drugs for happiness and well-being. Feeling depressed, get a script for a mood enhancer . . . feeling tired, get a pill for energy . . . want to have better sex, get some blue magic. What about the age-proven solution of removing or reducing the problems or stress factors affecting your life and then seeing if pharmacological agents are still needed?

Here, Miles and Hancock construct society as drug-infused, producing individuals who are dependent upon pills for health and happiness. They, along with Stu and Ollie, are critical of corporate and biotechnological attempts at constructing needs, desires, and easy markets for products. For Stu, Viagra marketing is not unlike the marketing he sees for antianxiety medications. In both cases, he says, pharmaceutical corporations construct problems, medicalize them, and attempt to fix them medically while ignoring important sociocultural factors in the realms of family, work, and relationships. As Ollie points out, consumers are "made crazy" by society and then manipulated into seeking medical solutions.

STU (thirty-six, white, homosexual, student): [Corporations] are telling us what the problem is—creating a problem—and [then] they give us a solution. We all have anxieties and relationship issues, and they do this to make it look like the way to solve your relationship issue is to take Paxil. The way to deal with your crazy family is to take Paxil. That way you don't have to address the relationship issues, substantive issues. I have a big problem with that.

OLLIE (sixty-four, black, heterosexual, printer): I think everything we do nowadays is overblown. I just see that society is just driving us crazy, making us jump through hoops and do things we really don't need to do. So a drug for everything—I think they—or not they—but the way things are set up, is to make you want to do things. Even if you don't want to do it, you are driven if you pay attention to what's going on. I'm not that kind of person. I won't let you do me that way. You won't be able to drive me that way. I just don't believe in it.

These men are clearly critical of Viagra's potential to enforce social and gender ideals. They refuse to "buy into" mythic masculinity, and they see through the problematic language used to describe medical progress as well as so-called widespread public health crises. In this way some men do resist and reframe masculinity, biotechnology, and medical science in ways that make sense to them. Rather than construct their bodies as troubled, with Viagra as a techno-fix or magical solution, these consumers see Viagra as problematic, contributing to larger social troubles. These skeptical voices, however, are easily drowned out by the overwhelming chorus of those who sing Viagra's praises.

## The Future of the Viagra Man

In our contemporary moment, enhancement technologies are not just instruments of self-improvement, or even self-transformation; they are tools for working on the soul. (Elliott 2003, 53). The new player in this enhancement tale is the man who has been told he is deficient or dysfunctional. With Viagra, a highly successful masculine empowerment campaign is underway, centered around a new late-twentieth-century tool, a magic blue pill, which promises to produce and enhance male bodies, confidence levels, and overall spirits. The male body and concurrently masculinity are constructed as in need of repair and become new sites for medical and biotechnological innovation and healing. In this context, the little blue pill is envisioned as a cutting-edge biotechnology and used as a cultural and material tool in the production and achievement of "true" manhood (Loe 2001). By associating Viagra with the potential for heterosexual potency, confidence, and control, Pfizer Pharmaceuticals has medicalized the attributes we associate with traditional and ideal masculinity (Riska 2000). In this way, Viagra presents a perfect case study in the medicalization of masculinity in America.

Social scientists Janice Raymond (1994), Nora Jacobson (2000), Kathy Davis (2005) and others have shown how medical technologies can be enabling and empowering in late modernity. For example, Davis finds that for women pursuing cosmetic surgery in the Netherlands, their goals are less about beauty and more about being ordinary. Likewise, for many men in my sample, Viagra becomes a tool for pursuing normality. But what happens when "normal" becomes mundane, as is the case for more than a handful of my informants, who consider using Viagra for "male enhancement?"

As more and more men "step up to the plate," to use Pfizer's tagline, and ask their doctor or their friends and Internet pharmacies for Viagra, the medicalization of masculinity increasingly becomes the norm. Folk artist Dan Bern's song "Most American Men" asks, "If everybody else is going to take [Viagra], do I need to take it just to stay competitive?" In a similar vein, social historian Lynne Luciano (2001, 165) warns, "By making the erection the man, science isn't enhancing male sexuality, but sabotaging it." As Viagra consumers in this chapter reveal, Viagra can and is being used to enforce and perpetuate an ideal masculinity and to discipline bodies to fit with cultural and gendered standards and expectations. Many consumers collaborate with medical professionals and pharmaceutical companies in an attempt to understand and fix "broken" bodies by constructing Viagra-infused bodies, or corporate corporealities.

But perhaps of more interest is that my data also reveal the struggle with the necessity for the Viagra-enhanced body and what that struggle represents. As Viagra consumers negotiate their relationship to this product, mainstream ideas about sexuality, masculinity, and health are both reinforced and redefined in important ways. For example, some men insist that "doing" masculinity does not require sexual performance. Others are critical of a society that increasingly promotes and depends upon biotechnology for achieving health and happiness. They have their own ideas about manhood, medicalization, and biotechnology that may or may not fit with Pfizer's approach. In general, this chapter reveals men complicating manhood by constructing not only corporate corporealities but also various and competing masculinities in Viagra's midst (Messner 1997).[21]

As most of us do, the men I spoke with are constantly negotiating social and cultural pressures to be healthy, young, sexual, and in control. For Pfizer, fixing the broken male machine is a simple process with the help of Viagra. Men in this chapter suggest otherwise, pointing out that the bodily "repair" process, the man, and the culture the man belongs to are more complex than Pfizer may acknowledge.

Erectile difficulties are real. But so are the fears that men have about such difficulties, as well as cultural ideals conflating potency, manhood, and individualism. Pfizer has a sizeable market for its product in those men suffering from erectile problems, those fearful of developing impotence, those interested in ensuring potency, and those intrigued by masculine enhancement. As Viagra consumers point out, by medicalizing masculinity, Pfizer and others may be "treating" erectile difficulties but at the same time pathologizing American masculinity itself and making it more elusive and difficult to achieve.

# 2

## Sex the Natural Way: The Marketing of Cialis and Levitra

### Chris Wienke

The introduction of Viagra, the first oral treatment for impotence, has changed the way men view problems with sexual performance. Today, men are more inclined to define and treat their performance problems as medical problems than ever before, thanks in large part to Viagra. Perhaps as a result of Viagra's success, as both a pharmaceutical product and as a cultural phenomenon, there is a now a burgeoning range of rival therapies for the treatment of impotence. Two such therapies recently received Food and Drug Administration (FDA) approval for prescription use: Cialis, an impotence treatment drug developed by the pharmaceutical companies Eli Lilly and ICOS Corporation, and Levitra, another pharmaceutical option being launched by Bayer and GlaxoSmithKline.[1] Like Viagra, both drugs treat impotence by increasing blood flow to the genitals under conditions of sexual arousal, thereby enabling the achievement and maintenance of a "normal" erection.[2] Their advent thus reflects an increasingly medicalized way of thinking about men's sexual problems and their treatment. Medicalization occurs when areas of life not previously considered medical are redefined as problems requiring medical analysis and management (Conrad and Schneider 1980). Impotence, or what health experts call "erectile dysfunction," has become one such example, with impotence medication exemplifying this trend (Mamo and Fishman 2001).

At present, Viagra, the blockbuster drug marketed by Pfizer Pharmaceuticals, dominates the impotence treatment market, vastly outselling
alternative therapies, including penile implants, vacuum pumps, in-
jectibles, and suppositories into the urethra. The drug, which annually
generates $1.5 billion in sales for Pfizer, has been used by over twenty
million men worldwide, easily making it one of the most popular prescription drugs in recent history (Doonar 2003). Available for prescription use only since 1998, Viagra has already become a household word
synonymous with treating impotence. However, with new drugs now
entering the market, Viagra's status as the treatment of choice appears
less certain. According to industry analysts, the emergence of Cialis and
Levitra marks the first serious challenge to Viagra's control over the anti-
impotence market[3] (Gannon 2003). Whether the makers of Cialis and
Levitra can mount a challenge strong enough to rival Viagra will depend
on the marketing strategies they use to sell these products. Both drug
makers promise to market their products aggressively through direct-to-
consumer advertising and plan to match or outspend Pfizer's ninety-
million-dollar advertising budget for Viagra (Howard 2003).[4]

This chapter analyzes the marketing campaigns for Cialis and Levitra
to see what kinds of promotional strategies are emphasized and whether
they offer a different medical discourse on impotence. The study focuses
on the major discursive themes related to the promotion of these drugs
and considers how they contribute to the project of medicalizing male
sexuality. I develop this focus through a discourse analysis of educational
and promotional materials about Cialis and Levitra. The materials analyzed include advertising and Internet promotional literature as well
as media coverage in popular periodicals. Analyzing such materials is
one way of sorting out the strategies used by drug makers to market
these products and illuminates the distinctive logic used to medicalize
this particular (sexual) aspect of masculinity. As sources of medical-
pharmaceutical knowledge, these texts constitute marketing sites for
potential consumers. Through analytical readings of these materials, the
chapter will shed light on the second wave of pharmaceuticals to enter
the male sexual consumer market.

I begin this chapter by examining the historical shifts in constructions
and treatments of impotence and the rise of medicalization as the sociocultural model of choice. Then, after a brief description of the data
collection process, I present the findings from my analysis of Web sites,
advertisements, and media coverage of Cialis and Levitra. Here I argue
that while the marketing campaigns for Cialis and Levitra employ most
of medicine's traditional discourses on impotence, they emphasize several additional discursive themes to help promote these drugs in the

competitive impotence treatment market. My findings reveal four general themes regarding the promotion of these drugs, which I identify as (1) technological advancement, (2) natural sex enhancement, (3) symbolic appeals to hegemonic masculinity, and (4) nonmedical, lifestyle usage. I suggest that these promotional themes have important implications for the medical project of constructing the sexually functional male body. In conclusion, I argue that these new drugs and the discourses they circulate introduce new standards for sexual functioning and medicalize areas of male sexuality not previously seen as requiring medical repair.

## Impotence and Medicalization

Historical and sociological investigations of impotence reveal how medicalization has transformed unacceptable erectile performance into a subject for medical analysis and management (Hall 1991; Mumford 1992; Tiefer 1994). Although impotence has been a concern for men for centuries, only recently, with the rise of sexology in the nineteenth century, has it been explicitly defined and categorized as a medical problem.[5] Prior to the late nineteenth century, impotence was often treated as an unwelcome experience, an unacceptable behavior, a personal trouble, an irregularity, even a sign of perversion. The focus was more on the behavior than on organic sexual differences. For example, in the 1800s, "an anonymous writer in the *Lancet* gave warnings against advising men with 'questionable powers' to marry . . . describing them as 'as a rule, inexpressibly nasty'" (quoted in Hall 1991: 115). This writer, like others at the time, attributed this behavior to the effects of long-continued masturbation and previous excessive intercourse, both of which violated the codes of sexual respectability and the ethic of self-discipline (Hall 1991). Only when impotence became redefined as a medical problem did people come to see it as a distinct, pathological condition associated with individual identity. When the focus shifted from the behavior to the individual man, impotence was no longer considered a perverted act. It was now considered a psychological or physical sickness that requires medical attention.[6] The pathologization of impotence that emerged at the turn of the century provides one instance of how the institutions of science and medicine have medicalized and controlled deviant male bodies and sexualities (see Foucault 1977, 1978).

The construction of impotence as a medical problem was, until recently, thought in most instances to be a psychological problem and thus the domain of sexology, psychiatry, and therapeutic interventions that emphasize treatment for the couple. In recent years, however, the diagnosis and subsequent treatment of impotence has moved to the physiological domain as biomedical experts isolated the physical mechanics of erectile functioning. In the following quote, Leslie Horvitz, a medical writer for *Insight Magazine,* reflects this shift in emphasis while at the same time framing impotence in a way that is very different from the terms used by the anonymous author of the 1800s quoted above:

> The penis contains two chambers, called the corpora cavernosa, filled with smooth muscles, fibrous tissues, veins and arteries. To achieve an erection, the smooth muscles must relax, allowing blood to fill the open spaces and expand the penis. Any illness or disorder that interferes with the normal function of the circulatory system can lead to impotence ... [including] heart disease, stroke, diabetes, kidney disease, chronic alcoholism, atherosclerosis, and vascular disease.... Smoking is a particularly grave factor since it impedes circulation over time.... [Impotence] also can occur because of injury... [and is] linked to prescription drugs for ailments such as hypertension and depression. (1997: 39–40)

One result of this shift in medical thought has been the development of a range of technologies designed to treat erectile dysfunction, from injections to erection pills to aphrodisiacs like Yohimbine hydrochloride to surgical implants. Indeed, the technologically enhanced erection has become the leading edge of America's multibillion-dollar impotence treatment industry. Initially, biomedical treatments were limited primarily to prosthetic implants, a type of surgery that enables erections with or without sexual stimulation and removes physical sensation. However, such treatments have been prone to malfunction and reoperation; thus few patients have opted for surgical treatments (Tiefer 2001). By the 1980s, penile injections (a type of therapy that produces an erection by chemical means) became common, although later studies showed high drop-out rates among patients using this method (Tiefer 2001). Today Viagra, the first oral medication to be approved for impotence, has become the treatment of choice. The drug, which costs approximately eight dollars per pill, is reasonably inexpensive compared to other treatment methods, and, given in pill form, is also less painful and invasive to use.[7] Although access to Viagra legally requires a physician prescription, public demand for it has resulted in loose medical regulation (Carpiano 2001). In fact, the diagnosis of impotence has recently become an almost entirely self-assessed condition, based on a fifteen-item impotence-evaluation instrument (Marshall 2002). The instrument, which was developed by the Center of Sex and Marital Health in New Jersey, is used widely by both specialists (urologists) and primary care physicians (family doctors).

With the advent of Internet pharmacies, which sell Viagra and other medications, medical-pharmaceutical treatments have become even easier to obtain. Such sites provide patients a way to bypass direct contact with physician intervention (Marshall 2002). In doing so, they eliminate the need for face-to-face counseling, allowing patients to avoid addressing other possible causes of their condition and other plausible treatment options (Carpiano 2001).

Social researchers have attributed the current wave of medicalized impotence and its treatment to a range of social and economic factors. According to Tiefer (1994), the contemporary investment in the biomedical construction of impotence derives from an indirect coalition among urologists, medical-pharmaceutical industries, mass media, and various entrepreneurs. These groups have actively promoted a medical view of impotence at the expense of other viable conceptual frameworks, such as political, feminist, and social constructionist (Gagnon 1977; Segal 1990; Parker, Barbosa, and Aggleton 2000). Cultural norms of masculinity, combined with phallocentric constructions of sexuality, have also contributed to the rise of medicalized impotence.[8] Within Western culture, images of manhood are closely tied to ideals of sexual potency and the ability to achieve an erection (Zilbergeld 1992). At the same time, sexual socialization teaches men to view intercourse as the primary component of sexual activity, and anything else as foreplay, afterplay, or special needs (Tiefer 1994; Fracher and Kimmel 1995; Potts 2000). Therefore, when men encounter erectile problems, they may feel like their masculinity is threatened and their sexuality is unnatural or deviant. Medicalized impotence offers men an explanation for their problems that lessens cultural stigmatization, thereby relieving men of blame and individual failure even in the face of impotence (Tiefer 1994). The availability of technological treatments, in turn, offers men the tools with which to manage sexual conformity and to preserve masculine power and confidence (Loe 2001). Consequently, men (and their partners) have become a receptive audience to quick-fix technological solutions as opposed to social or psychological remedies (Tiefer 1994; Fracher and Kimmel 1995; Carpiano 2001). Indeed, as Meika Loe (2001) has argued, the popularity of Viagra and other treatment technologies is in part a response to a crisis of masculinity in modern societies, stemming from the gains of women's liberation and female sexual empowerment. Richard Carpiano (2001) also attributes the popularity of these medicalized treatments to cultural and personal crisis, arguing that public demand for impotence medication played a bigger role in creating the Viagra craze than the medical field itself (see also Hepworth and Featherstone 1998).

In recent years, sexual-enhancement therapies like Viagra have become the focus of the pharmaceutical industry. The increasing privatization of biomedical research, the deregulation of the pharmaceutical industry, and the growing commercial appeal of "lifestyle" drugs have made it possible, and potentially profitable, for pharmaceutical companies to develop and market new medicalized sexual products (Tiefer 2004).[9] While several medicalized therapies have emerged to "manage" women's sexual problems, the medicalization of male sexuality continues to be the driving force behind sexual research, product development, and marketing (Loe 2001). The recent launch of Cialis and Levitra exemplifies this continuing trend. Hailed as viable alternatives to Viagra, these drugs have the potential to become the next blockbuster treatments for erectile problems.

## Methods

As a social researcher with an interest in male sexual medicalization, I wanted to examine the marketing campaigns for Cialis and Levitra to see if these treatments offer a different discourse from Viagra on medicalized impotence. To this end, I conducted a discourse analysis of texts offering promotional information about Cialis and Levitra. Discourse analysis involves a close reading of texts to explore the production and distribution of knowledge in society (Mamo and Fishman 2001). I use advertising, promotional materials, and media coverage in newspapers and magazines because these texts constitute marketing sites for potential consumers. In other words, these are the kinds of texts that consumers might read as they attempt to make sense of impotence, its treatment, and the availability of treatment options.

The materials analyzed include the official Web sites for Cialis and Levitra, print and television advertisements, and over 150 newspaper and magazine articles on Cialis and Levitra, spanning the time when knowledge of these drugs first broke to the immediate aftermath following their FDA approval in 2003. I analyzed the media coverage precisely because the mass media routinely publicize and promote new medical technologies for men's sexual problems (Tiefer 1994; Wienke 2000). As Teifer (1994: 368) writes, "By quoting medical 'experts,' using medical terminology, and by swiftly and enthusiastically publicizing new devices and pharmaceuticals, the mass media legitimize, instruct, and model the proper construction and discourse. People underline and save 'sex health' articles, and...bring in such material...[during patient-doctor visits]." I used Lexis-Nexis to locate articles offering information on Cialis and Levitra, specifically searching for those that offered details on pharmaceutical marketing strategies. I eliminated several types of articles from my final sample because the coverage made too sparse mention of the drugs to be of value or because they represented syndicated columns repeated in other newspapers under new headlines. Of the roughly 150 articles collected in my initial search, forty-six were selected for in-depth analysis. My sample included business news, commentaries, and science and health reports.[10]

In my analysis, I adopt Berger's (1977) argument that the meanings encoded into texts, such as advertisements or Internet promotions, contain a preferred reading. As readers, we can "make sense" of texts precisely because they suggest a certain set of possibilities to us, encouraging us to locate an intended or preferred reading of the texts and the encoded meanings contained within them (White and Gillett 1994). While texts cannot guarantee the decoding of those meanings, readers are unlikely to be able to ignore the preferred reading. As Duncan notes, "responsible textual studies do not assert without absolute certainty how particular texts are interpreted. But they suggest the kinds of interpretations that may take place, based on available evidence and likely interpretations of a particular text. Ultimately these interpretations must be judged on the basis of the persuasiveness and logic of the researcher's discussion" (quoted in White and Gillett 1994: 23).

My analysis of Web sites, advertisements, and media coverage of Cialis and Levitra reveals four general themes regarding the promotion of these drugs: (1) technological advancement, (2) natural sex enhancement, (3) symbolic appeals to hegemonic masculinity, and (4) nonmedical, lifestyle usage. In the first section below, I argue that the materials about Cialis and Levitra construct these drugs as state-of-the-art technologies that promise users optimal erectile results. Next, I argue that these texts promote a presumption about what is natural about male sexuality and represent Cialis and Levitra as technologies that return men to a "natural" state of sexual intimacy. In the third section, I explain how the imagery of professional sports is used in advertising texts to promote a symbolic link between these drugs and hegemonic masculinity. Finally, I argue that these materials construct Cialis and Levitra as lifestyle drugs for the improvement of male sexual satisfaction, whether or not users have "legitimate" sexual health problems. In outlining these discursive themes, I draw on exemplary texts and discuss how each theme, to varying extents, contributes to the medicalization of male sexuality. I suggest that, taken together, these themes work to reposition the medical boundaries of the "sexually functional" and "dysfunctional" male body.

## "We're Not Talking Your Daddy's Viagra": Cialis and Levitra as Technological Advancements

The marketers for Cialis and Levitra employ most of biomedicine's discursive strategies, portraying men's sexuality in biomedical terms, defining the causes of impotence as physiological, and touting medical intervention as the proper response to impotence. At the same time, however, marketers have advanced several additional strategies to construct their products as superior alternatives to other impotence technologies, especially Viagra. One way marketers have promoted Cialis and Levitra as preferable solutions is by appealing to modernist assumptions about technological advancement. The marketers for both drugs base the superiority of their products on their ability to outperform competing technologies in all areas of sexual functioning. To legitimate this claim, marketers have publicized the results of clinical studies that validate their drugs as faster acting, longer lasting, and having fewer side effects than Viagra, the current treatment of choice.[11] By making these clinical differences central to their promotional campaigns, marketers have discursively established Cialis and Levitra as state-of-the-art technologies while simultaneously constructing competing technologies as obsolete.

For example, unlike Viagra, which enables erections for a limited period of time (usually between two to four hours), marketers suggest that Cialis, after ingested, remains effective in the body for up to thirty-six hours. Because of its relatively long-lasting results, advertisers have labeled Cialis "the weekend pill." As one media report explains, the drug "can be taken on a Friday and its effects may still be felt on Sunday morning" (Foley 2002). The makers of Levitra, on the other hand, have distinguished their drug from Viagra by marketing it as faster acting. Clinical tests have shown that Levitra takes effect within fifteen minutes after ingestion, compared with forty to sixty minutes for Viagra.[12] This difference is important, marketers claim, because it "allows you a certain level of spontaneity" (quoted in Gannon 2003). In addition, both drugs are claimed to produce fewer side effects than Viagra, which some users complain causes abnormal vision, headaches, indigestion and diarrhea, and work even after eating a full meal, while Viagra works best on an empty stomach.

The theme of technological advancement was evident in most media stories on Cialis and Levitra. Such stories not only touted Cialis and Levitra as "new and improved" erectile dysfunction products but also depicted competing products as outdated technologies. For example, in addition to repeating findings from clinical studies, media stories often included testimonials by men who have tried different treatment options. An early 2003 article from the *Chicago Sun-Times* illustrates how this literary device adds legitimacy to the marketing theme of technological advancement. In the article, the author tells the story of Manfred Weber, a Viagra user who plans to switch to Levitra: "After more than 40 years of marriage, 'things weren't working so well anymore,' he says. He tried Viagra a few times, but it gave him headaches. After taking Levitra in a clinical trial, the headaches stopped. 'It brought my wife and I closer to each other again,' says Weber, 65. With that trial over, he is biding his time with an occasional Viagra until Levitra is approved in this country" (Fuhrmans 2003). The author of another article also uses the testimonial of a man who prefers one of the new treatment options over Viagra, in this case Cialis. In one of his quotes, the unnamed man appears to be parodying the tag line for a recent Viagra ad ("Let's just say [Viagra] works for me"). He says "I will stick to Cialis because unlike Viagra it works for 24 hours—that *certainly* works for me. It's great" (emphasis added; Young 2003). In media stories such as these, where individual accounts of satisfied customers are found, the media collaborates in publicizing and promoting the marketing theme of technological advancement: it compares new treatment options with Viagra and finds them to be preferable solutions precisely because they offer men the possibility of a "better" sexual performance.

In addition to testimonials, several media stories also included accounts from marketing researchers hired to oversee product focus groups. Such accounts explicitly reflected marketers' claims about technological advancement. A recent article on Cialis in *Business Week* illustrates the use of this strategy. In the article, the author relates the story of a researcher who was hired by Eli Lilly to gauge consumer reaction to Cialis. During one of the focus groups, the participants, whose husbands all suffered from impotence, were asked to watch a prospective TV commercial for the drug. The voice-over in the ad advised: "Introducing Cialis. You can take Cialis anytime and have up to thirty-six hours to respond to your partner, without planning or rushing." The researcher observed the group from the other side of a one-way mirror, while the group's moderator tried to flesh out the main source of the group's interest. As the researcher observed their reactions, she saw one of the participants leap out of her chair and shout "Thirty-six hours! Yeah!"

According to the report in the article, the researcher had never seen a focus group in her fifteen-year career of monitoring such groups get as excited as they did about a product. "It was a marketer's dream," she says (Arndt 2003). Apparently, what makes the drug "a marketer's dream" is that even participants in focus groups recognize it as a technological breakthrough that extends the male body's sexual capacities.

In this account, as in others provided to journalists by industry representatives, Cialis and Levitra are depicted as progressive discoveries in the scientific search for solutions to a sexual health problem. This theme, which is reflected in media reports and manufacturer publicity, contributes to the medicalization of male sexuality in at least two ways. First, it provides a justification for medicalization. The emphasis is placed on the novelty, sophistication, and advantages of these technologies. There is little in these materials that offers men an alternative to the scientific discourse of medicalized impotence. Instead, the new treatments are portrayed as sophisticated additions to the reining paradigm of medical management. Second, the materials that reflect this theme extend medicalization into previously undiagnosed areas of male sexual "health." The specific sexual concerns emphasized in these materials are extended to include the timing of erectile response, the duration of erectile readiness, and the side effects of erectile interventions. By emphasizing the efficacy of Cialis and Levitra in producing faster-acting and longer-lasting erections with fewer side effects, these texts broaden the clinical framing of male sexual functioning to include the ability to respond immediately to sexual urges, to respond to sexual urges without planning or rushing, and to function sexually with few unwanted health effects. In this way, the media and marketers collaborate in medicalizing areas of male sexuality not previously requiring medical help.

## Sex the Natural Way: Cialis and Levitra as Nature's Enhancements

In playing up these technological advantages, the narratives surrounding these products simultaneously play on cultural assumptions about what is "natural" about men's (and women's) sexuality. In addition to enhanced performance, the marketing campaigns for these drugs center on their products' ability to simulate a "natural" sexual response unencumbered by time or rational calculation. Unlike Viagra, which takes effect up to an hour before (and stops being effective a few hours after) sex is planned, marketers for Cialis and Levitra promise results that mimic the "natural" sexual cycle, which is spontaneous, worry-free, and uninhibited by external considerations. In doing so, marketers have discursively established a link between nature and technology. The marketing implies that, through these drugs, users will return to a natural state of sexual intimacy. Of course, the very idea of "natural" sex invoked in the marketing of these drugs is itself a sexual script, shaped by societal and cultural assumptions (Gagnon 1977). Associating sex with spontaneous feeling is thus a discursive strategy that constructs sex as natural.

The emphasis on Cialis and Levitra as technological enhancements for natural sexuality was apparent in the media coverage of these drugs. Media stories routinely quoted medical experts and pharmaceutical spokespersons in the promotion of this theme. The following quotes from Carole Copeland, a spokeswoman for Eli Lilly and ICOS, were found in the *New York Times* and the *Boston Globe*: "Men tell us that, when they take other pills, they feel like they're on a stopwatch and that adds to the pressure they already feel. They would like a treatment that would disconnect taking a tablet from intimacy" (quoted in Harris 2003a). Cialis, on the other hand, "offers a longer window of opportunity for intimacy, and that's what men and their partners say they miss most when they have erectile dysfunction: those special moments that just come naturally" (quoted in Goldberg 2003). Viewed in such terms, it would appear that Cialis restores control to the body and its bodily functions in ways that Viagra and other technologies do not. With Cialis, control returns to the body because the drug acts through the body's natural processes of arousal. A recent news report on Levitra reflects a similar sentiment regarding the relationship between control and nature, noting that "Viagra users are as controlled by the clock as a prisoner during conjugal visits: You have to wait two hours after a meal before taking it, then wait another hour for it to kick in, then hustle up and get your business done within four hours, before the little warden says visiting hours are over. Levitra, by contrast, doesn't interact with food, and works within 20 minutes" (McDougall 2003).

The advertisements for these drugs also emphasize the theme of technology as an enhancement for natural sex. This theme was particularly apparent in the ads for Cialis. In a promotional campaign entitled "Choose the moment," marketers for Cialis have created a number of television spots with scenes of couples snuggling and slowly caressing "to emphasize cozy, tender, or playful moments" (Arndt 2003). A soundtrack of easy, laid-back jazz accompanies these visual images. In addition, the scenes in the ads are lengthened so that the camera seems to linger with each couple, a subtle reminder that with Cialis there is no hurry. The voice-over advises: "When the moment is right, you'll be ready." A similar representation appeared on the home page of the Cialis Web site. The caption reads, "Cialis is here. Will you be ready?" Accompanying the caption is an image of a middle-aged couple bathing side by side in adjacent bathtubs—a signifier for romantic activity. Below the representation appears a heading entitled "What is Cialis?" under which a description of the drug is provided: "Cialis is a prescription medication...shown to improve erectile function...up to 36 hours following dosing" (Lilly ICOS, www.cialis.com). A recent online ad for Cialis makes the fusion of technology and nature even more explicit, claiming that the drug "works twice as fast as Viagra...[and] lasts 9 times longer...so you'll never miss the moment again." The visual accompanying the written text features a younger heterosexual couple, without clothes, gently holding and caressing one another. The reader is unable to tell whether the sexual "moment" has begun or ended. The image thus enhances the meaning behind the textual message: unlike Viagra, Cialis works in ways that reflect the body's "natural" urges, freeing couples to engage in spontaneous, worry-free lovemaking.

Marketing these drugs as enhancements to natural sex may seem contradictory, given that it is only through technological assistance that "natural" lovemaking is made possible. The spontaneity promised by drug makers depends on the use of technology, along with the medical assumptions that inform that use. The physiological effects of these drugs may produce the feeling of flexible, trouble-free lovemaking, but only within the confines of technological surveillance, regulation, and control. To reconcile this apparent contradiction, the marketers for Cialis and Levitra have reified their technology "as more *natural* than natural" (Mamo and Fishman 2001: 22). When sexually aroused, the body sometimes loses control (impotence), causing a breakdown in the sexual script of natural sexuality. With Viagra, control is restored to the body, but in an unnatural way, restricted by time and other considerations. Cialis and Levitra, on the other hand, incorporate technology within the "natural" body in a seamless way, such that it is difficult to tell where the body leaves off and the technology begins. Through this construction, the use of technology becomes the natural act (Mamo and Fishman 2001: 21–22).

The link between technology and nature in these marketing materials has other important implications for the medicalization of male sexuality, specifically with regard to constructions of sexual functioning. The materials suggest that sexual functioning involves more than the *mere* ability to attain and maintain an erection for the purpose of sexual intercourse. Rather, it involves doing so naturally according to the body's organic cycle of sexual arousal. By marketing these drugs as technologies capable of facilitating a "natural" sexual response, these texts present a new guideline for assessing functional male sexuality and its reparable deviations. Here "natural spontaneity" becomes a boundary point between sexual fitness and sexual deviation.

## "Tackling Men's Health": The Marketing of
## Cialis and Levitra through Popular Sports

With the possible exception of sex, few cultural idioms are invoked as often in advertisements aimed at men as that of the world of professional sports (Renson and Careel 1986; Grove et al. 1989). Corporate advertising campaigns for products ranging from beer to shaving cream regularly use sports to appeal to men. At the same time, professional sports provide advertisers an ideal setting for reaching large male audiences. Sporting events, especially televised ones, attract millions of male viewers each week (Sage 1998). Given this advertising tradition, it should not be surprising to find that the impotence treatment industry has turned to professional sport as a platform for marketing its products. Viagra's sponsorship of Major League Baseball is one such example. In fact, Pfizer recently phased out its previous Viagra spokesman, former presidential candidate Bob Dole, in favor of Rafael Palmeiro, the Texas Rangers' first baseman who recently hit his five-hundredth home run. Pfizer also sponsors a Viagra car on the NASCAR racing circuit and during many of the races provides a van where fans can receive free testing for erectile problems.

The marketers of Cialis and Levitra have continued this trend through sponsorships of other professional sports leagues and through campaigns headed by other sports celebrities. The makers of Levitra, for example, recently secured a twenty-million-dollar package with the National Football League (NFL), which will air television advertisements for the drug during games, and have hired Mike Ditka, the ex–NFL player and coach, as a spokesman. In addition to exclusive league sponsorship, the Levitra makers have cut individual deals with a number of NFL teams. The makers of Cialis, on the other hand, were recent benefactors for a racing yacht in the America's Cup and have sponsored NCAA men's basketball and the Professional Golf Association. At present, Cialis does not have a sports celebrity spokesperson.

As a cultural medium, sporting events are ideal for advertising because they are one of the few events for which a large number of men are regularly assembled, but it is the symbolism of sports that inscribes products in advertisements with cultural meaning. This is true in the marketing campaigns for impotence treatment drugs. In the case of Cialis and Levitra, marketers are using the symbolism of sports to appeal to "hegemonic masculinity": the socially dominant conceptions, cultural ideals, and ideological constructions of what is appropriate masculinity (Connell 1987). Competitive sports, especially contact sports like football, embody many of the valued characteristics of hegemonic masculinity. These include physical strength, skill, aggression, control, force, athleticism, and heterosexuality (Messner 1992). In this way, then, sports are not just a cultural medium but a masculine medium in which "the combination of skill and force" in athletic experience becomes a defining feature of masculine identity (Connell 1987: 85). Marketers of products like Cialis and Levitra depend on such symbolism to sell their products, thereby appealing to potential users' aspirations to attain or maintain hegemonic masculinity (Mamo and Fishman 2001: 23). In discussing Levitra's sponsorship of the NFL, a spokeswoman for Bayer explains: "We are talking to men in a language they can understand."

This language is evident in a number of recent advertisements for Levitra. As part of a promotional campaign entitled "Tackling Men's Health," the advertisements feature the football legend "Iron" Mike Ditka.[13] Known for his toughness, aggressive manner, and unrelenting resolve, Ditka publicly symbolizes all that is valued in current constructions of hegemonic masculinity—the highly skilled and powerful body, the supposedly virile heterosexuality, and competitive achievement. Ditka's presence, like Dole's before him, is intended to destigmatize erectile dysfunction. However, unlike his predecessor, whose image appeals primarily to older men, Ditka projects a more phallic-like image. In the ads, Ditka speaks frankly about his own difficulties with sexual health and his attempts to overcome them. At the same time, he uses his experiences in professional sports to connect with the targeted audience. The ads, which run the tag line "Stay in the Game," compare Levitra's use for erectile dysfunction to the physical sacrifices involved in athletic competition, including playing through pain and injuries. In one of these ads, Ditka advises "Any coach will tell you that you need to stay in the game." The statement, which should be familiar to anyone acquainted with the values of competitive sports, reflects a core lesson in traditional athletic socialization: sports involve physical sacrifice, even at the expense of pain. Within sport, physical sacrifice is glorified as a legitimate, even necessary means to achieving individual and team goals. Athletes are taught to play in pain, to sacrifice their bodies for particular pursuits, and that to do so is courageous and manly (Sabo 1995). This unrelenting emphasis on physical sacrifice in sport has contributed to the normalization of pain and the subsequent provision and legitimating of pain medication (i.e., "painkillers"), an occurrence that, in effect, medicalizes masculinity in competitive action (Messner 1992).

In the ad for Levitra, marketers have established a new twist on this old lesson: just as athletes need to manage physical discomfort to remain competitively active, men with erectile dysfunction need to manage sexual discomfort to remain sexually active. This twist deftly constructs Levitra as a legitimate, and perhaps necessary, recourse for male sexual action. In this way, Levitra becomes one more tool in the project of managing functional masculinity. Like painkillers for athletes, Levitra medicalizes masculinity. The drug transforms the limits of the male body so that men can be "men" again.

Another ad featuring Ditka aired exclusively during the 2004 Super Bowl, an event that regularly reaches 60 to 70 percent of the households watching television (Sage 1998). In the ad, Ditka discusses the differences between football and baseball, a subtle reminder that Levitra sponsors the former, and Viagra the later. Here Ditka compares erect manly-men to football, able to play in any weather conditions, as opposed to baseball, with fragile players who do not even play when it rains. "Baseball needs Levitra," says Ditka. The ad, which suggests an attempt by marketers to distinguish their drug from Viagra, uses a sports analogy to transmit a message about Levitra and its competitive rival. Apparently, Levitra, like football, is tough and enduring, while Viagra, like baseball, is sensitive to external conditions. This distinction discursively positions Levitra as the *more* masculine of the two products, and its medical effects as more potent.

In sports-themed ads like this one, the imagery of sports is used to symbolically link erection products to hegemonic masculinity. The ads, which appeal to men's aspirations to attain or maintain hegemonic masculinity, essentially promise consumers masculine achievement through the use of a pill. As in the example above, the ads attribute masculine characteristics to these products, essentially constructing them as tools for assembling masculinity (Loe 2001: 115). Here masculine identity itself becomes attainable with the help of medical intervention.

## Making Sex Better: Cialis and Levitra as Lifestyle Products

A recent television advertisement for Levitra features a young man, looking barely thirty, trying to throw a football through a tire. Initially, he misses, hitting the tire's side. However, after Levitra is mentioned, he shoots the ball straight through the tire again and again, and is joined by an attractive young woman, presumably his wife. The voice-over says, "Sometimes you need a little help staying in the game. When you're in the zone, it's all good." The ad, which has aired repeatedly over the past half-year of 2004, accomplishes several things in transmitting a message about Levitra. First, it effectively symbolizes the sexual activity which the product is designed to treat with no taint of obscenity or pornography. This is expressed through the image of a man penetrating a tire with a ball. Second, and perhaps more importantly, the ad reflects an attempt by the makers of Levitra to market the drug to a youthful, presumably "healthy," male demographic, men who, according to one advertising executive, "just need a little help with [their] aim." It is through the imagery and message of ads like this one that Levitra is constructed as a lifestyle drug. Such ads are intended to appeal to not only men with impotence but also large segments of the male populace, whether or not they have bona fide medical problems.

The construction of Levitra as a lifestyle product as opposed to a remedy for a health-related problem represents a shift in the marketing of impotence treatment technologies. For example, in Pfizer's initial advertising campaign, Viagra was marketed to mature audiences as a medical treatment for erectile failure caused by age-related conditions (Marshall and Katz 2002). In the original print and television advertisements, the company featured spokesman Bob Dole and images of white-haired couples dancing. Pfizer insisted at the time that it was not trying to encourage recreational use among otherwise healthy men. By contrast, GlaxoSmithKline and Bayer, the comarketers of Levitra, boldly admit their attempts to expand the impotence treatment market through appeals to recreational use. Unlike Pfizer, whose initial goals for Viagra were to treat impotence by helping men achieve penetration and ejaculation, Levitra's sellers stress the goal of sexual satisfaction (Harris 2003b). "We've done a lot of research on trying to understand what men want," says Nancy Bryan, vice president for marketing at Bayer. "And what they want is to improve the quality of their erections, to get one that's hard enough and lasts long enough for a satisfying sexual experience" (quoted in Harris 2003b). Another report explains: "the ads [for Levitra] have come a long way since the Bob Dole days. . . . That ad, with all of its Freudian implications, says everything you need to know about where the male sexual revolution is heading. ED 'erectile dysfunction' is old news. EQ 'erectile quality' is now the name of the game" (CBSNEWS.com 2004).[14]

Perhaps the most obvious illustration of this marketing strategy, wherein impotence drugs are repackaged for nonmedical uses, is found on Levitra's Web site. Although the home page of this Web site describes Levitra as a medical treatment for erectile dysfunction, in subsequent pages the site either opts for the term *erectile quality* (EQ) to describe the condition that the drug is intended to treat or else uses this term interchangeably with the medical term *erectile dysfunction* (ED). This apparent shift in terminology reflects a continuing trend in the medical-pharmaceutical construction of male sexuality (Marshall and Katz 2002). As stated in the introduction to this chapter, until recently, the term *impotence*, a psychological diagnosis, was used by medical professionals to describe the condition in which the male is unable to attain and maintain an erection sufficient for satisfactory sexual intercourse. Under this construction, the condition is understood as a psychological problem, and thus treatable with psychotherapeutic interventions. With the "discovery" of the physiological origins of the condition, however, impotence became erectile dysfunction, a biomedical diagnosis, and thus treatable with pharmaceutical interventions (Mamo and Fishman 2001). Replacing the term *impotence* with *erectile dysfunction* in the medical sciences was intended to reposition the condition as a physiological disorder and to lessen the pejorative stigma traditionally associated with it (Tiefer 1994). The term *erectile quality*, on the other hand, is entirely a marketing construction designed to appeal to larger segments of the public, not just those medically diagnosed.

A definition of EQ appears on a page linked to the home page of Levitra's Web site under a heading entitled "What is erection quality (EQ)?":

> In market research, men identified three things as essential elements of achieving a satisfactory erection, including: The ability to attain an erection; erection hardness; [and] the ability to maintain it for satisfactory sex. Taken together these make up erection quality (EQ). Many men have been, or will be, concerned with the quality of their erections at some point in their life. It may be an occasional difficulty in getting or maintaining an erection; it could be an erection that is just not as hard as it once was; or it may be a consistent inability to achieve an erection. (www.levitra.com)

Defined in these terms, EQ is a sexual condition that exists both within and beyond the medical category ED. By implication, Levitra may be viewed as a pharmaceutical treatment that works not just for medically diagnosed health conditions but for life-limiting conditions, however defined. The following four pages of the Web site describe "How an erection works," the "Things that can affect your erection quality," "How Levitra may help improve your erectile function," and how "Maintaining your erection quality (EQ) is part of maintaining your overall health" (Bayer, www.levitra.com). Reading through these pages, it becomes obvious that the focus of Levitra is not necessarily on the medical condition it has been authorized to treat, but on how the effects of that treatment will affect other aspects of one's life (Mamo and Fishman 2001); hence the term "erection quality."

Subsequent pages of the site include a section on "Talking to your doctor" about EQ, which provides helpful hints on what to say during and how to prepare for a doctor visit, and a section on "Information for partners," which, among other things, informs partners what men want in order to enjoy sex: "They want consistent, reliable erectile quality." In between these sections appears an "Erectile Function Questionnaire" in which readers are able to assess their erectile quality according to industry-specified standards, using it to gauge whether or not they exhibit signs of erectile problems. However, as I discovered in filling out the form, even scores that indicate no sign of erectile problems may not necessarily mean that there is no problem. In response to my results, the site read: "Your [score] . . . indicates that you have no signs of erectile dysfunction (ED). While you may not be having problems with your erectile function, you may still want to talk with your doctor if you have any concerns about your erectile quality (EQ)." The evaluation may thus provide the reader with reassurance regarding the normality of his erectile function (as in my case), but it also leaves room for speculation, especially in light of Levitra's efficacy at improving "erectile quality." The reader is left to decide for himself whether erectile normality is sufficient, or whether his already erect erection requires further "improvement."

As lifestyle drugs, Cialis and Levitra promise life-enhancing results. In particular, they promise sexual satisfaction in the form of a pill. The marketing of Cialis and Levitra as lifestyle drugs reinforces a medical-pharmaceutical model of male sexuality, with the emphasis of that model on penile erectility. The promotional materials represent erectility as a phenomenon capable of enhancement and improvement through technological intervention. Conversely, these texts reconfigure the intended user of erectile interventions. The intended user "is now configured not just as the man who, for whatever reason, is unable to get or keep an erection most of the time, but includes all those whose erections could be 'improved'" (Marshall and Katz 2002: 61). By repackaging these drugs for lifestyle use, marketers widen the application of their products to include areas of sexuality not previously considered in need of improvement, expanding their market in the process.

## Conclusion

Pharmaceutical company interest in male sexuality has grown rapidly since Viagra's popular emergence on the market in 1998. Spurred by Viagra's success, pharmaceutical companies are now on the lookout for the next miracle drug that can be manufactured, marketed, and sold to men. Today, Viagra, the pill that revolutionized impotence treatment, faces stiff competition from two new entrants to the market, Cialis and

Levitra. Although both drugs work in much the same way as Viagra, they promise to take male sexuality to a new level of performance and functionality. By pushing male sexuality beyond the limits of previous technologies, these drugs introduce new standards for functional sexuality and create new medically treatable deviations.

In some ways, the introduction of Cialis and Levitra reflects an old medical theme. As with Viagra, these drug makers rely on most of medicine's discursive strategies in marketing their products. Their marketing campaigns defend the legitimacy of impotence as a medical problem, uphold prevailing medical claims about the causes of impotence, and justify medical intervention as the proper response. In other ways, however, the marketing campaigns, in their attempt to distinguish these products from other technologies, offer a new discourse on impotence, medicine, and male sexuality. As this chapter has shown, this discursive move is significant because it essentially repositions the clinical boundaries of the sexually functional and dysfunctional male body. These drugs and the discourses they circulate promise to alter the male body and its sexual functioning in ways that Viagra and other technologies do not. Cialis and Levitra are constructed as technologies that enable the male body, or at least a part of it (the penis), to become sexually functional in ways that surpass the effects of other technologies. The sexually functional male body is now configured as a body that responds immediately when needed, responds without planning or rushing, works like nature (spontaneous, worry-free, uninhibited by external considerations), exhibits the ideals of masculine physicality, and is always sexually satisfied. Anything less is sexually dysfunctional and in need of medical repair.

As I have argued, the materials analyzed for this study represent Cialis and Levitra and their reported body-altering effects in several ways. First, they represent Cialis and Levitra as state-of-the-art technologies that offer users an optimal sexual performance. Users are promised fast-acting erections lasting long durations with few side effects. Second, these texts represent Cialis and Levitra as technological enhancements to natural sex. The marketing materials promise a return to natural, worry-free intimacy through the consumption of these products. This marketing strategy plays on cultural assumptions about what is natural about men's sexuality. In addition, these campaigns use the imagery of sports to symbolically link these drugs to hegemonic masculinity. Here the message emerges that one can attain masculinity in the form of a pill. Finally, they construct these drugs as lifestyle products that can enhance sexual satisfaction, whether or not users have bona fide sexual health problems. In this way, the marketing not only encourages medicalization for legitimate sexual problems but advocates the medical approach to nonmedical concerns. All together, these themes work to expand the domain of sexual fitness and the reach of medical repair.

In the years ahead, therapies that promise to solve men's sexual concerns, enhance their sexual performance, or make sex "better than the real thing" will continue to flood the marketplace (Mamo and Fishman 2001: 29). Indeed, several new therapies are already in development and could be available within two to three years, including a nasal spray, which works through the brain, stimulating sexual arousal; a topical cream, which has no major side effects, other than initial burning, stinging, or tingling; and a pill that dissolves under the tongue, which bypasses the digestive system, blocking the release of the adrenaline that obstructs sexual arousal (Allen 2003). With the increase in such therapies, it is likely that pharmaceutical drug development and marketing will play an even larger role in promoting medicalization, subjecting further areas of male sexual life to medical control and regulation. It is thus imperative that social scientists consider the implications of this newest stage in the medicalization of male sexuality.

# 3

# The Leaky Male Body: Forensics and the Construction of the Sexual Suspect

Lisa Jean Moore and Heidi Durkin

## Sperm as Evidence

As necessary components to certain types of sexual encounters, biological reproduction, and disease transmission, semen and sperm—quintessentially male bodily fluids—figure prominently in heterogeneous social relationships. Their depictions in a variety of texts display an understanding of these fluids as intimately linked with masculinity, even as actual men or masculine actors performing socially relevant activities. Consider the depiction of sperm in children's books—"sperm can swim so fast and so far" (Harris 1999, 22)—and in both allopathic and homeopathic medical textbooks—"one sperm *penetrates* the cell membrane" (Premkumar 2003, 436). Moreover, semen, left at the scene of a sex crime, has come to be seen as the gold standard of incriminating evidence about male action and intention, to be processed and distilled by bioforensic technicians. Indeed, in aggregate, seminal discourses present sperm cells and their male interpreters as solely responsible for complex social processes such as reproduction, disease transmission, incrimination, and exoneration.[1]

Across a range of texts and settings, semen is represented as engendered, malleable, agentic, emotive, instructive, sacred, profane, entertaining, controversial, empowering, dirty, clean, normal, abnormal, potent, impotent, powerful, incriminating, anthropomorphic, uniform, polymorphic, and deterministic (Moore 2002, 2003; Moore and Schmidt 1999; Schmidt and Moore 1998). Despite this variation, however, meanings attributed to semen are overwhelmingly deployed to reinforce—and elaborate—gender-based power relationships by, for example, implying that men have sexual power over women and men are unable to control their impulses.

This chapter illustrates the consistent albeit heterogeneous ways in which semen (and, by extension, men) are constructed in the course of forensic criminal investigations. Specifically, we demonstrate that through the rise of deoxyribonucleic acid (DNA) forensics techniques in criminal investigation, popular entertainment, and everyday life, sperm has emerged as a proxy for female testimony about male sexual action, agency, and motives and that sperm is increasingly positioned and understood as a symbol of male sexual action and agency itself. Just as women's motives, capacities, and agency have been reduced to their bodily fluids and reproductive capacities and processes, so are men's fluids being reduced to their sexual and reproductive capacities and processes. Just as women continue to be scientifically and culturally produced as leaky bodies (Shildrick 1997), so are men being produced as leaky bodies. This suggests that men are undergoing similar processes of medical and scientific reduction and subjugation that women underwent—indeed, that the medicalization of masculinity, while perhaps most visible in the publicly scientized world of the twenty-first century, has existed for centuries.

In the pages that follow, we explore the intersections of multiple bio-social-forensics worlds producing knowledge about sperm through new scientific techniques. The biomedical world of DNA technologies, the criminal justice world of forensics, and the popular world of entertainment all collaborate to create particular meanings about dangerous, amoral men and incriminating sperm. What these social worlds have in common is their construction and exploitation of sperm as a reliable "silent witness" to male sexual malfeasance and, sometimes, their innocence. In analyzing the biomedical, scientific, historical, legal, and popular documentation of DNA forensics as data, we illustrate the interplay between these texts and our social practices in the creation of discourses of masculinity, specifically, discourses that medicalize masculinity by rendering it reducible to and visible in bodily fluids that represent male action. In the case of sex crimes, a shift from testimony to DNA forensics has cast sperm as a silent witness to be manipulated by various professionals. (While we concentrate on the effects of this on men, it is important to note that this has consequences for women as well: with this emergence of DNA biomedical technologies, women are effectively erased. Because women are no longer needed to narrate their lived experience, this erasure is a convenient solution to the "age-old problem" of women as faulty, unreliable, or biased rape victims.[2])

Three different social worlds have established themselves around the manipulation of semen as evidence (the boundary object). First, today, federal, state, and local *crime scene investigators* probe locations of seminal residue—sheets, clothing, underwear, vagina, rectum—and analyze them for DNA markers.[3] Second, capitalizing on the technological imperative of these crime-fighting innovations, *sex crime entertainment television programs* incorporate cutting-edge DNA technologies without specifying the constraints of governmental (federal, state, or local) budget shortfalls. Finally, there is a growing field of *at-home semen evidence collection* to be used for personal sleuthing (i.e., checking the sheets or taking a wife's or husband's underwear if extradyadic encounters are suspected).[4] Because a long history of developing these practices precedes our current legal, medical, and popular practices, we begin our analysis with a summary of the history of semen forensics.

In the case of forensic sciences, the criminalization of masculinity has developed simultaneously with the medicalization of masculinity. The interdigitation of criminology and medicine is not a new phenomenon. Indeed, as Shelia Jasanoff explores, there is a long history of blurry borders between science and law. Through her interpretive analysis of a range of significant court cases, Jasanoff (1995, 8) determines that "the cultures of law and science are in fact mutually constitutive," that is, "these institutions JOINTLY produce our social and scientific knowledge [emphasis in original]." Our interpretation of forensics history argues that the long-standing criminalization of men is being institutionally and conceptually melded with—and supported by—the medicalization of masculinity.

After establishing our theoretical grounding, we describe our methodological choices for analyzing the myriad data about semen and DNA forensics. We then review the historical record of forensic discovery and use of semen as evidence in crime investigation. Moving our analysis to the hugely popular television franchise of sex crime entertainment, we interrogate both the popularization of DNA forensics techniques and popular representations of the biomedical application of these tools in the criminal justice system. Following this account of the sex crime entertainment industry, we briefly examine the cottage industry of mail order fidelity testing. Throughout our analysis of the biomedical, scientific, historical, legal, and popular documentation of DNA forensics, we highlight the role of these texts in the social construction of masculinity as sexually suspect and best scrutinized and regulated by forensics—a medical and criminal agency of social control.

## Leaky Male Bodies and Masculine Threats

Two substantive areas of scholarship provide a backdrop for our work on the medicalization of male bodily fluids. The first is the germinal work of the anthropologist Mary Douglas, who contends that "the body provides the basic scheme for all symbolism" (1966, 163). These bodily symbols located in and on the body represent profound sociocultural markers; as Douglas (1966, 4) writes, "I suggest that many ideas about sexual dangers are better interpreted as symbols of the relation between parts of society as mirroring designs of hierarchy or symmetry which apply in larger social systems." Meanings attributed to bodily fluids indicate sociocultural processes of ascribing meaning to social interactions—these collective representations are transmitted in part through medical-industrial complexes and health care encounters (both allopathic and homeopathic). Working in a similar vein, feminist philosopher Margrit Shildrick (1997) finds that female bodies are constructed within biomedical and bioethical discourse as *leaky*; the female body is messy, unbounded, shifting, porous, flexible, and unpredictable. Indeed, anthropological fieldwork demonstrates the cross-cultural experiences of women's bodies as polluting because of their leakiness—"a bleeding vagina and dripping nipples testif[y] to its inability to remain in control" (Tsoffar 2004, 10; e.g., Farmer 1988). Shildrick and Price (1999, 3) argue that this leakiness contaminates rational and bounded spaces—"As the devalued processes of reproduction make clear, the body has a propensity to leak, to overflow the proper distinctions between self and other, to contaminate and engulf." Although this leakiness has traditionally been depicted in pejorative terms, Shildrick's work attempts to resurrect leakiness as an asset in times of poststructural subjecthood, belonging to a subject that is nomadic rather than stable. These theories (à la Shildrick and Price, Tsoffar, and Farmer) about female leakiness can be a springboard for understanding sperm as soiling social spaces.

The second area is that of masculinity studies, which encompasses the work of interdisciplinary scholars who aim to disturb the taken-for-granted and essential notions of masculinity as arising from obviously natural male bodies and notes that while many versions of masculinity have existed through historical eras, not all masculinities are created equally. R. W. Connell (1995) has coined the term "hegemonic masculinity" to refer to a type of masculinity that is "constructed in relation to various subordinated masculinities as well as in relation to women." The ascendance of hegemonic masculinity, Connell argues, is supported by social structures in which masculinity is embedded—religion, politics, urban space, athletics, and popular culture—and this concept helps to explain that while different images of sperm and semen exist in different social worlds and thus produce different versions of masculinity, some of these images of masculinity elevate certain types of men, for example heterosexual, white, middle-class, reproductive, monogamous men "above" men who are homosexual, of color, lower class, nonprocreative or sterile, and nonmonogamous.

Two points of relevance to our work must be made here. First, the power of the natural (hard) sciences to *naturalize* these (and other) hierarchies is considerable because of their privileged epistemological position as exclusive producers of "official" knowledge. In a circular process, these practices and procedures rely on the presumed validity of socially produced knowledge. Firmly situated in the medical/scientific/legal nexus, forensic science claims to have an airtight lock on methods of determining male guilt or innocence. Second, the hierarchical ranking of men through hegemonic masculinity creates an inherent and ongoing competition for a singular and elusive top position. Patriarchal institutions, like the medical-industrial complex, the bioscientific enterprise, and the criminal justice systems, often pit men against one another in the pursuit of dominance, through which men represent other men as flawed, unworthy, or immoral. As is revealed in forensics discourses, men investigate seminal stains to prove the flawed character of other men by, among other practices, imbuing sperm cells with masculine attributes and foibles.

DNA testing of semen is performed routinely to identify perpetrators of specific crimes characterized by sexual activity. (Similar testing of female sexual fluids is neither as commonplace nor pursued as vigorously—semen analysis provides an additional means of social control over the actions of men but not of women.) Semen is thus defined, managed, and represented as evidentiary for the protection of women from men and as protecting men who would be falsely accused of deviant sexual behavior. Interestingly, while semen as evidence also has the potential to protect men from sexual violence from other men, not much is heard about this taboo subject. Thus the social contexts in which semen analyses are performed seem to be defined by hegemonically masculine notions of sex and crime and would appear to be used to punish certain types of sexual violence but not others. Semen and its biotechnical interpreters can define and identify criminal acts and actors and are thus central agents in the medicalization, criminalization, and control of masculinity.

## Methods

This chapter is part of a larger quest to create a formal grounded theory of semen as multiply constructed in our social worlds. We understand semen as a boundary object (Star and Griesemer 1989), that is, the same object, semen, is brought into different arenas, and its flexibility allows it to be used for local purposes and inscribed with local meaning by different social worlds (Clarke 1991). Meanings about semen accrue through practices and uses, and these meanings bleed into one another. At a forensic investigation, for example, a rapist is sometimes characterized as a "donor," neutralizing the stigma of the individual man and replacing him with a reproductive signifier.

Although this study does not claim to be either exhaustive or representative of the entire realm of semen and DNA forensics, we attempt to gather and triangulate data from three types of sources. Focusing our analytic lens on sperm itself provides interesting perspectives from which to interpret how sperm "is spent," "is reabsorbed," "swims," "spurts," careens, and crashes through ducts, penises, vaginas, test tubes, labs, families, culture, and politics. We reviewed forensic and criminalistic textbooks to grasp the history and principles of the field and coded and analyzed transcripts from television shows (three years of *CSI: Crime Scene Investigation*, two years of *Law and Order*, and two years of *NYPD Blue*) for their references to semen and sperm. After reviewing over two hundred Web sites advertising at-home infidelity testing services and kits between September 2, 2003, and November 21, 2003, we selected and analyzed eleven of these. A Google search for "infidelity kits" completed on September 2, 2003, listed over 2,700 sites, and of these hits at least one in ten of them led to Checkmate—the most popular infidelity kit. Each data source was assigned to two coders, who examined dimensions such as the description of sperm or semen, the frequency of references to sperm, the verbs used to animate sperm, and images of sperm.

These data were analyzed based on a modified grounded theory methodology. According to Anselm Strauss (Strauss and Corbin 1994), a key developer of grounded theory, it is through one's immersion in the data that these comparisons become the "stepping stones" for formal theories of patterns of action and interaction between and among various types of social units. Grounded theory is a deductive process whereby analysts incorporate as much data as possible in order for the formative theories to be used as deductive tools. This tool, the grounded theory, ultimately aims to incorporate the range of human experiences in its articulation and execution. As Strauss and Corbin (1994, 273) write, "Theory evolves during actual research, and it does this through continuous interplay between analysis and data collection."

Our methodology combines grounded theory techniques with content and discourse analysis as a way to develop theoretically rich explanations and interpretations of references to semen. Content analysis is the study of *social artifacts* (Babbie 1989), which are used to make inferences to the larger society (Weber 1990). Like other qualitative research, content analysis can be *exploratory* and *descriptive*, enabling limited insight into why significant relationships or trends occur. The aim is not to standardize facts into scientific units but rather to appreciate and demonstrate the range of variation of a particular phenomenon. Outliers, representations that do not fall neatly into the collection of the most common themes and concepts, are useful because they enable analysts to capture this range of variation and dimensions of the concepts. This process builds an understanding of the diversity of human experience.

## Sullied by Semen: Historical Foundations

Predating the formation of the forensic sciences, various scientific theories about semen and sperm were constructed, refuted, and refined. Clearly, the invention of the microscope was instrumental in making visible a world once imperceptible. Among the new wonders of the microscopic world were spermatozoa. Anton van Leeuwenhoek, (1632–1723) in a letter dated November 1677, confirmed that spermatozoa were present in male semen, came exclusively from testicles, and were not a result of decay or putrefaction (Florence 1895; Gaensslen 1983, 106). Although the significance of sperm was not yet clearly articulated, the excitement of this discovery is evident:

> Immediately after ejaculation . . . I have seen so great a number that . . . I judged a million of them would not equal in size a large grain of sand. They were furnished with a thin tail, about 5 or 6 times as long as the body, and very transparent and with the thickness of about one twenty-fifth that of the body. They moved forwards owning the motion to their tails like that of a snake or an eel swimming in water; but in the somewhat thicker substance they would lash their tails at least 8 or 10 times before they could advance a hair's breadth. (Leeuwenhoek as quoted in Kempers 1976)

This first scientific description of sperm, "the discovery," is linked to phallic imagery of snakes and eels swimming furiously rather than described as, for example, cells rhythmically undulating. Building on the work of Leeuwenhoek, researcher Nicholas Hartsoeker in 1694

theorized that the umbilical cord was born from the tail of the spermatozoa and the fetus sprouted from the head of a sperm cell embedded in the uterus (Spark 1988). Preformation or spermism was a belief
that the sperm contained a miniature preformed body. Semen is cast as
responsible for unilateral creation. Aura seminalis was a theory based on
the male providing only a vital stimulus (an aura or emanation) that
initiates the development of the ovum, placing a more spiritual role on
semen. Conventional wisdom during the seventeenth and eighteenth
centuries stated that women were "mere vessels" in the process of human reproduction. It was not until 1824 that it was discovered that
animalcules or small cells (spermatozoa) in seminal fluid fertilized female eggs (Pinto-Correia 1997).

Investigating DNA forensics requires a fluency in certain terminology
and practices. First, there is the distinction between *sperm* and *semen*. *Semen*
is fluid ejaculate, which contains the spermatozoa cells (sperm). In current crime scene investigation, there are different approaches that can be
used to find semen, including ultraviolet Wood's lights, which make semen fluoresce; biochemical tests for the presence of seminal fluid; and
visual or physical inspection of the crime scene (Kobus et al. 2002). These
are referred to as presumptive tests. Having identified a substance that is
believed to be semen, an analyst will subsequently perform additional
testing to confirm that the substance is indeed semen and extract sperm
cells to proceed identity testing. Usually the confirmatory test involves
microscopic examination and "Christmas tree staining" of the material to
identify morphologically recognizable sperm. Presumptive and confirmatory testing generally culminates in DNA testing. But how did forensic
science and the construction of sperm as evidence emerge?

Forensic science, the application of bioscientific disciplines to law
enforcement, developed momentum with the rise of Enlightenment
thinking in the late sixteen hundreds. During this time, the power of
ultimate arbitrator shifted from the realm of the divine to that of science. Forensics evolved as a natural progression of this newfound power
in that investigation and exploration of the Truth (facts) became essential. The desire for confidence in research capabilities provided an
environment ripe for proliferation of inventions, many of which would
facilitate investigation. As we demonstrate below, through the use of
scientific practices, early forensic investigators bestowed the morality of
man into the quality and quantity of their semen. What becomes clear
when reading the history of forensic sciences is an allegory where men as
scientists and semen as evidence work in tandem to uncover the Truth.

Through the production, procurement, and description of forensic "evidence," the Western biomedical-scientific world gains entry to

the criminal justice system, simultaneously lending new credibility to the claims making of legal practitioners. This "evidence" can either incriminate or exonerate. However, there seems to be an endemic cultural lag (Ogburn 1964) as the social, moral, and legal interpretations of crime scramble to keep pace with biomedical innovation. This lag fuels confusion about biomedical practices, mistrust for investigators, and overconfidence in the irrefutability of physical evidence. The migration of forensics terminology into our popular vocabulary further complicates meanings about identity, individuality, evidence, guilt, crime, and confession. Simultaneously, as forensic vernacular becomes more familiar to the nonscientist, expectations about DNA are both glorified and oversimplified. As Duster (2003) has demonstrated, throughout the twentieth century there has been an increasing propensity to see crime, mental illness, and intelligence as expressions of genetic dispositions.

## Early to Mid-Nineteenth Century

Tracing one genealogy of sperm as evidence leads to twelfth-century England, where Richard I established the Officer of the Coroner. The coroner was responsible for recording all criminal matters and investigating deaths due to unnatural causes. As the need grew for investigation of such deaths, coroners began asking physicians for assistance. Demand for physicians to be educated in investigative matters eventually led to the University of Edinburgh establishing a Department of Legal Medicine in the early nineteenth century. Prior to that, toward the end of the eighteenth century, modern chemistry emerged as a valid science, leading to discoveries that were applicable to crime investigation and detection. It was during this time period that the use of experts in the courtroom was first documented (Kind and Overman 1972).

When the presence of spermatozoa was recognized as the essential characteristic of a seminal stain, semen obtained a legal value. It was not until 1839 when Mathiew Orfila and Henri-Louis Bayard, a legal physician, established a means of methodological assessment of semen that semen was used as biomedical legal evidence. Before this determination, cases of sexual assault were determined by the expertise of midwives. The forces of medicalization and the rising esteem of rational, masculine machines of knowledge production usurped the role of the traditional female practitioner.

Orfila, a scientist most known for his work in toxicology, explored the characteristics of semen on fabric. When linen is "sullied by semen," then diluted in water for microscopic inspection, spermatozoa become crumpled and separated to the point of being unrecognizable. Orfila explained that the ideal situation to examine spermatozoa is soon after ejaculation when semen is placed on a glass slide: "For, independent of their form, which resembles that of a tadpole, they execute very marked movements and in the extreme, one can pronounce, solely after the existence of animalculi of this form, that the solution submitted to this examination is semen, for they are not observed with the same characteristics in any other liquid" (Orfila 1827 in Gaensslen 1983, 74). Bodily secretions other than semen on fabrics (women's discharge, secretions from venereal diseases, mucous, and saliva) were distinguished from semen by odor, coloring (or lack of coloring) when exposed to heat, and how quickly each dissolves in different solutions. Orfila's tests were ultimately rejected because of poor results, and it was not until 1839, when Bayard provided the first reliable microscopic analysis of semen on fabrics (Florence 1895; Gaensslen 1983, 112), that leaky semen could be accurately identified.

The simultaneous biomedical production of spermatorrhea was perhaps the first instance of the medicalization of leaky semen. In the middle eighteen hundreds, Western European physicians discovered, diagnosed, and treated this excessive discharge of sperm (from ejaculation, nocturnal emissions, urination, and sweating) caused by illicit or excessive sexual activity, which, they claimed, caused anxiety, nervousness, lassitude, impotency, insanity, and death. As historian Ellen Rosenman brilliantly writes (2003, 373), "semen was pathologized as the symbol of everything that is alarming about the body." The male body's inability to contain itself despite a conscious intention to not leak led to surgical treatments such as cauterization and the application of biomedical apparatus (such as the toothed urethral ring). Here, again, men are seen as controlled by their fluids, lacking self-control due to their inability to maintain bodily boundaries.

## The Early 1900s

Dr. A. Florence (1851–1927), a professor of medicine, created a standard for professionals to use in determining whether there is actually semen present at the scene of the crime. Florence (1895 in Gaensslen 1983, 104) described the fluid: "Semen (seed) is a thick, viscous liquid, a bit flowing, of an odor *sui generis* called 'spermatic,' and which has been compared to flowers of a chestnut tree, shredded hoof, sawn ivory, flour dough, gluten, etc. Its consistency is variable." Furthermore, Florence (1895 in Gaensslen 1983, 105) asserted a correlation between a man's semen and his sexual or moral practices.

> Its consistency is variable: thick, almost a gelatin, in a vigorous man after a long abstinence, it becomes very fluid, scarcely milky, in those who abuse venereal pleasures. In the first case, it is an opaque white, bordering on

yellow or grey, almost pearly, clotted, nonhomogeneous, because striations in an uncolored, transparent liquid, appearing dark by a phenomenon of refraction, engulf the masses of gelatin. In the second case, it is
rather homogeneous, more or less milky, a little translucent. In a degree
of even more considerable impoverishment again, after several repeated
acts of coitus in a short period of time, it is transparent and shows only a
few small whitish points or striations; at the same time the spermatic odor
becomes weaker and weaker and even null.

By implying that semen becomes weaker and less substantial the more
it is spilled or wasted, male fluids are tied to the notion of strength. By
the 1900s, writers believed in what Barker-Benfield (1976) has called the
"spermatic economy," according to which men must exercise sexual
restraint lest they waste and damage their seed and undermine their
physical strength. While medieval and early modern clerics interpreting
the biblical story of Onan found the fruitless "spilling of seed" to be a
capital crime, the scientific validation of the spermatic economy accounts, in part, for the proliferation of antimasturbation texts in twentieth century Western civilization. A Swiss physician, Samuel Tissot, took
an exclusively medical view, arguing that the unnatural loss of semen
weakened mind and body and led to masturbatory insanity. (His book,
published in 1758, was reprinted as recently as 1905 (Tissot 1760).)
Furthermore, the laws of the "spermatic economy" accorded that masturbation would take away from the impulse to perform civilizing work
that was the true manly calling. This conflation of semen with the relative perversion of a man is not merely a historical relic but is repeated in
later popular representations, as shown below.

## The Mid-Twentieth Century

In the late 1800s, the photograph was used to capture the criminal's
portrait. Alphonse Bertillon (1853–1914) refined the system by adding
the unique physical aspects of the individual to create a record that would
identify the criminal. By using the uniqueness of individual skeletal
variations, precise measurements were recorded. These measurements
along with verbal description of the criminal and any distinguishing
marks of the body were kept on record in a centralized police file
(Nickell and Fischer 1999). This was a significant advancement in providing a centralized database of criminals for criminal investigators
(Chisum and Turvey 2000). This system was used primarily to capture
the repeat offenders and apply a more scientific approach to the process. The Bertillonage "portrait parle" system and the use of stains as
evidence in the court began a shift from eyewitness testimony to the use
of physical evidence databases in criminal investigations.

One of Bertillon's students was Edmund Locard, whose exchange principle is widely regarded as the cornerstone of forensic sciences. This principle, first articulated around 1910, is based on theories of a cross-transfer of physical evidence between individuals and objects. Criminals, who soiled social spaces, could now be associated with locations, objects from crime scenes, and victims. Throughout the growth of forensics, the field becomes more substantiated as it is incorporated into law enforcement and popular imaginations—into academic curricula, literature (i.e., Sherlock Holmes in 1887), crime laboratories (France in 1910, California in 1923, and the Federal Bureau of Investigation's (FBI) lab in 1932), and state-endorsed agencies (the FBI in 1905).

In 1953, Paul Kirk published *Crime Investigation,* one of the first texts on criminalistics and crime investigation that encompasses practice as well as theory (Rudin and Inman 2002b). Building on Locard's transfer theory, Kirk likened the transfer evidence to a "silent witness." Florence's "irrefutable accusing witness" is a precursor to Kirk's silent witness: "Wherever he steps, whatever he touches, whatever he leaves, even unconsciously, will serve as silent evidence against him. . . . The blood or semen that he deposits or collects—all these and more bear mute witness against him" (Kirk 1953, 4). Kirk continued to speculate that the criminalist of the future might be able to identify perpetrators by the hair, blood, or 'semen he deposited,' which are probably unique to the individual. This recalls the legacy of sperm as a signifier of a criminal man:

> Blood abounds, it runs in the streets, a scratch makes it flow and a number of professions cannot be practiced without its blemish. It is not the same for seminal stains, whose presence in frequent cases has an absolutely precise significance and constitutes an irrefutable accusing witness. Their interpretation is extremely easy, for, rather often, the role of the expert consists in saying yes or no as to the presence of spermatozoa. (Florence 1895 in Gaensslen 1983, 104)

According to Kirk, where the semen is found can say something about the perpetrator. He urges criminalists to check areas other than the vagina for semen because "concomitant perverted sex activity" may have accompanied the crime (Kirk 1953, 95). Moralizing about the type of sex engaged in by the criminal further establishes the dominance of a heteronormative, procreative sex paradigm and constructs rape as a specific type of violence as well as a perverted sexual activity. Here, the sperm is soulful, for example, taking on new resonance when seen through the lens of the reduction of male agency to the drives, processes, and products of male bodies.

Before DNA testing, Kirk (1953) noted that there were excellent indications that the morphology of spermatozoa may have been characteristic of the individual man. He said that sperm are unique and strong and resilient (the implication is that it will take a real man to outsmart, identify, and extract the sperm from the material). Kirk noted that not all sperm of an individual are normal in appearance and the "variations from normal take several directions.... Distribution of various abnormalities and deviations is quite constant and ... a statistical summary may serve to identify the individual from whom the spermatozoa originated" (Kirk 1953, 210). If it is not possible to identify the criminal, it may be possible to use deviations to exonerate him. Kirk (1953, 668) details the analysis of semen stains on fabric, that cloth should be teased apart to separate as much as possible because sperm tend to be caught by cotton fibers and retained tenaciously. He suggests employing distilled water and diluted hydrochloric acid to soak an encrusted spermatozoon loose. However, the soiling properties of sperm become embedded in fabric, as in social relationships. Marveling at the tenacity of sperm, Kirk (1953, 668) reports, "The spermatozoa are not dissolved or damaged by any of these solvents, being one of the most resistant of all biological structures."

## Late Twentieth Century

In 1911, DNA was discovered, but it was not until 1953, when Watson and Crick unfolded the "secret of life"—the chemical structure of DNA—that the biolegal world would be transformed. DNA opened new frontiers in ethics, politics, religion, and commerce. Popular news media have added to the frenzy over DNA's potential affront to privacy. Mainstream literature suggests the power of DNA as a tracking device. We are encouraged to believe that DNA traces our heritage, our whereabouts, and our defects and told that 99.9 percent of every human being's genetic makeup is the same. Yet while DNA purportedly connects us all, it is used in forensics to identify and separate one of us from the rest.

DNA typing is a complex process that lacks a unilateral, rational, and consistent methodology, instead involving the (sometimes fractious) collaboration of many individuals and machines—a messiness hidden by an actor network teeming with experts (Halfon 1998). A stable network of medical, biotechnological, and legal experts erases and removes doubt from a multitiered system and propels it toward standardization. In the midst of this drive toward the standardization of "objective knowledge claims," DNA forensic testimony is situated in the highly polemic environment of a courtroom (Lynch 1998). While the bioscientific world is making claims of ultimate truth through statistical manipulation, attorneys are deconstructing their claims.

Until the mid-1980s, identity testing was generally conducted using serological tests, which identified proteins present in the seminal fluid. Interestingly, some men ("nonsecretors") do not secrete proteins into their seminal fluid, and as a result, their semen cannot be typed. Because of several other problems with the old serological tests, they are now considered fairly unreliable; since 1988 DNA testing has been the gold standard, and a variety of DNA tests are available for typing the DNA contained in the spermatozoa.[5] Of course, some men are aspermic and others have had a vasectomy, and semen from such men can be challenging to type, but some of the more powerful polymerase chain reaction–based DNA typing methods can determine a type from few DNA-containing cells present in the seminal fluid (other than spermatozoa).[6] There are a huge number of different DNA tests currently available for forensic work.

In 1984, Alec Jeffreys, a Research Fellow from the University of Leicester, discovered a truly individual-specific identification system and coined the term DNA fingerprinting (Jeffreys 1993). Two years later, this identification system was used for the first time in a criminal investigation. DNA profiling made its formal entry into the world of forensics with a murder case in a small town near Leicester where two girls had been raped and murdered. A teenage boy from the area confessed to the second murder and had been arrested. Police, frustrated and eager to solve the case, asked Alec Jeffreys to analyze the semen samples from both victims to verify the boy's guilt in both murders. The DNA profile verified that the same man committed the crimes and that it was not the teenager who had confessed. The boy was the first person proved innocent by DNA typing. The investigation continued with a DNA-based manhunt that involved screening all local men within a certain age range and eventually led to a man who matched the DNA profile signature. The implementation of this DNA fingerprinting had substantiated semen as a silent witness (Jeffreys 1993).

In a more current example of leaking semen and DNA testing, the Clinton/Lewinsky scandal quickly introduced the "semen-stained blue dress" as part of the everyday discourse. The transcript from the infamous Starr Report (Starr 1998) establishes that leaked semen, mistaken for spinach dip, can be difficult to "spit out" or decipher. Semen, even the semen of high-status men, is a messy substance, not easily contained, and when it is spilt in the wrong places, semen can provide the necessary evidence to indict individuals, as the following excerpt from the Starr Report shows:

Q. So at the time you didn't notice anything on the dress?

A. I don't believe so.

Q. Okay. What happened then the next time you wore the dress that led you to conclude that?

A. Well, I also—can I say here? I also—I think I wore the dress out to dinner that night, so which is why I'm not sure that that's what it is.

Q. Okay.

A. So it could be *spinach dip* or something. I don't know. I'm sorry could you repeat the question?

Q. Sure, when was the—when was it that you at least began to believe that maybe there was *semen* on the dress?

A. I really don't remember when it was the next time I went to wear the dress, but I gained weight so I couldn't wear the dress and it didn't fit. And I'm not a very organized person. I don't clean my clothes until I am going to wear them again.

Q. Did you notice there was something on the dress?

A. Yes, and at that point I noticed it and I though, oh, this is dirty, it needs to get cleaned. And then I remembered that I had worn it the last time I saw the President, and I believe it was at that point that I thought to myself, oh, no.

Cultural critics see Clinton's spilt seed as illustrative of a larger disruption of the unified notion of social order. Leaked semen has soiled the integrity of the office of the President of the United States:

> The leaking of fluids, rather than the completion of the act, its oral/ genital rather than genital/genital character, the quasi-onanistic spilling of the seed signified something far more disturbing to what we might call the image of the unified presidency, namely that this president was in his weakness willing to part with his precious bodily fluids. (Dumm 1999, 16)

Biological science, particularly forensics, simultaneously demystifies and obscures the description, purposes, and representations of semen, which is at first a mysterious and mythical substance. The social purpose of semen is produced and recast over several centuries. With exacting specificity, scientists have labored to interpret each sensory dimension of semen—imbuing them with moralistic relevance: color, taste, odor, consistency, shape, size, and volume. With the advent of DNA technologies, sperm cells contain the ultimate identifier and sperm reemerges as integral to yet another realm of social order.[7]

Throughout this section, we explored the social and scientific forces that medicalize masculinity through the medicalization of male sexual and reproductive fluids. These processes have occurred simultaneously, with men being constructed as sexual suspects and aggressors. The annals of seminal forensic sciences have not stayed within the realms of the medical-industrial complex or the criminal justice system. The television industry has increased the scope and breadth of this medicalization and criminalization of men.

## Lay Forensics: Popular and Consumer Forensic Science

### Ripped from the Headlines: Television Crime Shows, Sperm, and Sexual Deviance

Crime shows, a seasoned favorite, have generally fared well on network television. Through Web sites, conventions, and merchandise, fans still pay homage to shows such as *Dragnet, Adam-12, Hawaii 5-0, Quincy, M.E., Hill Street Blues*, and *Homicide*. Since its debut in 2000, CBS's *C.S.I.: Crime Scene Investigation* has consistently ranked number one in television viewership.[8] Using a successful formula of biotechnical forensic practices, deductive reasoning, interpersonal drama, and grisly, slow-motion reenactments, *C.S.I.* has surpassed its competitors *NYPD Blue, Crossing Jordan*, and *Law and Order* (including *Law and Order: Criminal Intent* and *Law and Order: Special Victims Unit*). So pleased are network executives with the show, they have created spin-off series, *C.S.I.: Miami* and *C.S.I.: New York*, as well as adding new shows *Cold Case* and *NCIS (Naval Criminal Investigative Services)*. Other networks are offering forensics shows for the Fall 2005 line-up including *Bones* and *The Evidence*.

What can explain the mass appeal of these sex crime entertainment programs? As they stimulate, exploit, and generate fear, crime shows claim to reflect real life. *Law and Order*'s storylines are often based on actual cases, hence the show's slogan, "Ripped from the headlines." It is one of the many shows that exemplify the increasingly fuzzy boundary between reality and reality-based drama on television. Most of the crime shows are really celebrations of the triumph of positivist thinking. Amidst all of the lies, deceptions, and partial evidence, the right deductive reasoning, testing, and fieldwork will reveal with certainty the moral deviant. These postmodern shows are locally produced but globally consumed and blur the boundaries between "reality" (actual grisly crimes quickly reported to a highly mediated public) and the canon of crime fiction; they are thus the dramatic grandchildren of Arthur Conan Doyle. What is at stake in these shows is the confounding of scientific discovery with moral pronouncement—the discovery of semen at a crime scene automatically indicts a "very bad" man. Again we are witness to the medicalization of masculinity via the forensic meanings attributed to the spilt fluid.

But scriptwriters aren't the only ones getting ideas from everyday lives of individuals. In 1998, after watching an *NYPD Blue* episode in which a rape victim saved the semen her attacker had left behind, a twelve-year-old Phoenix girl, using a cotton swab on herself, gathered sufficient DNA evidence to have her grandfather arrested (Safir and Reinharz 2000). Furthermore, within professional criminology circles, a new term, *the CSI effect,* has been coined to describe phenomena in which actual investigators are responding to the expectations of millions of individuals who consume television crime show dramas. Jurors educated by television programs have come to expect a certain amount of forensic evidence in every trial (Hempel 2003, Kluger 2002). Interpreting the plot lines and transcripts from these programs, *C.S.I.* figuring prominently among them, demonstrates the ways in which semen is both a silent witness as well as a go-to guy in most criminal investigations.

It is important to note that in all these episodes, semen is invisible, discussed but never seen, again a "silent witness." Furthermore, semen will only bear witness for those with enough expertise to draw out its testimony. The crime shows draw on real life and legal transcripts to suggest that DNA evidence is the product of specialized, technical, and scientific processes and is therefore inherently infallible. We, as viewers, are led to believe that the objective nature of such evidence makes it perhaps the only truly reliable evidence in a case.

## Anthropomorphized Semen

In this chapter, we use the term *anthropomorphism* as it has been used in previous work (Moore 2002)—that is, the act of attributing human forms or qualities to entities that are not human or singularly capable of attaining "personhood" (or fully human, for the sperm and egg of *Homo sapiens* are, in fact, "human"). While sperm in children's books are most commonly anthropomorphized as cheerful, smiling, determined tadpoles, *C.S.I.* uses terminology to make sperm cells or semen into different types of men. Sperm as evidence is most often benignly referred to as a "stain" or as the "donor" even in a murder or rape investigation.[9] In some episodes, instead of referring to sperm as an object, a vernacular of personhood is used, such as "these guys" (three times in three episodes) and "little soldiers" (two times in two episodes), or referring to sperm as part of a "ménage d'allele" (this term implies that the genetic information of alleles comes from more than two people. In other words, the dead women had sex with two or more men—a ménage à trois).

Generally, sperm are anthropomorphized to create an affinity for the cells and to liken them to men—for example, soldiers going to battle, or sex partners engaging in fantastic encounters. These representations imply some cognition and motivation on the part of the sperm or the man. As stand-ins for actual men, many sperm depictions do not degrade the character of man, but rather play on hegemonic ideals of men as soldiers and sexual schemers—hegemonically male agents. As anthropomorphism occurs along a spectrum of moral valuation, representations of sperm can be derogatory; for example, when the perpetrator is not a "real man" because he is incapable of "normal" sexual conquest.

Sperm, as little soldiers or guys, are in the service of their producers. For example, in "Boom" (season 1, episode 12), the little soldiers are actually able to exonerate one possible perpetrator (Nick, who is also a crime scene investigator). Investigating the murder of a prostitute, Greg is using a microscope to identify biological material. He sees Nick's sperm and dubs them "Nick's little soldiers." Catherine asks him, "When did you say this sample was frozen?" Greg answers, "About 10:15 A.M. Why?" Catherine shoots back, "These guys are all heads, no tails." Later, Catherine explains her theory to Grissom: "The sperm found in the condom was frozen at 10:15 A.M. It's all heads, no tails. It takes about seven hours for bacteria to eat away at the tails, placing the time of ejaculation at two A.M." Due to the life span of sperm and the method by which they disintegrate, Catherine is able to provide reasonable doubt that Nick murdered the prostitute.

Anthropomorphism can also be used as a ploy to degrade the male character's masculinity. Being a real man requires the capacity to have sex with women and not needing to rely on masturbation for sexual fulfillment. As we see, having "hardly any swimmers" in your semen may mean you are an excessive masturbator—unathletic and incapable of attracting women, the man in question is unable to be a donor and cannot attract a woman in whom to make a seminal deposit. Because of the familiarity with the etiology of low sperm count, a crime scene investigator (Nick) may even degrade his own claims to masculinity, as the following quick banter reveals.

Greg finds ejaculate that contains DNA outside a victim's window, which they characterize as "spank high." And even though a man may shoot his sperm high up on the window, Greg continues, "Well, I can tell you this about him: Really low sperm count. Sample hardly had any swimmers." Nick adds, "That's probably from excessive masturbation. Guy's been outpacing his ability to produce sperm." This comment draws smirks from his coworkers as they dub him "Spanky." Here, media representations call forth and legitimate images of strong, virile semen, which are called upon to achieve cultural standards of hegemonic masculinity.

## Semen as Decoy

In some instances, sperm are manipulated by men to entrap other men in their crime. A decoy is an imitation in any sense of a person, object, or phenomenon which is intended to deceive enemy surveillance devices or mislead enemy evaluation. In the *C.S.I.* episode "Strip Strangler" (season 1, episode 22), the guy is "planting hairs, planting semen," although where he is planting them is unstated (neither the woman's body nor her anatomical parts are visible or specified). Greg states, "The semen recovered at this morning's homicide matches the semen taken from the bed sheets of the last two female victims." Catherine, looking at the red-stained semen, says, "Freakiest semen I've seen in a while. Call me." In another scene it is called "indeterminate red stuff." The red stuff, ketchup, was mixed into the semen found at the scene of each of the Strip Strangler's crimes, concocted and placed by the perpetrator. Catherine ventures, "I guess we should've known, our guy was planting hairs, he was planting semen."

In these television shows, what is really sought is moral certainty through the reliance on medical knowledge: the more reliable the DNA evidence, the more certain one's moral judgment about the actions and intentions of its host. Crimes of sexual violence and deviance such as rape, incest, and sodomy evoke intense emotional responses from many segments of American society. In an increasingly culturally, ethnically, and economically diverse society, television has become a convenient dispenser of simple morality. While leaked semen on television figures prominently in morally charged messages about sexual deviance, the discourse around DNA evidence helps provide a calm, rational path to a moral high ground. Much as semen in children's books provides children with normative values regarding reproductive behavior (Moore 2003), semen in television crime series constructs stories of certainty, moral reprehension, and the punitive retribution exacted from violators. Moreover, these stories, again, depict semen as evidence of male malfeasance, applying a scientific—and medical—gaze to exclusively male fluids to interpret and evaluate their actions and intentions. Embedded in these fictionalized accounts of male sexual behavior is a construction of men as sexually suspect and of their male bodily fluids—the physical evidence of their masculinity—as both cause and proof of their lack of self-control.

## "So, Why Do You Have This Big Semen Stain in Your Underwear?"[10] The Home Fidelity Industry

Perhaps some of the fascination with these crime shows centers on the fact that semen does not just leak during violent crimes, but can also leak during furtive, intimate moments secretly shared between consenting adults. Leaked semen can soil the sanctity of marriage. The at-home infidelity testing industry, which provides at-home kits for semen detection and laboratory testing of "panties, nighties, sheets, condoms, tampons,"[11] has capitalized on the shift from testimony and intuition to physical evidence as trustworthy investigative resources. Infidelity tests for the layperson represent another trend in the CSI effect, where the lay forensic investigator is encouraged to draw definitive conclusions. The companies that benefit from this niche market both generate and rely on the suspicion of sexual infidelity, targeting men who suspect their female partners of sexual disloyalty. And indeed, according to testimonials, many people make important decisions based on the outcome of the tests. As ForenseX, an Arizona-based company, urges, "Send us your dirty panties."

www.infidelity.com boasts of being "The #1 Source for Semen Stain Detection Tests." An article from a London-based Web site (Krum 2001) states that in 2001 Checkmate sold a thousand kits a month; 85 percent of their clients were men, nearly half of customers have been married fifteen years or more, and 40 percent were over forty years old. This kit is primarily aimed at testing flowback, semen that drains into undergarments after intercourse for up to seventy-two hours. The test is specially formulated to detect certain enzymes produced by the male prostate gland and found in semen. The cost of at-home testing ($49.95 for testing ten articles) compared to hiring a private investigator is marketed as one of the product's major benefits. It also suggests that women who are cheating are usually in a rush and don't clean up very thoroughly, possibly leaving traces of semen on different parts of the inside of their clothing.

The sales pitches and slogans of these products are sensational. A cartoon on www.infidelitykit.com on June 3, 2003, illustrated a woman with a surprised look on her face saying, "I don't know how that semen got in my underwear!" Again, we see the passive woman who is a field for the sowing of seeds, invoking the age-old characterizations of women as whores. These sites explore the weaknesses of an insecure man, constructing men who might use them as being unable to afford a private detective or to lose in a messy divorce. These statements also construct two distinct types of man, who are adversaries. First, there is the stupid and foolish cuckold, who needs science to back up his suspicions. Second, there is the low-down dog who sleeps with another man's woman and then leaves the evidence behind. See these comments from promotional Web sites below:

- "Just imagine how many men who were doing laundry when they inadvertently came across a stain, they had no real way to identify" www.infidelitytestingtoday.com

- "Checkmate replaces Dog as man's best friend." www.infidelity testingtoday.com
- "Will give you scientific truth about the infidelity or fidelity of your mate" http://infidelitycheck.us/testing-a-woman.html
- "Don't be made a fool of by a cheating wife or a cheating wife's lover. Stop hurting and know the scientific truth." http://infidelitycheck .us/testing-a-woman.html
- "She brings the evidence home to you without even knowing it." www.infidelitytestingtoday.com
- "Make an informed decision." http://infidelitycheck.us/testing_a_ woman.html
- "Remember the Clinton Rule, check all clothing. Cheating is cheating." http://infidelitycheck.us/testing_a_woman.html
- "Did you know that semen, blood and saliva can be detected on clothing or bedding and that DNA technology can say who those stains came from or didn't come from?" www.cluefinders.tripod

While most of the marketing is targeted primarily to a male consumer, kits designed for testing men and marketed to women are also available. These sites claim that because men secrete semen up to two hours after intercourse or oral sex, semen will be in their underwear. There are no catchy headings on this page about a woman's best friend. Infidelitycheck.us states when testing a man, evidentiary confirmation of a semen stain *favors* infidelity. It also cautions that "a child could perform this simple in home semen test but an adult must interpret the results." The effect of testing a man is ambiguous and inconclusive. The same Web site states that evidentiary confirmation of semen stain in a woman's garment is *conclusive*—" the indications of infidelity are present."

Women are untrustworthy, but that is only because of the existence of other men and other sperm that want access to them. Infidelity kits allow for the creative and potentially deceitful manipulation of semen. For example, there is nothing preventing someone from getting hold of a woman's panties, having a male friend stain them, and then sending them in for testing.

The currently available technology employed by fidelity kits relies exclusively on the presence of semen. The authority to definitively answer questions of infidelity rests with semen. While women can be either suspected of infidelity or removed from suspicion, the only time a woman can get definitive results from this type of testing is if her partner is involved in homosexual activity. The heterosexual male is in the most advantageous position. To date, there are no definitive biological tests for women to employ to determine if their partners are participating in extradyadic sex.

These historical and scientific productions of semen as medically knowable and men as medically, morally, and criminally suspect have traveled from the public to the private. Seminal forensic science has flowed into the home. So just as jurors expect forensic evidence, everyday actors can become ethnoforensic specialists in their everyday lives. The traffic between the public realm of scientific knowledge production about semen and the private realm of the bedroom means that there is a clear legacy of sexual suspicion of men. Through scientific knowledge production, this suspicion has gained legitimation from scientific procedures and techniques. The sexual suspicion of men has traveled outside scientific circles to our popular culture as in television programs. This pop culture production of forensics entertainment and the seemingly unlimited potential to reach consumers through the Internet has allowed everyday actors to become pseudoscientists.

## Conclusions

Throughout the past three hundred years, semen has emerged as one of our most important totems. Semen is imbued with intense (often dichotomous) social meanings ranging from birth to death, disease, virility, sex, violence, love, hatred, and genetic heritage. It comes from the male body, is constantly produced throughout the life span of the man, and is ejaculated (with intention and by accident). The emergence of forensic science occurs at the intersections of processes of medicalization and criminalization. We now know that, being strong and tenacious, semen can endure in vaginas and fabrics; only collectible in the context of prior arrangements, it is nonetheless potentially messy and unpredictable, leaving recalcitrant tracks. We also know that while people who are the recipients of semen have a difficult time getting rid of it, when spilt, it leaves an evidentiary trail to one specific man. Finally, we know that by establishing methods of seminal detection, professional and lay forensic practitioners are able to locate semen, describe the type of sex men and women are performing (normal or perverted), and validate an act of intercourse. Indeed, semen can prove a man guilty or innocent of sexual excesses to which all men tend. In the medical/criminal gaze, sperm are sneaky and leaky silent witnesses; once coveted and assumed dangerous because of its ability to impregnate, semen, through biotechnological innovation, has become the equivalent of mobile identifiers. A man can be defined (as self-controlled or out of control) according to the actions of his sperm.

Just as women have been constructed as sexually undependable and vulnerable, men are now becoming scientifically constructed as sexually suspect—or, rather, cultural beliefs about certain men as sexually unreliable and suspect are being scientifically and medically legitimated. Furthermore, men are being constructed as driven and defined by their sexuality and male bodies—with their motives and essential "nature" recognizable by their bodily fluids—as female bodies have similarly been constructed. While it would appear as if the medicalization of femininity prefigured (or was concurrent with) the medicalization of masculinity, more research considering the simultaneity of these leaky bodies as evoking normative conceptions of masculinity and femininity must be conducted.

Again and again, semen is represented as having moral significance. The invention of DNA analysis has created another social arena in which moral stories about specific men and women can be told. Our analysis of sperm as evidence within the bioscientific historical record, the entertainment industry, and the at-home testing marketplace illustrates how sperm has become an integral component in the processes of adjudication. Perhaps the moral certainty of DNA comes not just from securing the guilty perpetrator, but also from a pervasive reproduction of gendered and sexed ideologies. We watch these shows and root for the "good guys" to avenge the "passive victims" (i.e., women) by getting the "bad guys." Sperm as DNA samples are among the tools used to reproduce these ideologies and hierarchies. Sperm are us, in a strange way; in them we see what we want to see and hear the stories we want to hear, about men and women. Even the jurors who want lots of evidence because they've seen it on TV (assuming they know the difference between entertainment and a real trial) want to be entertained and to have their preconceived notions about the world reproduced.

It is clear the solving of violent crime has shifted from testimony, narrative, and interrogation (which can be read as a "feminine" form of knowing) to the scientific rationality through manipulation of technology (which can be read as a "masculine" form of knowing). In this rationalization of interpretation, sleuthing is no longer an art or an interpretive experience; rather it exemplifies a quest for certainty. The presence of semen has become a basis for this certainty. In this process, we are witnessing the conflation of inference and deduction. Investigations are no longer reliant on the interrogation of a person but on bodily by-products of that person (blood, hair, cells, sperm, DNA). As is revealed in forensics discourses, men investigate seminal stains to prove the flawed character of other men by, among other practices, imbuing sperm cells with masculine attributes and foibles.

In sum, our work has explored the emergence and rise of the medicalization of male body fluids as it is entangled with the deployment of forensic science for criminal investigations. Not only does semen represent physical evidence, but semen also clearly becomes evidence of male intentions, actions, and weaknesses. We have illustrated how descriptions of semen, seminal stains, and sperm cells are articulated through a moral vocabulary of male actions and tendencies. These processes of articulation expand the medicalization of semen to the medicalization of masculinity itself. The historical and obdurate social and cultural constructions of men as sexually suspect and out of control are substantiated by their leaky bodies. Spilt semen reflects men's uncontrolled sexuality and moral pollution (their semen soils social spaces). Furthermore, the anthropomorphization of semen persuades us to see sperm cells and miniature men as tenacious, relentless, single-minded, and dangerous. Professional forensic sciences construct masculinity as an invader and polluter of space, which is then made evident by virtue of physical residue. In the popularization of this practice of constructing masculinity, lay social worlds now have access to the messages about and technologies to substantiate these messages.

More research into the ethnography of both professional and lay practitioners of forensic sciences could prove valuable to understanding the medicalization of masculinity. How do people actually use these devices to detect and describe seminal stains? How do people make meanings of seminal stains as evidence? What are the social consequences (both intended and unintended) of information about seminal stains? Additionally, a robust qualitative study of the sociolinguistics of seminal DNA forensics court transcripts would add to this history through contemporary case studies. In our own work, we intend to develop a sociological analysis of the Federal Bureau of Investigation's Combined DNA Index System (CODIS). National DNA Indexing is increasingly mandated and supported by local and state criminal statues. We would like to better understand how seminal evidence is used in this database and how actual men are then entered into CODIS in hopes of cold hits (i.e., matches between DNA from a crime scene with the alleged perpetrator).

# 4

# Medicalizing the Aging Male Body: Andropause and Baldness

Julia E. Szymczak and Peter Conrad

## Introduction

Aging men's lives and bodies are increasingly coming under medical jurisdiction. Images used to promote the latest erectile dysfunction medication, magazine articles about the best hair loss therapy, and television programs about successful aging consistently tell men to "see your doctor." The movement of aging from a natural life event to a medical problem in need of treatment (Estes and Binney 1989) is an example of medicalization. While earlier studies have pointed to the medicalization of women's bodies (Reissman 1983; Martin 1987; Riska 2003), we now see aging men's bodies becoming medicalized as well.

This chapter examines two clear cases of the medicalization of masculinity: one a commonly known bodily change, baldness, and the other an as yet lesser-known change, andropause. These cases raise interesting subtleties regarding the medicalization of masculinity. First, they point to a long-standing desire on the part of men and medical agents alike to achieve an old age that retains some of the essentially "masculine" and embodied qualities of youth and middle age—specifically, physical strength and energy, sexual vitality, and hirsutism. Thus the medicalization of male aging and baldness, while currently driven by the medical and pharmaceutical enterprises, is also fueled by men's own concerns with their masculine identities, capacities, embodiments, and presentations. Secondly, the medicalization of these "conditions" occurred only partially by design—while the pharmaceutical industry was actively seeking treatments for these conditions, current treatments emerged from research into other medical problems. Finally, these male "conditions" have only been partially medicalized. While medical and pharmaceutical enterprises have offered treatments for andropause and baldness, there is no consensus whether these constitute medical conditions, or if they do how their pathology is to be measured and assessed. These two conditions are provocative examples of the increasing medicalization of masculinity.

## Medicalization

While medicalization describes a process by which "nonmedical problems become defined and treated as medical problems, usually in terms of illnesses or disorders" (Conrad 1992, 209), analysts of medicalization have primarily been concerned with overmedicalization, noting that the widening jurisdiction of medicine over everyday life has potentially troubling consequences (Zola 1972). Critics are concerned that medicalization transforms wider aspects of everyday life into pathology, narrowing the range of what is considered acceptable. Furthermore, by expanding medical jurisdiction, medicalization increases the amount of medical social control over human behavior (Zola 1972; Conrad 1992). Normal life events such as birth, sexuality, aging, and death were increasingly medicalized in the past several decades (see Conrad 1992, 2000).

Medicalization is not an all or nothing phenomenon, but rather is bidirectional and occurs along a continuum. By *bidirectional*, we mean that there can be both medicalization and demedicalization, but the trend in the past century has been overwhelmingly toward medicalization. For demedicalization to occur, problems must no longer be defined as medical and medical treatments not deemed appropriate. The two clearest examples of demedicalization are masturbation (Engelhardt 1974) and homosexuality (Conrad and Schneider 1992); although after demedicalization there is always the potential for remedicalization (Conrad and Angell 2004), this would be very rare. However, most cases of medicalization are not complete, so we conceptualize this as "degrees of medicalization." Some problems are nearly completely medicalized, such as childbirth, death, and severe mental illness; others are partially medicalized, such as opiate addiction and menopause; and still others are minimally medicalized, such as sexual addiction and spouse abuse. While we do not know all the factors that affect the degrees of medicalization, it is clear that medical categories can shift on the continuum toward or away from more complete medicalization.

Medicalization often occurs through the actions of advocates who support and promote a medical definition of a particular trouble. Advocates can be physicians, social movements, organized lay groups, medical technology industries (pharmaceutical companies and medical supply manufacturers), or patients. Early studies of medicalization focused largely on physicians, social movements, and moral entrepreneurs as important agents in medicalization. But more recently the advocacy is shifting to corporate interests, especially the pharmaceutical industry and consumers (Conrad and Leiter 2004).

The balance between physicians and the pharmaceutical industry as agents of medicalization is shifting. While physicians are still the gatekeepers for many drugs, the pharmaceutical companies have become a major player in medicalization. In the post-Prozac world, the pharmaceutical industry has been more aggressively promoting its wares to physicians and especially to the public. This includes promoting blockbuster drugs like various psychotropics for a range of human troubles (from depression to shyness to learning problems) and Viagra and its competitors for sexual dysfunction to more modest promotions for problems like baldness and andropause. But in all cases, the creation of new markets by the pharmaceutical industry engenders broader forms of medicalization.

It is important to remember that the pharmaceutical companies do not create the markets by themselves. Often there is an extant consumer demand that the pharmaceutical industry shapes and even exploits in its promotion. For example, male sexual dysfunction was clearly a problem for some men before Viagra, but Pfizer has expanded the definition of erectile dysfunction in order to enlarge its market (Carpiano 2001). In so doing, it has medicalized a wider range of sexual troubles, so that now virtually any man can be a candidate for Viagra or its competitors. Similarly with other problems often associated with male aging, such as baldness, vitality, and loss of muscle tone, we can begin to see more medical treatments for the aging male body. Definitions of masculinity may encourage some men to see bodily changes as threats to masculinity and lead them to pursue treatments that will maintain their youthful body image. These men become consumers of products that promise to retain youth or at least repair or postpone unwanted bodily changes. The pharmaceutical industry is more than happy to supply treatments and develop a market for its products.

## Gender and Medicalization

Scholarly examinations of gender and medicalization have largely focused on the medicalization of women, ignoring the medicalization of men's lives. Some have argued that men are not as vulnerable to medicalization as are women (Reissman 1983): the substantial literature on the medicalization of childbirth, premenstrual syndrome, menopause, and anorexia in women (Wertz and Wertz 1989; Figert 1995; Bell 1990; Brumberg 2001) clearly shows that more of women's life experiences are medicalized than men's. Analysts have suggested several reasons for this. One of the reasons typically given for women's vulnerability to medicalization is the traditional definition of a healthy body. As Alan Petersen (1998a, 41) notes, "male bodies have been constructed through scientific and cultural practices as 'naturally' different from female bodies and [that] the bodies of white, European, middle-class, heterosexual men, have been constructed as the standard for measuring and evaluating other bodies." On the other hand, Catherine Reissman (1983) suggests that women are more vulnerable to medicalization than are men because their physiological processes are visible (menstruation, birth), their social roles expose them to medical scrutiny, and they are often in a subordinate position to men in the clinical domain. Reissman also argues that "routine experiences that are uniquely male remain largely unstudied by medical science and, consequently, are rarely treated by physicians as potentially pathological" (1983, 116).

However, while this may have been true when Reissman published her article in 1983, recent medical and scientific developments have engendered the medicalization of aging male bodies. Although it is not our intent to refute the claims that Reissman and others have made about women and medicalization, we would like to make a case for the increasing medicalization of men and to contribute to the understanding of medicalization as a truly gendered concept.[1] In this chapter, we examine two cases of the intersection of medical treatments, masculinity, and aging male bodies. We first examine the scientific identification of the male hormone testosterone and the "discovery" of andropause, purportedly caused by abnormal decrease of testosterone with age. Numerous medical testosterone based treatments were offered to alleviate this "disorder." Male hair loss, or baldness, is a common occurrence in aging men. Various elixirs and treatments have been introduced over the years, but in the past two decades new surgical and medical treatments have brought baldness further into the jurisdiction of medicine. Together these cases illustrate how medicine, expectations of masculinity, and the physiology of aging contribute to the medicalization of aging male bodies.

## Age, Masculinity, and the Body

The medicalization of aging men's bodies is relevant to a range of disciplines besides sociology. Masculinity theorists, gender scholars, and anthropologists are concerned with the social processes and pressures that produce and constrain masculinity. The medicalization of men's aging bodies, through pressure to conform to certain standards of health, is one such source of constraint. A lack of discussion about the social factors that pressure men's lives, including medical factors, contributes to an incomplete picture of contemporary masculinity. Just as feminists consider the intersection of women's bodies and medicine to be an important issue, masculinity and gender studies can benefit from understanding the medicalization of men's bodies.

In addition to masculinity, such an analysis considers both age and the body as focal concerns and sheds light on a number of intersecting sociological themes. First, through the lens of medicalization, we can see a reflection of negative social beliefs about and fears of the aging process in men. We live in an ageist society where the aging process is resisted and often feared. Instead of accepting the natural progression of the life course, we medicalize old age in an attempt to control it (Marshall and Katz 2002; Katz and Marshall 2004; Gullette 1997). While researchers have paid attention to the aging process in women, particularly as it pertains to menopause (Friedan 1993b; Lock 1993), aging men have been overlooked, for several reasons. Edward Thompson (1994) suggests that older men are invisible, in part because of the stigma that is placed on men as they disengage from traditional social roles and become more dependent. The longer life expectancy of women and reduced percentage of men in older cohorts may also play a role in this invisibility. In addition, feminist writers (e.g., Sontag 1978) point to a double standard of aging, which suggests that men benefit from the aging process while women are stifled by it. As some have suggested, "sociocultural constructions of femininity place considerable value on physical attractiveness and youth, and aging therefore moves women away from these cultural ideals" (Halliwell and Dittmar 2003, 676). This chapter confronts the double standard of age and argues that a majority of men may not experience an increase in masculine traits as they age. Rather, the growing market for testosterone and hair loss treatments suggests that many men want to resist the aging process and may attempt to gain control of it by embracing its medicalization. If the desire for products to reverse the signs of age is any indication, men do not revere old age as a time in their lives when their masculine characteristics increase but instead are concerned about their decline. Thus, as we will discuss later, men often collude in the medicalization of their capacities, characteristics, and functions.

Medicalization can also provide insight into the sociocultural construction of the body—a burgeoning field (Gatens 1996; Turner 1992). There is a great deal of scholarship dedicated to understanding the body as a social and cultural artifact (Sault 1994; Scheper-Hughes and Lock 1987). The body is the site where aging occurs, or as Christopher Faircloth (2003, 16) suggests, "the body visibly marks us as aging." Understanding how medicine acts upon the aging body through definition, control, and surveillance is a valuable step towards the creation of a fuller picture of the male experience of age. While aging can be understood on many levels, the body provides a salient frame of reference to comprehend the process. Age is characterized by bodily change and there is evidence that "the body [can] provide a key frame of reference for the male experience of health" (Watson 2000, 87). By looking at the different biotechnologies that "treat" the aging male body (here, testosterone and Propecia, Rogaine, and hair transplants) we can understand how it becomes socioculturally constructed. As Laura Mamo and Jennifer Fishman (2001, 14) suggest, "within the biomedicalization framework, medical technologies are part of programs and strategies of inscription that indicate the exercise of a rationalized, disciplining and regulating of bodies." The infiltration of biomedicine into everyday life through commonly used medical treatments redefines "healthy" and "normal" with regard to bodily function. Men experience and understand their bodies differently when the aging process is constructed as pathological. Medical treatments for baldness and andropause are part of a larger trend towards the discipline and regulation of male bodies.

## Andropause: Running on Empty

Testosterone is the most intriguing of the male hormones. Physiologically, it is claimed, testosterone increases sex drive, musculature, aggressive behavior, hair growth, and other traits traditionally considered masculine. Healthy men maintain a relatively high normal level of testosterone throughout early and middle age, but bodily production of testosterone may naturally decline with advancing age. For the last century, some physicians and other advocates have claimed that the age-related decline in testosterone levels results in a pathological condition known as andropause, which requires testosterone supplementation. Currently, older men are being prescribed testosterone replacement therapy for a set of vague symptoms, often referred to as andropause, male menopause, the male climacteric, or androgen deficiency in aging men (ADAM). A recent Institute of Medicine report estimates that "more than 1.75 million prescriptions were written in 2002, up from 648,000 in 1999" (Kolata 2003). Despite the widespread use of testosterone replacement therapy, there is a dearth of information and clinical studies about its risks and benefits. Amongst many in the scientific community, including the National Institute on Aging and the National Cancer Institute of the National Institute of Health, there is "growing concern about an increase in the use of testosterone by middle aged and older men who have borderline testosterone levels—or even normal testosterone levels—in the absence of adequate scientific information" (Institute of Medicine 2004, 1).

Uncertainty characterizes current medical knowledge of both the safety and efficacy of testosterone therapy and the existence of a male menopause. This uncertainty is not new, as scientists and physicians have debated the existence of andropause for over a century. A brief exploration of the history of testosterone therapy and andropause reveals that the pharmaceutical industry, endocrinologists, the media, and men in general have promoted a medicopathological definition of aging. With its perceived potential to return the aging male body to a state of socially valued youthful vigor, testosterone has an almost magical attraction. Current media attention, the development of new pharmaceuticals, and the push to explore male aging and testosterone in medical terms are contributing to the further medicalization of the aging male body.

## Historical Context for the Emergence of Testosterone Therapy

The discovery and isolation of testosterone undoubtedly contributed to the movement of male aging into the medical gaze. Although most of the scientific progress surrounding testosterone occurred during and after the nineteenth century, "both folklore and medicine had explored the sources of maleness, seeking ways to promote strength, vitality, and potency" before then (Rothman and Rothman 2003, 132). The medical definition of male aging had its origin in the work of the scientists who pioneered the field of endocrinology. One of the most important ways that scientists made connections between testosterone and masculinity was through observations of castrated men: men without functioning testicles do not exhibit typical "male" attributes. The recognition that the testicles had some powerful effect on the male body predated the discovery of testosterone. Rothman and Rothman (2003, 132) describe nineteenth-century common knowledge relating to the testicles and masculinity:

> After all, as every farmer knew, the testes affected energy and muscularity; to castrate a rooster produced a capon—fatter, softer, and less active. To

castrate an aggressive farm animal (a horse, dog, or bull) rendered him more docile and manageable. Indeed, popular lore recognized that men castrated whether by accident or on purpose . . . lost their manly characteristics.

Thus, according to this logic, an increase in the function of the testicles would amplify, enhance, or replace male traits from an undesirable level to a satisfactory one. Although they did not yet know that testosterone was produced in the testicles, many scientists, all of whom were male, applied this logic in exploring the testicles of a variety of animals.

It was not until 1889 that the endocrinologist Charles Edouard Brown Séquard made the connection between testosterone and aging. Brown Séquard completed a series of controversial experiments on himself. Motivated by a general feeling of malaise, weakness, and fatigue that had persisted for a few years, he injected himself ten times with "a solution composed of testicular blood, testicular extracts, and seminal fluids from dogs and guinea pigs" (Rothman and Rothman 2003, 134). The results were spectacular and dramatic: Brown Séquard reported that he was now able to work long hours in the laboratory, "his muscle strength, as measured on a dynamometer, increased dramatically, his urinary jet stream was 25 percent longer, and his chronic constipation had disappeared" (Rothman and Rothman 2003, 134). This sparked much interest in medical treatments for aging within both the scientific and lay communities. After a report of his presentation appeared in a French newspaper, "a geriatric horde descended on [his] laboratory at the College de France, demanding that he share his miracle potency restoring elixir with them" (Friedman 2001, 251). Some physicians in France and the United States were quick to adopt Brown Séquard's formula in the hope of rejuvenating their aging male patients. Although Brown Séquard's experiments could never be reproduced and he was eventually denounced as a quack, he was the first person to connect male aging to a biological process and to suggest a medical remedy for it.

Physiologists and early endocrinologists continued to be extremely interested in the science behind male physiology at the turn of the twentieth century. Not surprisingly, researchers were more interested in masculinity than fertility as "they defined the male not so much by his ability to reproduce, but by his manliness" (Rothman and Rothman 2003, 136). This concern with masculinity may have contributed to the medicalization of male aging and to the medicalized construction of andropause. In women, menopause is characterized by the cessation of fertility, a socially valued trait. This loss of fertility is considered the primary pathological event in the definition of menopause. Although men do not experience a decline in fertility when they age, they may notice a decrease in some of their allegedly masculine characteristics, such as libido, strength, and physical performance. Medicine, mirroring society, values these traits, and, as a result, provides a pathological definition for their diminution or disappearance.

Endocrinologists prescribed a variety of testicular extracts to male patients, which were identified as useless by the scientific community when the male hormone was isolated in 1935. The accurate isolation of testosterone and the ability of pharmaceutical companies to synthesize it were accompanied by increased optimism within the medical scientific community. As Rothman and Rothman assert, "the newfound ability to produce the male hormone in the laboratory...sparked an even more zealous effort to establish its clinical uses" (2003, 151). Testosterone became a drug in search of a disease to treat. The excitement and increased optimism surrounding testosterone is particularly evident in medical journals following the 1935 discovery: published articles illustrated the dramatic effects that testosterone therapy could have on aging men. Many of these articles began by describing the pre-treatment patient as desperate. In an early issue of the *Journal of the American Medical Association* (*JAMA*), for example, Dr. August Werner wrote "in addition to markedly diminished sexual libido and inadequate penile erections, these patients, prior to treatment with testosterone propionate were disturbed, anxious and broken in spirit" (1939, 1442). Patients who had not yet received testosterone therapy are described as pathetic, broken men, with little ability to function in a society that demanded so much of them (Kearns 1939, 2257). By portraying the so-called male climacteric as a dire condition with potentially devastating consequences for male virility, physicians created a telling case for treatment.

Early pharmaceutical companies had a great deal at stake with testosterone. The optimism and excitement that surrounded the isolation of testosterone was easily translated into marketing strategies that targeted physicians. Companies such as Schering, Oreton, and Ciba promoted the use of testosterone to the medical community in a variety of ways. Schering produced a "clinical guide for physicians about male sex hormone therapy" (Rothman and Rothman 2003). Initially indicated for the treatment of sexual underdevelopment, hypogonadism, and testicular failure, Schering promoted testosterone therapy for the treatment of a broader scope of ailments, primarily the male climacteric. Pharmaceutical companies' promotion of testosterone for male menopause was profit driven, as "sexual underdevelopment was too rare to constitute a substantial market" (Rothman and Rothman 2003, 138), and they worked to develop a wider market for testosterone, with advertisements targeting physicians portraying testosterone as a magic pill that could work wonders for middle-aged male patients. A 1924 advertisement from the *Endocrine Herald* promoted the use of Orchotine, a testicular extract. The advertisement proclaimed that Orchotine was "The Modern Treatment of Mental and Physical Sub Efficiency For Men." The text of the advertisement suggests to physicians that the use of this wonder drug will, beyond a doubt, fix problems that afflict their aging male patients, such as fatigue, mental and physical subefficiency, and sexual apathy.

## Andropause: Disease or Myth?

Andropause is not a clear-cut, easily identifiable or definable condition. In a broad sense, andropause is defined as the age-related decline of testosterone levels in men that is accompanied by various symptoms, such as fatigue, lowered libido, and depression. The confusion surrounding the condition is "evident in the disputes over what to call it—andropause, veropause, male menopause, ADAM, and the male climacteric" (McKinlay and Gemmel 2003). This conceptual confusion has existed for some time, as physicians and scientists have debated the use of each of these terms. A review of the current scientific literature on andropause reveals that describing the age-related decline of testosterone levels in men as "male menopause" and using terms like *andropause, male menopause,* and *the male climacteric* is misleading because, in Louis Gooren's (2003, 350) words, "terms like male menopause or andropause more or less suggest that, similarly to women, all men go through a profound decline of their androgen production from middle age on, but it should be stressed that the age related decline of androgens in men follows a totally different pattern in comparison to the menopause." In other words, *andropause* and *male menopause* are physiologically incorrect terms because, unlike women, men do not universally experience a cessation of gonadal function and reproductive capability. In fact, "aging in healthy men is normally not accompanied by abrupt or drastic alterations of gonadal function, and androgen production as well as fertility can be largely preserved until very old age" (Nieschlag and Behre 1998, 437–438). Some in the medical community have suggested that the more accurate term *partial androgen deficiency in aging males* (PADAM) be used. This search for a scientific-sounding and accurate term is indicative of the process of medicalization, where a legitimate name for a condition promulgates its diagnosis.

While scientists agree that some men may experience a decrease in testosterone with age, the measure and meaning of testosterone levels remain contentious issues. Measuring testosterone levels is not straightforward: debates continue over whether it is the level of "free," bound, or total testosterone that is the most significant measure (Stas et al. 2003), and concerns that testosterone levels can vary from hour to hour and that "periodic declines can occur in some otherwise normal men" (American Association of Clinical Endocrinologists 2002, 442) fuel the debate as well. Thus, "there is currently no gold standard laboratory test" to determine testosterone levels (Tan and Culberson 2003, 16), and no agreement as to what measurement to use to arrive at a diagnosis of andropause. The American Association of Clinical Endocrinologists (AACE) suggests that "an important research goal is to establish a consistent method for determining free testosterone levels and to verify the results so that these levels can be more widely used and trusted" (2002, 442). In short, standardizing ways to measure testosterone levels and creating agreement on what levels are considered abnormal will facilitate a diagnosis of andropause and contribute to increased rates of treatment—a crucial step in the medicalization of masculinity.

Moreover, while there is a basic understanding of testosterone decline and aging, scientists and clinicians know very little about the mechanisms behind the decline and its connection to the physical manifestations of aging. It is clear that testosterone decreases with age, but whether or not this decline means that a man has a pathological condition such as andropause is not known. That professional societies such as the AACE are pushing for a resolution of diagnostic uncertainties, the acceptance of a standard laboratory analysis, and an accurate label to replace andropause is clear evidence that the medical and scientific communities are contributing to the medicalization of aging men's bodies. Indeed, despite the "humbling chasm of ignorance about testosterone therapy," as many as 1.5 million men are taking testosterone supplements (Vastag 2003, 971). The availability of testosterone as a supplement in a convenient form will increase the chance that healthy men will use it to help them "treat" the symptoms of aging.[2]

## Modern Pharmaceutical Companies and the Medicalization of Male Aging

Although testosterone therapy for the treatment of male menopause declined in popularity for most of the second half of the twentieth century, it never completely disappeared. Indeed, while the situation today is still somewhat ambiguous, the idea of a male menopause and the use of testosterone replacement therapy are reemerging, driven by technological advances made in the pharmaceutical realm and by the distribution of these drugs for an increasing range of male troubles, both of which facilitate medicalization.

First, the mode of delivery for testosterone has evolved over the past few decades. By providing a highly effective and convenient form of the drug, more men are likely to participate in treatment, and pharmaceutical companies continue to search for more convenient and attractive treatments. Oral preparations of testosterone, in the form of pills, are relatively easy to take but are problematic because they do not maintain a constant level of the hormone and may cause liver damage. Injections are uncomfortable for everyday use and "produce a sharp spike of the hormone, and then a fall, and these fluctuations are often accompanied by swings in mood, libido, and energy" (Groopman 2002, 1). Patches, worn on the abdomen, back, thighs, or upper arm, maintain a steady level of the hormone but may be uncomfortable or fall off. The most recent form of testosterone, a clear, odorless transdermal gel, can be rubbed into the shoulders once a day without any irritating effects. The main gel on the market today is AndroGel, a product of Unimed, an American division of the Belgian pharmaceutical company Solvay. The United States Food and Drug Administration (FDA) approved AndroGel in February of 2000. Shortly after the FDA approval Robert E. Dudley, president and CEO of Unimed, stated that "we believe that doctors and men who are waiting for a more convenient testosterone treatment will regard AndroGel as a very attractive alternative to existing testosterone replacement therapy" (Doctor's Guide Global Edition 2000).

Secondly, while AndroGel is currently only FDA approved for well-defined conditions associated with hypogonadism, such as Klinefelter's Syndrome,[3] "pharmaceutical companies often obtain FDA approval of a new product for a niche population with a relatively rare disease, hoping to expand later to a larger and more profitable market" (Groopman 2002, 3). This "off label" use of drugs is common medical practice and occurs when a physician prescribes a drug for conditions other than those for which the drug is approved. FDA regulations do not allow AndroGel to be advertised for any nonapproved uses, but pharmaceutical companies can use other avenues for promoting their product. For example, "they can run ads that 'raise awareness' of a condition without mentioning the proprietary therapy by name and they can align themselves with . . . well known physicians whose views are thought to have influence among their peers" (Groopman 2002, 3), and Unimed/Solvay has used both of these tactics to promote the use of AndroGel in aging men. Perhaps the most interesting technique is a patient checklist titled "Could You Have Low Testosterone?" on AndroGel's Web site (www .androgel.com). The questionnaire is derived from a 1997 "Androgen

Deficiency in Aging Men Questionnaire"; the questions are vague and mirror many life changes that occur as men age. Questions such as "Have you noticed a recent deterioration in your ability to play sports?" and "Are you falling asleep after dinner?" hardly seem like clear medical symptoms, yet the implicit promotion of AndroGel turns these common life events into symptoms of a medical problem and suggests that a physician review the checklist.

## The Allure of Testosterone

Although pharmaceutical companies promoting andropause have been prominent advocates for the medicalization of male aging, they are not alone. The promise of testosterone therapy has an almost magical allure for many people, including clinicians, their patients, and even the lay public. Testosterone is often portrayed as a miraculous substance, with amazing power to restore or enhance masculinity. The metaphors for testosterone in the public media illustrate the magical light within which the male hormone is often viewed. Men become complicit in their own medicalization with the promise that such treatments can produce astonishing results.

An advertisement for AndroGel from the March 2003 issue of *Clinical Endocrinology* represents another way in which testosterone is framed to physicians and their male patients. The advertisement depicts a gas gauge with the arrow pointed to Empty. The text states "Low Sex Drive? Fatigued? Depressed Mood? These could be indicators that your testosterone is running on empty." Here, testosterone is depicted as fuel for the male body that can be used up; the body does not naturally replace the material essential to sustaining its gender. Playing on the body-as-machine metaphor, the brightly colored dial illustrating two poles—Empty or Full—suggests that men and their physicians can simply "fill up" with testosterone supplementation to regain sex drive, energy, and optimism—essentially masculine qualities. Testosterone supplementation is promoted as something that many men will need as part of the regular maintenance of their body—not depicted as a rare condition, here andropause emerges as a mundane, typical, and predictable aspect of the daily life (and lived bodies) of men.

Testosterone therapy is also an attractive subject for the press. Different print sources publish stories that begin with headlines like "Testosterone: Shot in the arm for aging males" (Preidt 2002) or "Are You Man Enough? Testosterone can make a difference in bed and at the gym" (McLaughlin and Park 2000). These pieces almost always begin with the personal story of a man who was tired at work, uninterested in sex with his wife, failing on the football field/at the gym/on the squash court and whose life turned around after his physician prescribed testosterone. Using a metaphor redolent with images of man as a sleek, powerful, and fast machine, one journalist wrote, "if you happen to be a man, the very idea is bound to appeal to your inner hood ornament, to that image of yourself as all wind sheared edges and sunlit chrome" (McLaughlin and Park 2000, 58). This statement reflects a cultural preoccupation with reinvigorating the male body as a series of working parts that come together under the influence of "rocket fuel" (Friedman 2001). The millions of aging male baby boomers are an attractive market for both the media and pharmaceutical manufacturers (Friedan 1993b; Hepworth and Featherstone 1998). Coupled with the real and imagined aging male concerns with body failure, it seems likely that we will see testosterone replacement therapy as an important step in the medicalization of aging male bodies in the next decade.

## Baldness: Plugs and Drugs

Losing one's hair or going bald is a common bodily occurrence that can cause anxiety among aging men. While remedies ranging from tonics and elixirs to bear grease have a long history, and medicine has long been concerned with hair loss, baldness has only recently begun to become medicalized. Although the medical profession is reticent to call baldness a disease, the medicalization of baldness is gaining momentum in the light of new medical treatments for hair loss. Here, too, we see the invention and availability of medical therapies driving the process of medicalization.

### A Brief Look at Historical Treatments for Baldness

Throughout history, men have been concerned with hair loss, as evidenced by an impressive range of remedies, potions, and concoctions used to treat baldness. One of the first known written medical records, the Ebers Papyrus, dates back to 1500 B.C. and contains eleven recipes for the treatment of baldness. One recipe "advised the sufferer to apply a mixture of burned prickles of a hedgehog immersed in oil, fingernail scrapings, and a potpourri of honey, alabaster, and red ocher" (Segrave 1996, 3). Baldness treatments were understood in magical, mythical terms. For example, in the sixteenth century A.D., the alchemist Paracelsus prescribed an elixir that purportedly contained "blood from women in childbirth, the blood of a murdered new born baby, and 'vipers' wine'" (Cooper 1971, 153). The treatment of baldness was left to alchemists who created concoctions that were shrouded in mystery.

Until the late nineteenth century, there was little medical interest in the cause or potential treatments for baldness: medical science had limited legitimacy in an area where traditionally "the care of hair was left in the hands of charlatans, and treatments involved a mumbo jumbo of alchemy, magic, and superstition" (Cooper 1971, 157), and since most of the remedies for baldness were ineffective, medicine had little to offer for the treatment of hair loss. However, the late nineteenth century saw the emergence of several medical theories about baldness. Physicians and scientists conceived of a myriad of different causes of baldness, ranging from the logical to the bizarre. One of the most popular theories was that hats caused baldness because "they compressed the circulation system, thus reducing nourishment to the hair" (Segrave 1996, 14). Many physicians speculated on the hat theory, suggesting that the shape of the skull or the style of the hat were to blame. Accessing the new germ theory to present a pathological view of baldness, M. Sebouraud, a French physiologist, announced at the 1897 meeting of the Dermatological Society of Paris that a microbe caused baldness. Medical journals warned that "combs should be boiled regularly and frequently, and under no circumstances should members of precociously bald families use other combs or brushes than their own, or allow them to be used on them, in barber shops, unless they are assured of their sterilization beforehand" (*JAMA* 1903, 249). Late-nineteenth-century dermatologists believed that irritating the scalp through blistering would cause hair regrowth. The procedure, known as vesication, "was believed to produce pooling of blood in the scalp, which provided more nourishment for the follicles there, causing hair regrowth" (Segrave 1996, 52). Other treatments included vacuum caps and electrical shock treatment. Men subjected themselves to painful treatments like vesication and electric shock in the hopes of medically producing hair growth. Interestingly, none of these alleged causes were specifically gendered.

## Current Medical Understanding of Baldness

Despite or perhaps because of the quackery of the past, modern biomedicine has shown a keen interest in researching the causes of male pattern baldness (referred to in the scientific literature as "androgenetic alopecia"). Despite the fact that a MEDLINE search we conducted for articles from 1985 to 2003 on androgenetic alopecia produced 356 citations, and despite the fact that the term "androgenetic alopecia" evolved from the understanding that male baldness (alopecia) is dependent upon male hormones (androgens) and genetics, there is disagreement over whether androgenetic alopecia is actually a disease. One textbook states, "the human species is not the only primate species in which baldness is a natural phenomenon associated with sexual maturity" (Dawber and Van Neste 1995, 96). Other medical agents believe that "androgenetic alopecia becomes a medical problem only when the hair loss is subjectively seen as excessive, premature, and distressing" (Sinclair 1998, 865), with some distinguishing between androgenetic alopecia and hair changes that accompany "natural" aging, known as senescent baldness. The dermatologist David Whiting writes, "the clinical and histologic evidence for senescent alopecia is not clear cut and is still disputed" (1998, 564). However, the ambivalence scientific writings express over the identity (or lack thereof) of male baldness as a distinct pathology coexists with the medicalization of male pattern baldness as seen in the definition of androgenetic alopecia as a distinct entity from hair loss associated with "normal" aging.

Indeed, a science of hair loss has recently developed within this partially medicalized context: researchers have found that the male hormone dihydrotestosterone causes the hair follicle to produce the fine, unpigmented hair common in baldness. Growing evidence shows that male pattern baldness runs in families and has a genetic basis: a gene called "sonic hedgehog" has been implicated in baldness. A *Science News* article declares enthusiastically that "scientists suggest that a gene named after the combative [video game] character could prove a potent weapon in the battle against a fearsome foe: baldness" (*Science News* 1999, 283). A recent study published in *Nature Biotechnology* (April 2004) suggests that stem cells may be helpful in curing baldness. Such findings have been significant in providing a medical basis for baldness and its treatment.

According to a definition mentioned earlier (Sinclair 1998), androgenetic alopecia becomes a medical condition when hair loss is excessive. Determination of what constitutes excessive hair loss is subjective, yet medicine has created standards of hair loss through visual representations and quantitative means. Medical textbooks and journal articles contain diagrams that visually depict the progression of baldness, known as categorical classification systems. These diagrams represent categories of increasing severity from mild to severe hair loss. Surgeons and dermatologists commonly use them, and this system "has become the standard of classification for hair restoration physicians" (Stough and Haber 1996, 15).

Descriptions of baldness are awash in medical terminology. Consider the following description, which corresponds to a Norwood level V classification:

> *Type V.* The vertex region of alopecia remains separated from the frontotemporal region of alopecia. The separation is not as distinct as that in

type IV because the band of hair across the crown is narrower and sparser. Both the vertex and frontotemporal areas of alopecia are larger than those in type IV. (Stough and Haber 1996, 16)

The language of this description is medically precise and does not assign subjective value to the phenomenon. Other diagnostic criteria exist, including measurements such as hair density, hair length, hair diameter, and cosmetically significant hair, defined as "a hair with a defined thickness and length, usually >40$\mu$m and at least 3 cm long" (Van Neste 2002, 364). Medicine has attempted to quantify the exact length and diameter of a hair that would be considered attractive. Although the use of medical terms and measurements seems to remove the value judgments of baldness, the standards are still subjective and influenced by sociocultural expectations. Even M. D. Van Neste, a clinical dermatologist, admits to the capriciousness of this measurement when he writes, "fashion may . . . limit the application of the method depending on what hair style is desirable for the patient (e.g., a close hair cut is the currently popular style compared with longer hair in 1970)" (2002, 364).

## Current Treatments for Baldness

Modern medical, surgical, and pharmaceutical technology has yielded treatments for baldness that differ from the snake oils of the past in their efficacy and are currently the driving force in the medicalization of baldness; however, while effective, the drugs Rogaine and Propecia and hair transplant surgery are not miracle cures for baldness, but may be costly, painful, and useful for only some men. Despite such limitations, these treatments have been verified by the medical community, including the Food and Drug Administration, and are thus considered legitimate medical treatments. The cost of these treatments is significant, particularly for Rogaine and Propecia. Estimates from 1999 indicate that men spent nine hundred million dollars on medical treatments (Rogaine, Propecia, and hair transplant surgery) for baldness (Scow, Nolte and Shaughnessy 1999). Brand-name Rogaine costs three hundred dollars for a year's supply, and Propecia costs six hundred dollars (Scow, Nolte and Shaughnessy 1999). Because these two treatments must be continued indefinitely lest hair loss return, pharmaceutical companies are encouraged to develop and market these expensive and lucrative hair growth drugs. Moreover, hair transplants can cost anywhere from two thousand dollars to over ten thousand dollars depending on how many hairs are transplanted (Fischer 1997)—here too, many patients will require repeat surgeries to maintain the transplant, creating a lucrative market for hair restoration surgery.

*Surgical Treatments*   There are three surgical treatments for male pattern baldness: transplants using a plug or graft technique, scalp reduction, and scalp flaps. As P. Bouhanna and J. C. Dardour assert, "the basic principle of the surgery of baldness consists in distributing the paucity of material as uniformly as possible" (2000, 29). Hair restoration techniques have limitations since baldness is a progressive condition: a transplant on a man in his thirties may look good at the time, but twenty years later his hair pattern could change significantly, rendering the cosmetic benefits of the transplant obsolete. Thus, although conceived of as a medical treatment for baldness, surgical procedures do not "cure" baldness but simply mask it. Textbooks and surgical atlases recognize this limitation. Marritt and Dzubow (1996, 30) contend that "hair restoration" is a misnomer, writing, "sadly, hair restoration has nothing at all to do with the restorative process. Hair cannot be restored or resuscitated, only rearranged."

Hair transplantation using plugs or grafts involves removing a section of the scalp from a part of the head that still has hair and sectioning this piece into "plugs" or "grafts" with a few follicles each. The plugs are then transplanted to the front of the scalp in an attempt to create a "natural" hairline. According to the surgical hair restoration literature, the creation of an "aesthetically pleasing" hairline is of utmost importance (Khan and Stough 1996), as is "naturalness." A goal of this surgery is to make it appear as if it were never done; one article even warns against "lowering the hairline to a position of youth . . . If the hairline is restored in a middle aged person to the level of hair when they were 18 or so, it looks very unnatural" (Muiderman 2001, 142). This paradox characterizes the field of hair transplant surgery. Overall, the procedures available today are only moderately effective, with side effects including scarring, infection, and rejection of donor grafts. As a result, hair restoration surgery has had limited appeal as a medical treatment for baldness. The cutting edge of medical interventions for hair loss resides in pharmaceutical treatments.

*Rogaine*   The pharmaceutical company UpJohn was not seeking a baldness cure when it happened upon minoxidil, the active chemical in Rogaine. In the mid-1960s, researchers found that minoxidil lowered heart rate. FDA approval followed for the drug, known as Loniten, in 1979 for the treatment of severe high blood pressure. Loniten was not expected to be a high-profit drug, since it had a relatively specific target group. However, during clinical trials for hypertension, researchers had noticed that one patient had grown new hair on the top of his head. This growth was significant because it was dark, thick terminal hair; the kind that is lost in baldness. When the media picked up research reports about this side effect of minoxidil, interested volunteers deluged dermatologists and physicians. As an associate of Dr. Howard Baden, a Harvard researcher involved with early trials of minoxidil, says, "it wasn't even necessary to advertise for volunteers. All you have to do is whisper in the corridors that you're doing a study of male baldness and you get all the volunteers you want" (Segrave 1996, 148). Clearly, the demand for an effective medical drug for male baldness was tremendous.

In the mid-1980s, even though the FDA had not approved the drug for treatment of baldness, many physicians were prescribing Loniten for their balding patients. This off-label use was so widespread that a 1986 survey estimated that "American dermatologists were prescribing topical minoxidil to over 100,000 patients per year" (Segrave 1996, 153). It was clear that this growth was not due to an expanding hypertension market. In December 1985, UpJohn presented their newly researched baldness treatment, Regaine topical solution, to the FDA for approval. After UpJohn modified its product information and changed the name of its minoxidil to Rogaine (which the FDA felt was less misleading than Regaine), the FDA granted approval on August 18, 1988.[4]

The availability of Rogaine changed dramatically on February 12, 1996, when the FDA approved both the over-the-counter sale of the drug and the production of generic formulations of minoxidil. Determined to stay a leader in the hair growth market, UpJohn released a 5-percent stronger formula of Rogaine in 1997 and launched an advertising campaign emphasizing the strength of the new formula and of the men who use it. A 1999 advertisement features the tennis player John McEnroe promoting the "return" of Rogaine. The advertisement tells consumers that McEnroe "attacked" his bald spot and "beat" it. It also poses the question, "Is John the first man to snatch victory from the follicles of defeat? Far from it." The message being communicated here is that using Rogaine can help men conquer their baldness by aggressively attacking it. Other Rogaine promotional materials utilize the slogan "stronger than heredity" and depict a bald father sitting next to his son with captions like "I love Dad. I'm just not in a rush to look like him." Rogaine is depicted as a drug that can give men power and control over a bodily change that was once perceived as inevitable. This is a seductive message, and one that reconfigures male aging as a vulnerable, though tenacious, foe.

*Propecia*   Rogaine's potential for profit was diminished when, on December 22, 1997, the FDA approved Merck's hair loss pill, Propecia. Researchers stumbled upon the hair growth properties of the drug

finasteride while it was being tested for use in men with enlarged pros-
tates. The effectiveness of finasteride for preventing hair loss has been
evaluated in three studies comprising a total of 1,879 men (Scow, Nolte,
and Shaughnessy 1999). Results are promising in that the drug is effective
in preventing baldness in the early stages of androgenetic alopecia.
Current scientific understanding supports the early use of Propecia because in most cases of androgenetic alopecia, "prevention and maintenance are the most realistic therapeutic options" (Ramos e Silva 2000,
729). Propecia works well for men who have just begun to notice signs of
baldness but will not regrow hair, and because it cannot reverse significant hair loss, it is not even technically a cure for baldness. To maintain
the benefits of Propecia, men must take the medication for the rest of
their lives, or they will revert to the normal progression of balding.

Propecia targets self-conscious men who are troubled by their hair
loss, telling them that their impending baldness is preventable. Early
Propecia advertisements depicted a man with a slight bald spot and a
troubled, hopeless look on his face gazing into a bathroom mirror,
seeing a reflection of himself as totally bald. The text of the advertisement reads, "If you think losing more hair is inevitable, think again."
Another Propecia advertisement depicts a man with a bald spot staring at
a dome. The text reads, "You don't need reminders about your hair loss.
You need something to deal with it." Empowerment to attack hair loss
and regain control is a central theme seen in both Rogaine and Propecia
advertisements: even if a medical solution is not fully effective, the fact
that one exists is enough to make men potentially empowered to do
something about baldness. This is the attraction of drugs like Rogaine
and Propecia, which contribute to medicalizing hair loss by providing
men with medical treatments to conquer a troubling "disease."

## Psychosocial Construction of Baldness

Psychological effects of baldness serve as one of the main justifications
for the treatment of hair loss as a disease. Medical textbooks and journal
articles on the subject of treating baldness often have a separate section
on psychosocial concerns or the effect of hair loss on quality of life. As
Valerie Randall asserts early on in her chapter on androgenetic alopecia:

> In our youth oriented culture, the association of hair loss with increasing
> age has negative connotations and, since hair plays such an important
> role in human social and sexual communication, male pattern bald-
> ness often causes marked psychological distress and reduction in the
> quality of life, despite not being life threatening or physically painful.
> (2000, 125)

While such psychosocial connotations may or may not be accurate, making this connection allows Randall to justify treating hair loss as a disease, albeit a psychological one. Indeed, some physicians cite the negative psychological correlates of baldness as the justification for medical treatment of hair loss. Emanuel Marritt, a hair restoration surgeon, sees this as his medical responsibility: "that 'simple office procedure' has, in reality, just handed me a life sentence of follicular responsibility. The weight of this awareness is not only humbling, it can be at times, simply overwhelming" (1993, 4). While Marritt's views on treating hair loss are influenced by the fact that he specializes in a more invasive procedure than does a dermatologist prescribing Propecia, he expresses an increasingly common viewpoint: hair loss is a serious problem worthy of medical intervention.

Given the Western cultural view of hair loss, it is not surprising that men may hold negative views of baldness. A recent advertisement for Hershey's chocolate depicts the progression of baldness in a man with the text "change is bad." Although it has nothing to do with baldness therapy, the advertisement reinforces the view that bodily change due to age is not welcome and is stigmatized. Baldness often represents a loss of masculine traits and can affect male self-esteem. Psychological studies document the negative impact baldness can have on male mental health. Pamela Wells, Trevor Willmouth, and Robin Russell (1995) found that hair loss in men is associated with depression, low self-esteem, neuroticism, introversion, and feelings of unattractiveness. There are of course cultural counterexamples of bald men. Actors like Yul Brenner and sports stars like Andre Agassi or Michael Jordan are not considered unattractive because they are bald. These are examples of men who have embraced baldness and shaved their remaining hair. They have, in a sense, taken control of their hair loss. But these counterexamples stand in contrast to the generally negative views of baldness as an undesirable condition and one increasingly deemed appropriate for medical treatment.

## Concluding Remarks

Andropause and baldness represent aspects of aging male bodies that have become partially medicalized in recent years. As new pharmaceuticals are developed and medical science understands more about the physiological basis of aging, it is likely that medicalization will continue. Men and masculinity have often been omitted from medicalization analyses, in part due to the belief that men are not as vulnerable to medical surveillance and control as women. But, as this chapter demonstrates, such a belief is no longer tenable.

Medicine has long been an avenue for women to resist aging bodies and reclaim fading youthful features. Now this avenue is available and becoming increasingly appealing to men. Youth and youthful manifestations of the body are paramount, as "contemporary expectations about health, fitness, and sexuality have pushed men to maintain youthful performance in all aspects of their lives" (Luciano 2001, 204). Medical treatments can help men achieve this youthful appearance, if not performance.

While both andropause and baldness are medicalized aspects of aging male bodies, they show some contrasting features. Male testosterone levels decline as men age, but it is unclear what this means. Unlike menopause in women, andropause has no distinct markers or "symptoms." Although claims have been made regarding the benefits of testosterone replacement therapy, there is precious little evidence of any efficacy or improvement from such treatments. Baldness, on the other hand, is a distinct physiological condition, similar in some ways to a disease or disorder; it appears to have a genetic basis and creates what could be called a "bodily dysfunction" but, until recently, was not considered a medical disorder, nor were medical treatments available for it. With the advent of surgical and pharmaceutical treatments, however, hair loss has been increasingly medicalized; while not yet conceptualized as a disease, baldness is an actual bodily change that can be treated through medical interventions. In a sense, andropause has a medical name but unclear symptoms and no efficacious treatment. In contrast, baldness has clear symptoms and a range of medical treatments, some of which have achieved success.

In both cases, we see the infiltration of biomedicine into everyday life through definitions or treatments that redefine "healthy" and "normal" male bodily function. Men experience and understand their bodies differently if the aging process is constructed in pathological terms. The maintenance of masculinity is often connected to the functioning of the male body. As body function declines, self-conceptions of masculinity may be imperiled. This may invite men to seek medical solutions to repair or retain the body's abilities, especially in western culture where "all of us are encouraged to believe that our problem, aging, is natural, inevitable, awful, but controllable" (Gullette 1997, 231).

This male anxiety about aging and masculinity, while not ubiquitous, is sufficiently common in American society to create a strong market for medical solutions. Given the growing number of aging baby boomers in our generally youth-oriented culture, it is not surprising that male bodies are increasingly being seen as potential markets for medical solutions. The advent and promotion of products like AndroGel, Propecia and Rogaine, and Viagra, Levitra, and Cialis may just be the beginning of a new medicalization of aging male bodies. The potential market expands when one considers that certain types of body maintenance and prevention must begin long before the onset of "old age" (Katz and Marshall 2004). Pharmaceutical promotion of so called "lifestyle drugs" that "treat conditions understood not as life threatening, but rather as life limiting" (Mamo and Fishman 2001, 16) is likely to be one of the forces pushing toward the medicalization of male bodies. The combination of corporate promotion and consumer demand together make medical definitions and treatments of human problems increasingly likely (Conrad and Leiter 2004).

Male concerns with aging bodies are propelling men to seek medical solutions for declining signs of masculinity. These threats to traditional characteristics of manliness are not universal, but seem to be increasing as pharmaceutical and medical entrepreneurs seek to establish markets, amplify male anxieties, and provide solutions to the problems of aging men. The medicalization of aging male bodies requires the joint action of men who seek solutions for perceived masculinity decline and the medical treatments that are offered to reinvigorate significant attributes of such masculinity. The huge success of Viagra and the partial medicalization of andropause and hair loss may be only the beginning. With the baby boomers coming into their sixties, one may expect an expansion of the medicalized categories and treatments for various ailments associated with aging men and masculinity.

# 5

## Dissecting Medicine: Gender Biases in the Discourses and Practices of Medical Anatomy

Alan Petersen and Sam Regan de Bere

### Introduction

Medicine, like other disciplines, has been the subject of numerous histories. Official histories, written by members of the profession itself, tend to be stories of continuity and inexorable progress, involving great feats and heroic figures. The past is portrayed as leading inevitably to the present. Such histories, like those written by victors of battles, tend to confirm the rightness of the present; to show that things could not or should not have been otherwise. For example, the rise of anatomical dissection is seen to have brought enlightenment about the workings of the body, while the birth of germ theory is seen to have paved the way for the penicillin revolution and the saving of lives. Social scientists, on the other hand, have drawn attention to the social production and social relations of medicine, to the exercise of power, and to winners and losers in political struggles (Richardson 2000; Sappol 2002; Starr 1982). Social science histories, while not always overtly "critical" of the present, tend to unsettle the self-evidence of our ways of thinking and acting by showing them to be "socially constructed" and therefore by no means inevitable. Feminist histories of medicine have been largely of this kind.

Feminists contend that the history of medicine and anatomical sciences has been a history of a *gendered* practice. A rich corpus of feminist historical scholarship has revealed how, since its birth, scientific medicine and anatomical practice has controlled women's bodies and lives, and the male-dominated medical establishment has taken over women's healing practices and suppressed women healers (e.g., Ehrenreich and English 1973, 1979; Thompson 1999). Women's behaviors and conditions are portrayed as having been "medicalized," in that events previously defined in nonmedical terms, such as childbirth and abortion, became medical events (Reissman 2003; Oakley 1984; Rose 1983; Wallsgrove 1980). Consequently, medicine and medical practices have been key sites for feminist struggles to regain control of women's bodies and women's health and healing. For example, the emergence of activist groups, such as the Feminist International Network Resisting Reproductive and Genetic Engineering, the development of women's health centers, and the turn to complementary healers and "holistic" care have been some of the practical responses to what has been described as the medicalization of femininity. We would argue that exposing processes of medicalization and revealing their effects, is integral to the effort to recover the feminine and human dimensions of medicine that appear to have been lost over time.

Feminist work has been insightful and influential, helping to highlight the poor treatment and injustices suffered by many women due to medical interventions. However, in their tendency to focus almost exclusively on the control of *women's* bodies and lives, feminists have tended to overlook how the gender system of medicine intervenes in the bodies and lives of both women *and* men. By positing women as subjects of medicalization, feminists have tended to render women as passive victims of medical ascendancy and thereby to perpetuate the very assumptions about women that feminists have sought to challenge (Reissman 2003, 47). Thus far, there has been little focus on women as active agents within medical systems, on counter-discourses, and on exploring the potential for resistance to medical norms.

This chapter attempts to fill this gap by examining the engendering of medical anatomy, and asks whether recent developments in the philosophy and practice of anatomy reflect a "feminization" of medicine. Anatomy is a particularly useful domain within which to explore the production of and changes in the gender norms of medicine and to evaluate the significance of discursive shifts in medical practice. Anatomical dissection has long been seen as a defining feature of the medical profession and for student doctors (who are mainly male), provides evidence of a developing professional status (see, e.g., Richardson 2000;

Sappol 2002). The transference of anatomy from the hands of the barber surgeon to those of the professional surgeon physician signified the emerging importance and credibility of medicine as a scientifically and intellectually driven pursuit, and an emphasis on empirical research placed anatomical dissection at the very heart of medical science. The teaching of anatomy through dissection has since become the mainstay of modern medical education, a symbolic initiation that distinguishes medical professionals from practitioners of other established sciences. That anatomy is central to modern medicine's identity is underlined by the strong reaction by sections of the medical profession to recent suggestions to dispense with the use of cadaveric dissection in medical education (Stansby 2004; Mitchell and Stephens 2004).

In this chapter, we focus on the anatomy profession in terms of those who work within it, those whose bodies are worked upon, and the anatomical learning that has resulted. We take a genealogical approach to exploring the gender, class, and racial biases inherent in the anatomy profession (see Foucault 1977, 1978). We argue that societal transformation has continually informed and transformed a clearly gendered anatomy profession, along with the medical profession of which it is core. Discussion is structured through reference to discursive practices in three key spheres: professional membership, research and teaching practice, and anatomical knowledge. Our genealogical approach therefore not only helps us to understand gendered medicine. It also helps us to consider how such understanding can be facilitated (or constrained) by applying a "masculine" or "feminine" sociological gaze to the topic at hand. In order to achieve this, we draw on a largely feminist critique of modern "masculinized" anatomy before raising questions about the possible "feminization" of the profession, via more humanistic, egalitarian, and feminist discourses. The evidence presented in the chapter demonstrates that the latter issue is a complex one and one worthy of further analysis and sociological debate.

## The Gendering of Anatomy
### Professional Membership

Throughout most of its history, anatomy—including its teaching and practice—has been constructed and portrayed as a quintessentially masculine pursuit. Women were excluded from medical schools and from the dissection room until the second half of the nineteenth century. Indeed, few universities in any European countries accepted women (or racial minorities) for admission to study, and those women who graduated remained barred from the public realm (Schiebinger 1990, 400).

In the United States, by 1893–1894, women represented 10 percent or more of the students at nineteen coeducational medical schools (Starr 1982, 117). The growth of coeducational schools at first produced only a small increase in the percentage of female doctors between 1880 and 1900, from 2.8 to 5.6 percent—though in some cities the proportion was higher; for example, 19.3 percent in Minneapolis and 13.8 percent in San Francisco. However, the representation of women was even worse in England and France. Whereas at the turn of the century, in the United States there were seven thousand female physicians, England had just 258 and France only 95 (Starr 1982, 117).

As Paul Starr notes, in the United States, the growing number of women in medicine did not occur without resistance from men in the field. Women were viewed as especially unsuited to dissecting cadavers, which was seen as somehow polluting of a natural femininity. While for women, anatomical studies offered the possibility of escape from traditional gender roles and obligations, including marriage, for men, women's involvement in dissection challenged the masculinist coding of anatomical dissection (Sappol 2002, 88–89). And women who did dissect were "masculinized" in that they assumed the characteristics of men. As Michael Sappol (2002, 90) notes, "The 'in-group' men were imitated by a female 'out-group' who wore their hair short like men, were 'serious' (eschewed female frivolity and feminine dress), and abandoned the normative female role." In coeducational settings, female dissecting rooms served to govern a similar homosocial order to that operating among male students, which was challenged only with the rise of feminism in the 1970s (Sappol 2002, 90).

This "masculinization" of the subject of anatomy was integral to the development of the identity of an emergent scientifically based medical profession. Undertaking dissection served as a male bonding ritual by allowing novice practitioners to demonstrate to one another and to others their shared essential difference from women who, like the dissected cadavers, were constructed as passive objects of men's instrumental reason. Dissecting-room antics among male anatomy students served to socialize neophytes into masculine culture. Sappol (2002, 81) describes "the high-spirited camaraderie among medical students, who often enough performed rituals of professional and scholastic solidarity via copious consumption of alcoholic beverages and tobacco, in addition to their dissections." Pranks involving body parts were common in the eighteenth and nineteenth centuries, and bodies and severed limbs were often displayed to visitors or taken home. These sometimes involved the snatching of bodies from graveyards and even from death vigils (Sappol 2002, 84–87).

## Research and Teaching Practice

The professionalization of scientific medicine has gone hand in hand with the growing control over women's bodies and women's healing. Medical education has been traditionally a male *rite de passage* that is necessary for the development of the mind and the production of the learned practitioner (Porter 2003, 34–35). Even when universities eventually opened their doors to women, the theory of complementary opposites, which predominated from the late eighteenth century, provided a barrier to women's involvement in public life (Lloyd 1984). This theory suggested that women and men were essentially different but complementary in all aspects, and that women's natural role was as childbearer, carer, and supporter of their husbands (Yalom 2001). Women who challenged this traditional order were either ostracized or masculinized. In some cases, women attempted to pass themselves off as men in the effort to advance themselves in a male-dominated social order (see, e.g., Trumbach 1994). In the case of medicine, however, there were few enticements and little material support to enable women to enter the profession. In the nineteenth century, as now, relatively few women were privileged enough to undertake the long period of uninterrupted medical training required to become a licensed practitioner.

The predominance of the male practitioner in the history of anatomy education and practice is only part of the story of the "masculinization" of anatomy. The knowledge and the teaching of anatomy reflect the male worldview of white European males. As Roy Porter (2003, 34) argues, from the twelfth century and the founding of universities and the recovery and retranslation of learned medicine from Islamic sources, the goal of formal scholastic education has been the acquisition of rational knowledge within a philosophical framework. Men who undertook medical education undertook a prolonged university education to render them expert in the liberal arts and sciences. Only a certain strata could afford the long arduous training required to instill the requisite cultural capital. The ideal physician was a saintly, austere, dignified figure who could be readily distinguished from the "quack," who was a "money-grabbing pretender," and the nurse and midwife who were caricatured either as inebriates or as gossipy (Porter 2003). In learning how to view and act upon the body rationally and dispassionately, novice physicians developed those qualities judged to be desirable in medical practice, detachment, objectivity, and emotional control—those qualities most closely associated in modern Western culture with masculinity. The emotional culture of medicine, like male emotional culture, values "level-headedness" and eschews any displays of vulnerability or expressions of uncertainty, which can undermine claims to authority.

As Larsen and Pleck (1998, 56) explain, in their analysis of male emotional communication, "By giving the appearance that they are unwavering, by not displaying weakness, and by creating the impression that their decisions are made with rationality and efficiency, men maintain and strengthen their power in a relationship." In undertaking dissection, the male medical student acquires and demonstrates a mastery over both the subject and himself (Sappol 2002, 80). Like sports and warfare, dissection serves as a root metaphor of male culture in that "it expresses a competitive, Social Darwinist moral order" (see Larsen and Pleck 1998, 51). Anatomical science has mirrored this vision of the moral order. As Londa Schiebinger (1990) notes, the development of anatomical knowledge was generated in a context of fascination with the classification of difference. The European men who dominated science during the eighteenth century—the "great age of classification"—both controlled what was recognized as and produced legitimate knowledge. They wrote natural history from their point of view, using the European male as the standard of physical and scientific excellence (Petersen 1998a).

Anatomists sought to establish a schema for dividing humankind based upon categories such as age, sex, nationality, nourishment, and susceptibility to illnesses, lifestyle, and clothing. Of these, sex and race emerged as central categories of analysis. In seeking to characterize and classify the races and the sexes, anatomists faced the critical dilemma of where to rank the black man (the dominant sex of an inferior race) in relation to the white woman (the inferior sex of the dominant race; Schiebinger 1990, 389). As Schiebinger notes, for anatomists, "the question was how these subordinated groups measured up to the European male" (1990, 404). Anatomists have sought to identify irreducible physical markers of difference (e.g., hair and skull shape and size) by which one could judge intellectual and moral abilities and thus rank humankind. It was believed that growing debates about equality could be settled by reference to anatomy rather than to ethics (Schiebinger 1990, 405). Consequently, anatomists found "evidence" that confirmed that white women and black people lacked intelligence. Because these groups were excluded from centers of learning, they could say little about their actual capacities (Schiebinger 1990, 404).

Despite evidence that social hierarchies have structured scientific debates, anatomical knowledge continues to be presented as objective knowledge; that is, as unaffected by the worldviews of the European males who have produced it. Because of their connection with femininity, emotion and empathy have been seen as potentially disruptive of scientific medicine's professional self-image and of medical practice. From the Middle Ages, the developing scientific worldview of medicine posited the body as a machine that could be broken down into its component parts and understood without reference to the mind of its "owner" (Capra 1983). This Cartesian mind/body dualism has been underpinned and supported by a series of further dualisms: subject/object, nature/culture, masculine/feminine, and reason and emotion. The process of learning to view the body as a machine, particularly through dissection, is integral to the process of learning the norms of masculinity; that is, how to conduct one's self without "becoming emotional" (i.e., feminized).

## Anatomical Knowledge

Anatomical texts have played a key role in teaching medical students and lay publics decontextualized knowledge about the body-machine. Studies of anatomy textbooks widely used in medical education, covering different periods, have shown how the male has been portrayed as the standard human body against which the female is implicitly measured (e.g., Giacomini, Rozée-Coker, and Pepitone-Arreola-Rockwell 1986; Lawrence and Bendixen 1992; Moore and Clarke 1995; Schiebinger 1986, 1990; Petersen 1998b). The male body has been found to be greatly overrepresented in standard chapters of anatomy texts, with a more equal representation of males and females evident only in urogenital (gender-specific) chapters (e.g., Lawrence and Bendixen 1992; Giacomini, Rozée-Coker, and Pepitone-Arreola-Rockwell 1986, 416–417). As Mita Giacomini and colleagues (1986) argue, this greater visibility of males serves to pathologize women's bodies by implicitly conveying the message to students that women's bodies are exceptional and abnormal. It suggests that women are mysterious and that female patients are less deserving of diagnosis than are male patients. The more equal representation of women's bodies in the reproductive chapters when viewed in the context of the entire textbook suggests that the important features of women's bodies are those associated with the specialized and limited functions of sexual partner and mother (Giacomonini, Rozée-Coker, and Pepitone-Arreola-Rockwell 1986, 417–418).

A study of gynecology texts, covering 1943 to 1972, revealed that a basic image of woman and her "normal" adult role in a marital relationship had changed little during that period despite the emergence of new data challenging such views (e.g., Kinsey 1953; Scully and Bart 1973, 286). For example, as late as 1965, gynecology texts referred to the vagina as the main erogenous zone (Scully and Bart 1973, 285). In their study of anatomy texts used in medical education in the United States between 1890 and 1989, Susan Lawrence and Kai Bendixen (1992) found that anatomy texts have remained generally consistent in how "the" human body has been depicted during the whole of the twentieth century. In their illustrations, vocabulary and syntax, the anatomy texts depict male anatomy as the norm against which female structures are compared, continuing long-standing historical conventions of setting the male as the central model of human anatomy. Chapters tended to employ a male-centered organization or used male-only descriptions, thus reproducing male anatomy as the standard to which the female is implicitly contrasted. Most comparative statements compared the female to the male structure, either directly or by using the female term in parentheses after the male expression (Lawrence and Bendixen 1992, 931).

Other research has confirmed that anatomy has remained relatively stable and impervious to the challenges posed by feminists and sexologists. In their study of the visual representations of the clitoris in anatomy texts during the twentieth century, Lisa Jean Moore and Adele Clarke (1995) found female anatomy to be less visible than male anatomy (e.g., the clitoris was sometimes missing in diagrams). Further, women's sexual response was inextricably linked with reproductive function (Moore and Clarke 1995, 271, 284, 289–291). In their more recent study of cyberanatomies, Moore and Clarke (2001) found a continuing bias against the clitoris, which remains largely invisible or portrayed as nonagentic in this media. Although the Internet would seem to provide the potential for alternative anatomical representations to counter the traditional biomedical genre, as the authors conclude, "popular alternative genital anatomies, including feminist anatomies, remain comparatively rare, isolated and difficult to locate" (Moore and Clarke 2001, 85). Further, Alan Petersen's (1998) study of *Gray's Anatomy* from 1858 (first edition) to 1996 shows that anatomy has remained largely impervious to broader public debates about sexual inequalities and gender representations during this period. Both textual descriptions and illustrations were found to reflect an assumed two-sex model described by Thomas Laqueur (1990), whereby the male body is posited as the standard against which the female is implicitly judged as inferior. In descriptions of sex organs, pelvises, and skulls and the brain, differences are emphasized, using homologies and language that confirms the male as the norm or standard for comparison.

The sex portrayals revealed by the above can be understood in light of a broader discourse about complementary difference that has predominated in the West since the late eighteenth century. According to Laqueur (1990), this period ushered a significant shift in anatomical representation, from the one-sex to the two-sex model that continues to shape thinking about gender and difference. The one-sex model, which can be traced to the ancient Greeks, posits the female as an inversion of the male. In many early drawings and paintings, for example, the uterus is depicted as an inverted penis. With the rise of the complementary thesis in the eighteenth century, however, female anatomy began to be depicted as different from—but complementary to—male anatomy. The rise of the two-sex model, argues Laqueur, occurred at the very same time as the rise of liberal democracy, when women began claiming equality in the public sphere. Anatomists joined philosophers and other scholars in arguing that women were essentially different from men, which justified their exclusion from involvement in public life. Anatomical drawings henceforth began to emphasize difference rather than similarity.

Other scholars have made similar observations to Laqueur's. Schiebinger (1986), for example, has shown that beginning in the 1750s, a body of literature appeared in France and Germany urging a finer delineation of sex differences. In her view, the search for sex differences around this time led to the drawing of the first female skeletons in England, France, and Germany between 1730 and 1790 (see also Schiebinger 1990, 396). This reflected a tendency to look to science as the arbiter of social questions, for example in relation to women's rights and abilities, and represented a shift from earlier centuries when anatomists were relatively indifferent to the question of sex differences (Schiebinger 1986, 49; Martin 1987).

## The Recent Humanistic Turn in Medical Education

Whilst the dissecting room has traditionally provided a key site of learning and a symbolic initiation to the medical profession, recent initiatives have advanced arguments in favor of introducing medical students to anatomy through alternative methods that focus more closely on individuality, sensory experience, and embodiment in general—goals that correspond more with the tenets and goals of humanist feminism than those of masculine hegemony. British medical and health care services have recently witnessed rapid and often quite radical change (British Medical Association 1991, 1995). The response of medical educators has been one of reflection and curriculum reform, the latter involving an emphasis on quality and effectiveness, clinical skills, humanistic treatment and care, ethics and patient rights, improved doctor/patient communication, professional development, cultural diversity, and the role of new technologies (General Medical Council 1993). Such debate has also precipitated a review of anatomy teaching and of dissection specifically (Marks, Bertman, and Penny 1997;

Dangerfield et al. 1996). What is significant about such a review is the rearticulation of the schematic and, particularly, "masculinist" discourses underpinning anatomy that we have explored earlier, arguably as a result of feminist critiques of the last thirty years. Calls to develop a more "humanistic" medical education, articulated in documents such as the United Kingdom's *Tomorrow's Doctors* (General Medical Council 1993), reveal a concern to recover that which is seen to have been lost in the development of scientific medicine and dualistic thought; that is, practitioners' care and concern for the "whole person" that, these critiques contend, predates the male gaze in medicine that emerged during the Enlightenment.

New medical educational policies have been increasingly cognizant of cultural issues including ethics, social stratification, and perceptions of life, death, and dying. There is evidence of curricular change in favour of incorporating learning about the social context of medicine and about its roots in an imperialist, sexist, and class-based period of Western historical development (Kleinberg-Levin 1990). Some new medical schools in the United Kingdom (mirroring some in the United States) have incorporated specific teaching of gender, ethnicity, age, and sexuality issues, as well as humanistic approaches to death and dying (McLachlan et al. 2004; Scott 1994; Marks, Bertman, and Penny 1997). Such developments have heralded the first real move towards an integration of humanistic and, significantly, more egalitarian (indeed, feminist) issues into a traditionally masculinized and clinically detached profession. While medicine has traditionally been a masculine enterprise, feminist critiques over the last thirty years and their relative uptake in popular culture, appear to have had some impact on policy design— all of which has implications for how anatomy is taught.

One particular aspect of this has been debate about the relative benefits and disadvantages of using human cadavers in teaching anatomical knowledge (Gregory and Cole 2002). The simultaneous advent of new technologies has provided a number of viable alternatives to cadaveric dissection (Dyer and Thorndike 2000; McLachlan et al. 2004) that may be labeled "live and virtual anatomies." These largely unpublicized methods comprise a variety of approaches to understanding the body, including the use of life models, real patients, and peer examination for surface anatomy; radiological imaging; technological simulations, replications, and three-dimensional animations of gross anatomies (Rosse 1995; McLachlan et al. 1997; Aziz et al. 2002); and, more recently, body painting and light illumination techniques that transpose internal organs on to the relevant areas of living (usually students') bodies (Peninsula Medical School 2004).

**Figure 5-1.**   Body Painting at Peninsula Medical School, UK, 2004

Both dissection and nondissection methods have generated their own controversies in anatomy. Many fears have been related to cultural preoccupations with the "identity" of medicine and with dissection as a symbolic rite of passage for raw recruits to the profession (Porter 1997; Dyer and Thorndike 2000; Persaud 1967). Of course, this challenges the masculinism that has for so long served to socialize raw recruits into the masculine culture of the dissecting room. It threatens the symbolic male bonding rituals that have cemented the masculine identity of the anatomy profession since its birth. Current objections to live and virtual anatomy are often leveled at the need for students to experience "real" death from the outset as well as the need to observe cadavers to gain scientific anatomical knowledge, but it could also be argued that this is merely an extension of traditional masculinist anatomy discourses. Critics have attempted to counterbalance this view through reference to more appropriate clinical settings and to contact with dying patients, their families, and their friends.

The new emphasis on these experiential aspects of health and illness are important in that they represent a break with viewing the body as mere object and with the empiricism and universalism under which anatomy has been traditionally practiced. Whereas anatomy has been associated historically with abstract analysis of dead, inanimate bodies, the new live and virtual methods are designed to introduce future doctors to issues of personality and social character, lived experience, various interpretations of bodily feelings and sensations, and cultural difference. As one new United Kingdom medical school has put it, "Anatomy is life, anatomy is not death" (McLachlan and Regan de Bere 2004). Such discourses are more akin to those that traditionally underpinned more female areas of medical treatment and care, such as midwifery and obstetrics, yet they are now being applied to a traditionally masculine enterprise.

Reflecting the individualization of the body, plastic models (lifelike models that may communicate the idea of living, breathing human beings more effectively than real, but dead, human corpses (Aziz et al. 2002; Stillman, Ruggill, and Sabers 1978) now come in various shapes and sizes, including different sexes, ages, skin tones, and even hairstyles. Many have been fitted with audio systems that reproduce human "noises" such as coughing, complaining, vomiting, and so on. Reports from anatomy tutors employing such techniques demonstrate that students often respond as they would to real patients, holding hands and developing a sense of empathy for their hypothetical suffering (de Bruxelles 2002; BBC News 2002).

In what might be seen as a return to the pre-Enlightenment emphasis on care and treatment of humans as individuals (as opposed to the pursuit of pure medical knowledge and scientific discovery), anatomy has been charged with reviewing the role of bodily exploration. Many anatomists and medical educators suggest that consideration of the changing nature of our bodies, the ways in which we inhabit and seek to learn about them, and the methods we employ to do so lead us in the direction of increased live and virtual anatomy. These are methods that allow for an appreciation of difference, of embodiment, and of lived experiences. The integration of the humanities in some medical education curricula has recently turned attention to the social construction of the seemingly natural and purely biological. Whilst the humanities do not refute the fact that bodies clearly have a corporeal reality—they sweat, move, decay, and ultimately die—they also view them as social and cultural entities. The human body is increasingly seen as both a source of social identity and a site upon which people can inscribe who they are or who they wish to be. Issues of gender, ethnicity, age, sexuality, and ability/disability have come to the fore. Many new programs of anatomy teaching, both in the United Kingdom and abroad, have responded accordingly (Aziz et al. 2002; Dangerfield et al. 1996; Dyer and Thorndike 2000). Many argue that these more humanistic dimensions of live

**Figure 5-2.**   Body Projection at Peninsula Medical School, UK, 2004

and virtual anatomy are well placed in a new curriculum that emphasises the centrality of the patient and medical ethics. This is a departure from the emotional detachment from patients that was practiced by the godfathers of anatomy and thus both a direct challenge to the masculine medical gaze and an exhortation for medicine to embrace a more humanistic, feminine/feminist approach to the body.

## Performance Anatomy

Developments occurring *outside* the institutions of medicine have also helped bring into question what have long been held to be self-evident truths of anatomical practice: that the body and its workings can be objectively, that is, "dispassionately," known through science and that knowledge of the body is the exclusive preserve of a single professional (and male) group. Of particular note in this respect is the debate surrounding "performance anatomies," which focuses on the potential of "performative" explorations of the human body in informing both academic and lay knowledge. Often, these works have been performed as scientific *and* artistic processes of what has been termed by the contemporary media "education, entertainment, and edification." Here, bodies have been portrayed as living sites for "life projects" within late modernity whereby through health and fitness regimes, surgery, and so on, we inscribe into our flesh a range of statements about our identities (Featherstone 1991). Developments in health technologies (clinical and cosmetic surgery, artificial body parts, reproductive technologies, a wealth of contraceptive devices, etc.) and other scientific adventures and misadventures (genetically modified foods, genetic cloning, synthetic diseases and "superbugs") all have implications for bodies and embodied identities. So, while early anatomical studies were presented to a cynical public as "revelations" of the natural human state, contemporary studies have taken into account the implications of new technologies not only for examining bodies but also for the state of the bodies that are to be examined.

An explosion of studies, experiments, and exhibitions on the anatomical body has recently caught the public imagination and begun to feed popular discourse. Many initiatives have represented the fragmentation of society, exploring issues of gender, sexuality, ethnicity, lifestyle, and a challenge to normative depictions of the biologically determined body. The artist Orlan, for example, used surgery and digital enhancement to reconstruct her face along the lines of different cultural expressions of femininity, and in so doing provided a feminist critique of the status of the body in the cultures from which she borrowed her inspiration (Clarke 2000; Ayres 1999). In a similar vein, the artist Stelarc explored transhuman aesthetics, presenting the technically modified body as an evolutionary structure through which new forms of sensory experience could be used to transcend issues of gender, ethnicity, age, and other "bodily" differences (Zurbrugg 2000; Farnell 1999). The most widely debated and controversially received performance anatomy work of late was perhaps that of the anatomist Gunter Von Hagens. His public autopsy and graphic exhibitions of over two hundred real but plastinated bodies simultaneously drew in, delighted, and appalled: it captured the attention of anatomists, medical professionals, the media, and the lay public in equal measure.

In terms of our genealogical analysis, there is an important distinction to be made between these types of works. Whilst much SciArt[1] anatomy represents a move towards what some have labeled postmodern anatomical study, it could be argued that Von Hagens's performance anatomy and the Visible Human Project (VHP)[2] have marked a partial return to the more historically enduring aspects of dissection-based anatomy and medical culture. SciArt works can be distinguished by their emphasis on deconstructing the personal, cultural, and political dimensions of anatomy, therefore often questioning and reappropriating issues of gender, ethnicity, and other classifications. This discursive

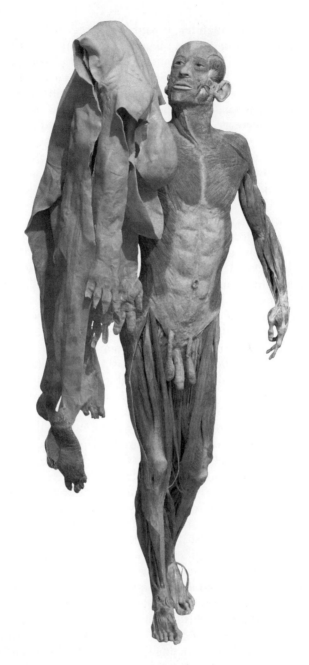

**Figure 5-3.** Body worlds pictorial.
Copyright Gunther von Hagens, Institute for Plastination,
Heidelberg, Germany (www.bodyworlds.com)

practice involves critical reflexivity and self-awareness and is an obvious break from the fundamental, masculine, scientific principles of the Enlightenment period in which formal anatomy was born. However, the VHP and Von Hagens's autopsy and exhibitions of plastinated corpses reflect more clearly the dispassionate, detached scientific endeavors of early anatomy. Here, as then, the anatomist has been concerned with the traditionally masculine qualities of detachment, objectivity, and emotional control.

It is the requirement of medicine for rational knowledge, scientific methodology, and value-free "level-headedness" that has also brought negative responses to Von Hagens and the VHP. If we consider our previous discussion, this does not signal any discursive break with the past. Controversy surrounding early anatomy theatres and public dissections can be usefully seen as representing a discursive shift from mystical to rational knowledge and schematic scientific medical explanation that culminated in biologically based social classifications. Late modern anatomical discourses then placed an emphasis on ethical considerations relating to the gendered, class-based, and racialized derivation of cadavers for dissection as well as unorthodox methods of acquisition— often from the lower or "criminal" classes. And later, such shifts extended to challenging the hegemony of a medical profession that had long been seemingly unaccountable to the public it was supposed to serve.

Press coverage has now provoked a reconsideration of these age-old issues, albeit in relation to a new set of social conditions. Here we have witnessed a shift from modern, scientific, fixed universal explanations to a sense of the postmodern (but then a seemingly partial backtrack in terms of the work of Von Hagens and the VHP). High-profile media agendas have begun to raise issues of human rights, and ethical issues concerning the derivation of "criminalized" bodies—executed felons in the United States used for the VHP (Curtis 2000; Waldby 2000) and Chinese executed felons who have allegedly provided a large number of plastinated human specimens (Channel 4 2001). In a similar vein, there has been controversy over the use of cadaveric tissue in body modification, sex-change operations, and other surgeries (Roach 2003), further bioethical concerns over "biobanking,"[3] and the lack of human rights shown to the children involved in the "Bristol Babies" scandal and the Alder Hey affair (Phillips 2004; Bauchner and Vinci 2001; Hume 2003), high-profile scandals in which bereaved parents discovered their children's organs and tissues had been retained without their knowledge or consent. The contemporary relevance of such anxiety is evident in the Human Tissue Bill that was brought to the House of Commons in June,

2004. These are issues that have shaped recent anatomy, and they should be considered a rich social backdrop against which contemporary gender, age, sexuality, ethnicity, lifestyle, and other forms of difference can be explored within a genealogical framework.

What is interesting here is that contemporary critics have made vociferous assaults on many different forms of performance anatomy, espousing seemingly "traditional" values and advocating a return to the status quo of autonomous medical disciplines and professions and to more traditionally defined and biologically classified human bodies. Let us consider again the idea of the autonomous, clinically detached, and spatially removed higher echelons of the emerging medical profession. It is perhaps telling that those with more traditional attitudes towards performance anatomy have referred to the "trivialization" of medical science caused by bringing anatomy to those outside of those protected ivory towers. What relevance, then, does such anxiety have for contemporary gendered medical discourses and practices? If one is to view anatomy as a profession experiencing identity crisis, then it becomes imperative to reconsider our understanding of it.

## Challenging a Masculine History?

The source of contention of performance anatomy has been the "novelty" of engaging science, medicine, and art within a single anatomical project. One might hypothesize that it is precisely this integration that could facilitate a deeper appreciation of the complexity of human bodies and of the experiences of those living within them. Its implications for medical understanding and treatment of embodied individuals without discriminating along gender, ethnic, or class lines are already becoming clear in innovative moves towards integrating the arts and humanities into anatomy courses in contemporary medical education. However, such innovation has alternatively been viewed in a more pessimistic light, particularly by those with more traditional (and perhaps masculinist) leanings.

Live and virtual methods may herald a breaking with masculinist discourses within medicine, in that they shift the emphasis from dead cadavers and archetypal "male" anatomies to living anatomies and the experiences of individuality and personalized embodiment based on gender, age, or ethnic lines. They also challenge traditional discourses towards other "different" bodies, or those that fall outside of the normatively prescribed standards for "healthy" bodies. In modern anatomy, "difference" was perceived as the result of abnormality or pathology, and more sociocultural differences were explained accordingly, just as they were in relation to gender relationships. In terms of what we might now call disability, this was perhaps most evident in the spectacle of the "freak show," where the "different" body was presented as a deviation from the divinely created "perfect" body—a particularly persuasive argument during the religious fervor of the Victorian era, where freak shows flourished on the lay circuit outside of the more respected and legitimate institution of medicine that used only "normal" bodies to explore anatomy (Richardson 2000). Such perspectives are relevant to our discussion of discursive change when they are positioned against contemporary constructions of multiple "bodies." More recent approaches include references to pluralism, difference, and hybridization: the individualization of bodies and society. As such, disabled persons and groups have been able to reclaim and rearticulate normative discourses and participate more fully as valid, but different, embodied individuals. Clearly, this reclamation contrasts with the "abnormal" or "pathological" labeling that was once based on a more prescriptive, early anatomical approach and the hysteria of the freak show.

Take as an example the recent placing of a pregnant, female, disabled anatomy sculpture in Trafalgar Square sitting amongst the more traditional statues of male national heroes. In the light of our previous remarks about the "normal," "healthy," "natural" body, this reflects a change in attitude by some towards the inclusion of different anatomies in mainstream society. As the artist, Alison Lapper, stated, "It is so rare to see disability in everyday life—let alone naked, pregnant and proud." And critics have argued that Lapper's "Pregnant" celebrates the human spirit on a very large scale. "The work considers questions of idealism, heroism, femininity, prejudice and identity," said Greg Hilty, director of visual arts and literature at the Arts Council England, London (Greater London Authority 2004).

Nevertheless, the "Pregnant" event has caused much controversy amongst those less willing to part with traditional views on gender, bodies, and "different" anatomies (Lane 2004). Such novelty has been variously described as vulgar, a homage to political correctness, and a travesty of meaningless modern art. We can perhaps relate to this an anxiety caused by scientific, artistic, and medical changes that have divested society of some of its more biologically determined, normative, and masculinist traditions. We might even view it as evidence of a discursive shift in medical, scientific, and artistic thinking—material consequences of changes in discursive norms. Performance anatomy does not merely replicate anatomical structures in a traditional modern way that abstracts the physical from the personal, social, and political experience of the body. Rather, it invites emotional responses and provides space for the viewer to "imagine" different anatomies and varied sensual experiences. Here lies the distinction, and the novelty, of contemporary performance anatomy.

We might also view the prevalence of more feminist performance anatomy as a discursive shift in itself, this time in relation to theorizing scientific culture. It reflects a society more tolerant of more egalitarian critique and more aware of gendered relations. The controversies surrounding such works demonstrate the importance of such issues and their provocation of anxieties relating to both medical and popular culture. As such, they are intriguing to those interested in studying the gendered evolution of anatomy. On the one hand, there are those who draw on contemporary discourses and advocate more humanistic approaches that are grounded in feminist critiques of traditionalist, masculinized medicine. Others, in contrast, reject feminist critique or "novelty" and argue in favor of a return to the traditional principles of modern science.

Such novelty is worth considering in a genealogical sense. Novelty implies an element of change and, as Whitely (1999) asserts, novelty in science (and, by implication here, the core of scientific medicine—anatomy) is challenging and disturbing. Innovation challenges established ways of doing things. It often engages other changes in social, economic, cultural, and political realms, for example, in gendered and racialized medical discourses. More importantly still, it has vast potential for reorganizing existing distributions of power within the medical profession and related fields. The advent of live and virtual anatomy and performance anatomy therefore brings uncertainty and vulnerability to the historically developed practice of anatomy, to the culture of medicine itself, and to the wider society that patronizes it.

## Conclusion

In light of the recent developments described, we may ask: To what extent are we moving towards a more humanistic, gender-neutral anatomical practice, and how far might this represent the "feminization" of a traditionally masculinized culture? What prospects are there for developing new, less masculine-biased approaches to the body and novel ways of portraying and teaching anatomy? And, at the same time, what are the implications of different masculinist and feminist perspectives for studying gendered medicine? Recent feminist challenges to the idea of scientific objectivity and certainty and to modernist conceptions of the body and its depictions provide the opportunity to consider the issues at stake in established ways of thinking about and intervening into bodies. New technologies and practices of anatomy, such as live and virtual and performance anatomies, allow publics to imagine that there is nothing inevitable or universal about medical approaches to the body. The practices of medicine are being opened to public scrutiny and criticism as never before. The Internet, television, and other media are the source for proliferating images of bodies unavailable to earlier generations.

Publics are arguably becoming more inured to blood-and-guts images of dissected bodies and increasingly knowledgable about the diverse techniques of body modification available in the medical marketplace. They would appear to be becoming not only more consumerist in relation to the body but more critical and discerning about medicine and its practices. In the United Kingdom, aforementioned debates surrounding events in Alder Hey and Bristol Royal Infirmary and the public outrage of the Harold Shipman case[4] reveal an apparent decline of public trust in the institutions of medicine, and in science more generally, and the publics' greater willingness than in the past to openly question medical procedures. The "threat" from such awareness is threefold: to modern scientific autonomy and normative ideas about gender and other classificatory systems, to purely biologically deterministic theories in medicine, and to current philosophical approaches to "knowing" the human body, its workings, and its social significance. As such we are reminded to consider the importance of exploring new, alternative, and rearticulated medical (expert and lay) attitudes towards anatomy in relation to aesthetics, gender, sexuality, spirituality, age, cultural memberships, pleasure, and other pertinent issues.

Feminist studies have contributed to highlighting the various ways in which medicine has constituted and controlled women's bodies and minds through its history and have helped raise our consciousness of the gendered character of medical practices. However, the masculine biases of medicine and the medicalization of men's bodies and lives have remained largely hidden behind the cloak of neutrality and dispassionate detachment, and recent developments in medical education have gone largely unstudied in a sociological sense. Whether or not such developments have heralded a discursive shift from "masculinized" to "feminized" medicine is a matter for debate and begs for further exploration.

# 6

## Making the Grade:
## The Gender Gap, ADHD, and
## the Medicalization of Boyhood

Nicky Hart
with Noah Grand and Kevin Riley

### Child Socialization and
### the Gender Relations of ADHD

This chapter explores the gender relations of attention deficit and hyperactivity disorder (ADHD), the most prevalent form of childhood disability in North America. The incidence of ADHD increased at a stunning pace during the 1990s. We know this indirectly from the exponential increase in the production and distribution of the medicine used to treat ADHD children. Methylphenidate, better known as Ritalin, is the synthetic amphetamine drug prescribed to suppress the symptoms of ADHD. Between 1994 and 1999, its production rose by 800 percent and since more than 90 percent of it was consumed in the United States,[1] we can be sure that an epidemic of ADHD was developing in North America. The scale of the increase is extraordinary and raises questions that go well beyond the orthodox sociological framework for explaining ADHD.

Sociologists have conceptualized ADHD as the medicalization of childhood deviance. It has been seen as a label for singling out, diagnosing, and treating disobedient children. The labeling perspective emphasizes the socially constructed nature of the disorder and gives priority to the process of social control and especially to the interests of those who have the power to define and treat deviants—in this case, physicians. Since the independent reality of the disorder is under question in this approach, sociologists have tended to stay away from research that treats the disorder as if it were real. Consequently, we know very little about the social characteristics of ADHD children and their families apart from one inescapable empirical observation—ADHD is predominantly a disorder of boyhood.

Most of the children who get labeled ADHD are male. The ratio of boys to girls in the sample drawn by Peter Conrad for his seminal (1976) study "Identifying Hyperactive Children" was fourteen boys to every one girl. This was above his estimate of the population ratio in the mid-1970s, which was ten to one. Since then the gap has narrowed principally in response to revisions of the American Psychiatric Association's *Diagnostic and Statistical Manual of Mental Disorders* (*DSM*; see below), which broadened the behavioral criteria for diagnosing ADHD. There is still no administrative apparatus for systematically monitoring the social composition of the child population diagnosed with and treated for the disorder, but the inclusion of the symptoms of attention deficit alongside hyperactivity was probably the most important factor increasing the chance of girls being labeled ADHD. Any trend in this direction accelerated after 1991 in response to legislative changes that classified the disorder as a bona fide learning disability.[2] Recent estimates put the ratio of male to female cases at three or four to one, which means that 75 to 80 percent of children currently afflicted by this learning disability are still male.

The gender gap in the child population with ADHD is matched by a very significant and opposite differential among adults initiating the labeling process. While young males form the great majority of those labeled, it is overwhelmingly adult females, their mothers or teachers, who make the first determination that a child's behavior falls outside the normal range of what little boys do. Though this differential obviously reflects the adult female's more immediate involvement in the day-to-day management of children, recent research indicates that mothers and fathers frequently disagree on the "pathological" nature of their sons' behavior (Singh 2004). In other words, many fathers of ADHD children are reluctant to acknowledge their sons' disability, and some may even believe that a positive evaluation is reached more in the interests of the mother or of domestic calm than of the child. The predominant role of the mother seeing the problem and then bringing children for medical evaluation seems to be of long-standing provenance.[3] Conrad noted it in his 1976 monograph "Identifying Hyperactive Children," though he did not take it further. His observation stands as an important benchmark of the fact that the mother has always been at the forefront of the medicalization process. She is the primary agent of socialization, and it now seems that she has played the pivotal role in the rapidly increasing prevalence of ADHD. The kindergarten or elementary school teacher comes next. Women comprise more than 85 percent of the teaching profession in grades K through 6, and there is persuasive evidence that the teacher has also been a major player in the rising numbers of children under medication. In fact, one study has estimated that teachers are numerically more important than anyone else initiating the labeling of learning disabled children (Sax and Kautz 2003).

From these preliminary observations we can see that the social relations of ADHD occur within the context of child socialization. They bring together little boys and those responsible for their primary training as social beings. The discourse representing ADHD as a learning disability reinforces this way of framing the phenomenon. Sociologically we can conceive of ADHD as a term meaning "resistant to socialization." As we will see, its symptoms are all associated with the lack of motivation to engage in learning social skills and a willful resistance to submit to adult supervision. Its most troubling component, impulsivity, brings us to the core of social learning—the failure to be aware of the consequences of action and therefore to develop the capacity for moral reasoning. This makes ADHD a profoundly sociological phenomenon, a classification of individuals by their inability or limited capacity to be effective social actors.[4] What is also remarkable is the idea that this social disability can be managed by a powerful medication. In effect, Ritalin may be conceptualized as a technological substitute for internalized morality. Like magic, Ritalin promises to succeed where parents and teachers have failed, to produce the effects of self-discipline and emotional control—the fundamental prerequisites for social interaction.

While the concept of deviance remains a useful tool for making sense of the epidemic of ADHD, it is important to be specific about who gets labeled. ADHD is a profoundly gendered phenomenon. The vast majority of children who get labeled and processed as ADHD are boys, and the scale on which the process is now occurring leads to the argument that what we are witnessing verges on the medicalization of boyhood.[5] In other words, large-scale efforts to suppress the symptoms of ADHD point to an increasing intolerance of puerile behaviors that have been conventionally excused on the grounds that "boys will be boys." Targeting these behaviors and defining them as deep-seated psychiatric pathologies involves a reformulation of gender norms and a virtual transformation of cultural knowledge. Understanding the forces driving this trend calls for a detailed examination of the disorder itself and of the social composition of the afflicted population.

This chapter reviews the social and geographical parameters of the ADHD epidemic in the United States. As we will see, the available empirical evidence reveals that the resort to Ritalin as a tool of child socialization is geographically uneven. It is much more pronounced in prosperous white communities where education is a high priority, where children of both sexes perform above the national average in standardized tests, and, most important, where the gender gap in educational achievement favoring females is at its widest. This distinctive social pattern lends no support to the biomedical representation of ADHD as a congenital abnormality that is the fundamental rationale for treating small children with powerful psychostimulant drugs. The ecological pattern is more consistent with the view that ADHD is a social barometer of parental anxiety about child development and especially the development of sons. In the pages that follow, this evidence will be laid out and evaluated, but first we set out our argument for representing ADHD as a case of deficient or underdeveloped socialization.

## ADHD: Deviance, Disability or Deficient Socialization

Representing ADHD as a case of "From Badness to Sickness," as did Peter Conrad and Joseph Schneider (1992) in their bestselling textbook on medicalization, can be misleading. It conjures up negative images of serious rule-breaking behavior and sends the sociologist in search of violent breaches of norms, that is, vandalism, bullying, intimidation, and gun- and knife-toting practices on school premises. This kind of conduct is not the stuff of ADHD, although child psychiatrists sometimes warn that untreated ADHD may well result in adults who are a menace to the community (Barkley 1990). Dire predictions aside, pediatricians have actually developed another quasi-clinical terminology to describe more egregious norm violations associated with "barbaric masculinity." The terms *conduct disorder* (CD) and *oppositional defiant disorder* (ODD) have been developed specifically for rule breaking, which comes closer to capturing youthful male criminality than do the qualities associated with ADHD.[6] In making sociological sense of ADHD, we would do well to look closely at its symptoms and what they represent in sociological terms. The appropriate place to start this process is the *DSM*. Figure 6.1 sets out the checklist for identifying ADHD in DSM-IV, revised in 1994.

The hybrid character of ADHD is brought out well in the division between inattention and hyperactivity/impulsivity in Figure 6.1 It is noteworthy that the symptoms of inattention now take priority in the

A. **Either** (1) or (2):

    1. six (or more) of the following symptoms of **inattention** have persisted for at least 6 months to a degree that is maladaptive and inconsistent with developmental level: *Inattention*

        a. often fails to give close attention to details or makes careless mistakes in schoolwork, work, or other activities

        b. often has difficulty sustaining attention in tasks or play activities

        c. often does not seem to listen when spoken to directly

        d. often does not follow through on instructions and fails to finish schoolwork, chores, or duties in the workplace (not due to oppositional behavior or failure to understand instructions)

        e. often has difficulty organizing tasks and activities

        f. often avoids, dislikes, or is reluctant to engage in tasks that require sustained mental effort (such as schoolwork or homework)

        g. often loses things necessary for tasks or activities (e.g., toys, school assignments, pencils, books, or tools)

        h. is often easily distracted by extraneous stimuli

        i. is often forgetful in daily activities

    2. six (or more) of the following symptoms of **hyperactivity-impulsivity** have persisted for at least 6 months to a degree that is maladaptive and inconsistent with developmental level: *Hyperactivity*

        a. often fidgets with hands or feet or squirms in seat

        b. often leaves seat in classroom or in other situations in which remaining seating is expected

        c. often runs about or climbs excessively in situations in which it is inappropriate (in adolescents or adults, may be limited to subjective feelings of restlessness)

        d. often has difficulty playing or engaging in leisure activities quietly

        e. is often 'on the go' or often acts as if 'driven by a motor'

        f. often talks excessively
          *Impulsivity*

        g. often blurts out answers before questions have been completed

        h. often has difficulty taking turn

        i. often interrupts or intrudes on others (e.g., butts into conversations or games)

B. Some hyperactive-impulsive or inattentive symptoms that cause impairment were present before age 7 years.

C. Some impairment from the symptoms is present in two or more settings (e.g., at school [or work] and at home).

D. There must be clear evidence of clinically significant impairment in social, academic, or occupational functioning.

E. The symptoms do not occur exclusively during the course of a pervasive developmental disorder, schizophrenia, or other psychotic disorder and are not better accounted for by another mental disorder (e.g., mood disorder, anxiety disorder, dissociative disorder, or a personality disorder).

**Figure 6-1.** Criteria for Diagnosing ADHD

*Source*: http://www.surgeongeneral.gov/library/mentalhealth/chapter3/sec4.html, Table 3-3. *DSM-IV* criteria for Attention-Deficit/Hyperactivity Disorder

*DSM-IV.* This reverses the historical chronology of the condition that began its clinical life under the heading "hyperkinesis." It was a relatively rare condition in the mid-1950s. As Conrad (1975, 14) observes, hyperkinesis got very little attention before the Food and Drug Administration (FDA) approved Ritalin to treat childhood behavioral disorders. This happened in 1961, and by the end of that decade, articles on hyperkinesis began appearing in the popular press. Within a few years of its official sanction and with the elaboration of the disorder to include attention deficit disorder greatly assisting the trend, ADHD emerged as the most common psychiatric disorder of childhood.[7]

But the symptoms of inattention laid out in Figure 6.1—not paying close attention, not listening to adults, leaving work unfinished, avoiding chores, and being easily distracted—are quite unexceptional in young children. Using this checklist, any child could qualify for medication, as the symptoms exemplify typical childhood behaviors before socialization and early education have formed the motivation and disposition to engage in purposeful activity in a classroom setting.

The same may be said of the signs of hyperactivity/impulsivity even though these behaviors are more likely to be disruptive to others. This suggests that the symptoms of ADHD are not intrinsically abnormal or deviant but rather include some of the normal yet irksome traits of small children that frequently annoy parents and teachers and therefore stimulate efforts of control—fidgeting, showing off, being boisterous, uncooperative, and overactive, and ignoring instructions. These symptoms also involve less disruptive conduct like failing to concentrate, not applying oneself sufficiently, and daydreaming. Because each of these forms of conduct can be "natural" in small children, to earn a diagnosis of ADHD, the child must display them with greater frequency and in more than one setting. This is why the *DSM-IV* prefaces each instance of the relevant misbehavior with the word *often.*

Because children who get labeled with ADHD are more successful in resisting or evading their parents' and teachers' efforts to eradicate undesirable, disruptive, or annoying behavior, it might be said that they fail to grow up at a reasonable pace and thus represent a failure of socialization not in the sense of feral children who have never been exposed to socialization but rather as those who have so far successfully resisted the parents' efforts to keep them in line. When they get to school, they are a "headache" for the teacher. Medication may thus be an easy substitute for the lack of sustained parental discipline and consequently the absence of internalized self-control that turns out to be a serious liability in a learning situation both for ego and for the rest of the class. We can thus appreciate why ADHD has taken on the mantle of a learning disability: in a very fundamental sense, it represents a failure of normal socialization.

The "symptoms" that bring forth a diagnosis of ADHD can be summarized under the heading "raw childish behavior in social interaction." They involve inappropriate and uncontrolled reactions, insensitivity to other people (adults and children), failure to read symbolic cues and respond appropriately, and undeveloped skills of emotional control. The checklist of the *DSM* reads like a state of delayed or arrested socialization—children who are behind in the process of learning how to comport, confine, and constrain themselves in social relationships. The undeveloped state of socialization most often comes to light when children make their initial transition from the private to the public sphere of social interaction. While the first day at school has always been the first challenge for small children to demonstrate their developing competence as social beings, in recent years, the age of entry into school has fallen as socialization in the private sphere became less labor intensive with married women's rising rates of participation in the paid labor force. As a result, small children are now required to develop and display satisfactory interpersonal skills earlier in their lives, at least compared with the golden age of the male breadwinner/female homemaker. It is of some sociological importance to ask if the rise of ADHD is a consequence of declining resources for child socialization in the private sphere of life. On this hinges the issue of whether ADHD is more appropriately seen as a learning disability or an instance of deficient socialization.

Lowering the age of entry to the public sphere as represented by the school appears to be more of a challenge for boys than girls. While all children are entering school-like environments at younger ages, little girls seem to be significantly more adept at learning how to manage the emerging self in demanding social settings. Observational research in the kindergarten finds girls more sociable than boys, more sensitively oriented to other children, and in general better equipped at an earlier age to manage their selves in social interaction (Maccoby and Jacklin 1987; Archer and Lloyd 1982; Thorne 1993). Boys, by contrast, are more self-absorbed and more interested in manipulating objects than in developing and managing their relational skills. Interestingly, when ADHD was first emerging as a clinical label, the female's relational reputation was seen by psychoanalytically oriented feminism to be a social disability—a case of arrested individuation that left the average female ill equipped to compete in a culture valorizing "possessive individualism" (Macpherson 1962). Inspired by object relations theory, Chodorow (1978) interpreted the more relational "nature" of women as the result of a failure to achieve a complete psychic separation from their same-sex nurturers.[8] But the evidence that little boys are more vulnerable to ADHD might suggest an alternative hypothesis to Chodorow's, namely that early individuation may impose unrealistic demands on the embryonic male personality. If the symptoms of ADHD are appropriately conceived as a delay in the acquisition of age-appropriate relational skills exacerbated by being pushed into the public sphere at younger ages, the administration of Ritalin or similar psychoactive medicines emerges as a substitute for the "natural" process of learning to internalize the techniques of self discipline required for effective performance of interpersonal relationships. If medication becomes a perpetual prop, delayed socialization may turn out to be a permanent state of arrested development in the social persona.

Ritalin is a narcotic drug that can only be administered to small bodies in small doses at repeated intervals throughout the school day.[9] The effects of small doses last for a limited time, and it is widely reported that when the effects wear off, the symptoms of ADHD return with a vengeance. In consequence, parents who can only spare "quality time" for their children tend to rely on continuous medication during waking hours to produce the effect of civilized social relations during the limited time that they have to spend with their children. Continuous medication reinforces the impression that ADHD is a congenital abnormality, but the same experience may logically also be equivalent to a condition of underdeveloped socialization that is actually perpetuated by the continued administration of Ritalin as an artificial substitute for internalized standards of self-discipline.

This risk was more clearly understood in the early experimental phase of Ritalin's use as a parenting and teaching aid. Then the temporary effects of the drug were an advantage, creating windows of Ritalin-free opportunity after school and during holidays when various members of the family would have a chance to catch up with teaching and learning age-appropriate skills of social interaction.[10] Since 1990, the collapse of the modern family[11] and its characteristic sexual division of labor means that these social spaces have increasingly disappeared, and there is now nobody at home who has the time, energy, and motivation to engage in child-focused social interaction. In this context, Ritalin offers itself as a technological substitute for traditional parenting, and as if to fit the circumstances of the post modern nuclear family, many child psychiatrists in the pro-ADHD camp now insist that ADHD is not an age-related learning disability but a lifelong affliction requiring lifelong medication. The alternative interpretation suggested here is that the administration of powerful narcotics to the child's developing psyche is a technological substitute for conventional socialization and that it leads to a lifelong deficit of learned social skills. In this scenario, Ritalin substitutes for self-help in the civilizing process; it is a biomedical technology substituting for labor-intensive socialization. This is why it may be appropriate to list Ritalin alongside Prozac and other "modern" medical narcotics as the psychopharmacology of modernization.

## ADHD as a Social Fact: The Changing Trend and its Social Distribution

The United States is home to the largest number of children with ADHD in the world, and as we have seen, a very rapid increase took place in the 1990s. This section summarizes what is known about the prevalence and social composition of the disorder, specifically its social distribution and rate of increase.

How big a problem is ADHD in the United States? This is an important question, obviously essential for gauging the rising trend, yet the answer is elusive. For the last three decades, people writing about ADHD have characteristically reported between 3 and 7 percent of elementary school children afflicted with ADHD. Peter Conrad used this range in 1976, and Laurence Diller followed suit in 1998. Yet we know from the increase in production of Ritalin and other ADHD drugs in the 1990s that the stability of this national estimate is scarcely credible. As it turns out, its source is poorly documented and its empirical basis difficult to ascertain.[12]

Determining the overall rate of ADHD diagnosis and treatment in the United States is a difficult, if not impossible, task because it is not a reportable condition. Though politicians have frequently expressed concern over the escalating rate of ADHD, they have not set in place an apparatus to monitor the number of new cases. Consequently there are no systematic data collected and reported at the point of diagnosis and treatment,[13] nor are there any reliable national statistics. The much-quoted estimate of 3 to 7 percent itself encompasses as few as 1.8 million or as many as 4.2 million children. Individual studies over the past decade give even wider estimates—anywhere from 1.7 percent to 16 percent, depending on the population examined and the methods employed (Goldman et al. 1998). Given the absence of statistics based on registered cases, the best source of data comes from the National Child Health Interview Survey (NCHS), which has inquired into the incidence of ADHD since 1997. Their estimates are reproduced in Table 6.1.

In 1997, 5.5 percent of children were reported by their parents or guardians as being afflicted with ADHD. It is not clear how many of these were under medication. By 2002, the incidence had risen by one-third to

**Table 6-1.** Rates of ADHD in the NCHS, 1997–2002, ages 3–17 years—all children

| Study year | ADHD Prevalence |
|------------|-----------------|
| 1997 | 5.5% |
| 1998 | 5.9% |
| 1999 | 5.6% |
| 2000 | 6.6% |
| 2001 | 6.3% |
| 2002 | 7.2% |

*Source*: National Center for Health Statistics, 2004.

7.2 percent, adding up to 4.3 million children between the ages of three and seventeen years. Within this age band, only 1 percent of children aged three to four had an ADHD diagnosis in 2002, as opposed to 6.8 percent of children aged five to eleven and 9.6 percent of children aged 12 to seventeen (National Center for Health Statistics 2004). In each case, the prevalence rate is proportionately higher in males: overall, an estimated 10.3 percent of boys as opposed to only 4.0 percent of girls—a gender ratio of 2.7 to 1 (National Center for Health Statistics 2004). Six years earlier, the gender gap stood at 3.3 to 1.

These survey data are based on the "lay" person reporting their own or a child's disability.[14] Their main virtue is the coverage of a broad cross-section of the population based on a single point of data collection. In other words, this is not an attempt to concoct a single estimate from evidence generated in different school or clinical settings. But can we rely on the honesty and accuracy of self-reported survey data? Do ordinary people tell the truth about what might be seen as the "failings" of their children and, by implication, of themselves as parents? Can these data serve as a reliable measure of the true rate of diagnosis by medical professionals? The answer to this question is a definitive no. A national survey estimate will contain several kinds of biases that either depress or inflate the true incidence, whatever that might be.[15] On the one hand, there is the very real tendency to underreport stigmatizing conditions, while on the other, we cannot rule out the possibility that parents impressed by the unruliness of their children may describe them as ADHD when in fact no official medical diagnosis and no prescription for medication has been made. Notwithstanding these problems, the rising trend almost every year in the NCHS data in Table 6.1 does suggest that however incomplete or inflated, the incidence of the disorder was rapidly rising in the decade spanning the beginning of the new millennium. The same conclusion is backed up by one-off surveys generated from medical records. Using a commercial database of physicians' diagnosis and prescription practices, Swanson, Lerner, and Williams (1995) discovered a 2.48-fold increase in the annual number of outpatient visits for ADHD between 1990 and 1993 from 1,687,000 to 4,195,000.[16] The NCHS findings also include a breakdown of the incidence of ADHD by some social variables. They reveal the disorder to be more concentrated in the white population, among families covered by private health insurance, and among single-parent female-headed families.[17] This source leaves no doubt that ADHD was rising on a steep curve in the nation as a whole after 1990. It confirms that U.S. children are at much greater risk of entering drug therapy than their counterparts anywhere else in the world. (Outside the United States, less than 1 percent of the child population is treated for ADHD). Yet national estimates derived from survey samples such as this can mislead more than enlighten by creating the false impression of uniformity with steady annual increases. As we will see, the degree of regional variation is so large that we learn more about the ADHD phenomenon in the United States and its causes by focusing on the kinds of communities that report either very high or very low rates of treatment.

Some of this regional data comes from one-off surveys carried out in specific school districts. One of the best and most widely quoted was conducted in Virginia in 1994. LeFever, Dawson, and Morrow (1999) had the opportunity to examine school records to establish who was actually taking Ritalin at school among children grades 1 through 5 in two school districts in southeastern Virginia in 1994. They found 8 percent of children in one district and 10 percent of children in the second district receiving daily medication on school premises with the rate of medication increasing steadily from grade 1 to grade 5. Since their method of gathering the data leaves out children whose daily Ritalin consumption is not controlled by school personnel, these estimates are unlikely to represent the full extent of reliance on Ritalin for the management of child behavior by teachers and parents.[18] It is known that some, especially older, children self-administer the drug at intervals throughout the school day. Even so, this study revealed that the school authorities were responsible for supervising the medication of between 18 and 20 percent of boys in the fifth grade in one of the school districts.[19]

Studies like that of LeFever and her colleagues invariably report the well-known gender difference in ADHD diagnosis and treatment. Generally boys are diagnosed and treated for the condition at rates between three and four times higher than girls. In a survey of parents in a rural county in North Carolina, Rowland, Lesesne, and Abramowitz (2002) found that 10 percent of all children in the sample had been given a diagnosis of ADHD—15 percent of boys and 5 percent of girls. In their Maryland study, Safer and Malever (2000) report a male to female ratio of administration of medication of 3.5 boys for every 1 girl in elementary schools and four boys to every girl in secondary schools.[20]

The most systematic evidence of regional variation in the incidence of ADHD comes from production quotas for methylphenidate supervised by public authorities. This is the same source of the much-quoted exponential rise in Ritalin production. The Drug Enforcement Agency (DEA) sets annual production quotas for the legal amount of controlled substances. Since these are based on and limited to demands for domestic pharmaceutical production and sale, they provide a useful estimate of the volume of psychostimulant substances being consumed by the U.S. population on a year-to-year basis, and they reveal a large regional variation in the consumption of Ritalin.[21] The DEA data have been analyzed at a county level by Bokhari, Mayes and Scheffler (2004). These authors compared the social characteristics of 3,030 counties above and below the mean country consumption level of 3,359 grams per 100,000 population in 2000[22] and concluded that relative affluence is the most effective indicator of communities where children are likely to be identified for drug therapy. High-consumption counties are more populous, though the ratio of adults to children is below average, per capita income is higher, unemployment rates are lower, private schooling is more prevalent, and access to medical care is more assured (higher ratios of physicians to the population and more HMOs).[23]

The social distribution at the county level is confirmed at the aggregate level of the state. In the year 2000, an average 4.5 kilograms of Ritalin (and "look-alike" drugs) was consumed per hundred thousand individuals in the United States, but some states recorded much higher or lower rates of consumption than others. The five states with the highest rates of methylphenidate and other related drugs prescribed to treat ADHD in 2000 were Delaware, New Hampshire, Rhode Island, Vermont, and Massachusetts. In these states between 6 and 7.4 kilograms of Ritalin were consumed (per hundred thousand population) compared to a range of 1.7 to 2.2 kilograms in the five lowest-use states: Hawaii, New York, Nevada, California, and New Mexico.[24]

Table 6.2 presents a series of simple but revealing averages. In the five states recording the highest consumption (6.5 kilograms) of Ritalin in 2000, on average 80 percent of the student population is white. It is only 40 percent on average in the five states with the lowest consumption of Ritalin (2.2 kilograms).[25] These data strongly reinforce the impression

**Table 6-2.**   Race and per capita school funding in states with high and low rates of Ritalin consumption

| Where | Ritalin use, in kilograms per 100,000 individuals | Percent white | Per capita school funding |
|---|---|---|---|
| National average | 4.5 | 60% | $7,507 |
| Delaware | 7.4 | 60 | 9,116 |
| New Hampshire | 7.1 | 95 | 7,415 |
| Rhode Island | 6.2 | 73 | 9,480 |
| Vermont | 6.2 | 96 | 9,315 |
| Massachusetts | 6.0 | 76 | 9,677 |
| High-use state average | 6.5 | 80 | 9,001 |
| Low-use state average | 2.2 | 40 | 7,413 |
| Hawaii | 1.7 | 20 | 6,712 |
| New York | 2.1 | 55 | 10,905 |
| Nevada | 2.2 | 55 | 5,910 |
| California | 2.3 | 35 | 7,111 |
| New Mexico | 2.7 | 34 | 6,425 |

*Sources*: U.S. Drug Enforcement Administration ARCOS database, 2000 for data on Ritalin use. U.S. Department of Education, National Center for Education Statistics, the NCES Common Core of Data, "State Nonfiscal Survey of Public Elementary/Secondary Education," 1988–1989 through 2001–2002, and Projections of Education Statistics to 2013 for information on student ethnicity and per capita funding.

that high-use states are predominantly white and disproportionately privileged in socioeconomic terms. Table 6.2 also shows that high-use states record higher per capita expenditure on education—an average of $9,001 per annum, whereas low-use states with their larger nonwhite student bodies allocate only $7,413 per annum per student. New York is the exception in Table 6.2—a low-use state with the highest per capita investment in education in the United States. The generous funding of New York disguises huge inequality in per capita expenditure of special needs students and those who do not claim eligibility under the Individuals with Disabilities in Education Act (IDEA; see pages 156–157).

The above average expenditure per capita on education in high-use states is associated with high levels of educational achievement. This comes out clearly in statistics generated by the "No Child Left Behind" Act. In 2001, states were required to participate in various national testing programs to keep receiving certain types of federal funds. The

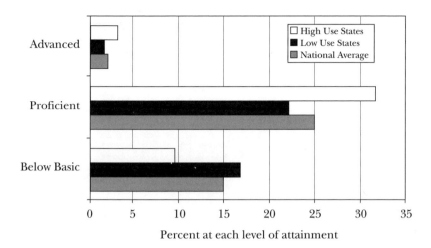

**Figure 6-2.**   Writing achievement levels in high and low use states, grade 4, 2002

*Sources*: U.S. Drug Enforcement Administration ARCOS database, 2000 for identifying high- and low-use states. U.S. Department of Education, Institute of Education Sciences, National Center for Education Statistics, National Assessment of Educational Progress, 2002 Writing Assessments for testing results.

act provided more funds for sampling on a state-by-state basis, increasing the reliability of data starting in 2002. Students' writing was tested in the fourth, eighth, and twelfth grades. The results for elementary students, fourth graders, are used in Figure 6.2. Students were graded on an abstract three-hundred-point scale. These results were translated into four levels: below basic, basic, proficient, and advanced for each grade.[26] The results for high- and low-use states are displayed in Figure 6.2 for writing scores below basic, proficient, and advanced.

High-use states clearly have more high achievers, and they have fewer children performing at below basic levels. For example, in high-use states 31.5 percent achieve proficiency in writing, and less than 10 percent fail to achieve the basic level. In low-use states, the comparable figures are 22 percent at the proficient level with nearly 17 percent failing to achieve the basic level. These distinctive characteristics come out clearly in Figure 6.3, with attainment in high-use states above the national average for proficiency and below it for students who fail to make the grade even at the basic level. Once again, low-use states exhibit the opposite profile. They have above-average numbers of students performing at below basic

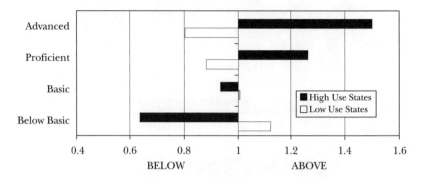

**Figure 6-3.**   Educational attainment in high and low use states, compared to the national average [ratios, where 1 is the national mean]

*Sources*:  U.S. Drug Enforcement Administration ARCOS database, 2000 for identifying high and low use states. U.S. Department of Education, Institute of Education Sciences, National Center for Education Statistics, National Assessment of Educational Progress, 2002 Writing Assessments, for testing results.

level and fewer students who make the grade (i.e., the national average) at the proficient level.

Ironically, the strong impression conveyed by these data is that ADHD is systematically more pronounced in prosperous communities where children perform above the national average in standardized tests. This flies in the face of the popular perception of ADHD as a learning disorder of poor, underprivileged, and badly behaved minority children, a perception encouraged by thinking about ADHD as the medicalization of deviance. Nationally, ADHD is currently lower among African Americans and Latinos. It is also lower among Asian Americans. The lack of correlation with poverty and the medically uninsured casts considerable doubt on biomedical representations of ADHD as a product of congenital abnormalities that are now and always have been strongly correlated with socioeconomic disadvantage. Though the composition of the ADHD population may be heterogeneous to some degree, the social characteristics that distinguish high-use counties are those where the risk of birth injury and congenital disability is lowest.

These observations may reflect relatively recent shifts in the social composition of communities and, by implication, families using Ritalin as a tool of child management. Adam Rafalovich (2001) has attempted to trace the nosological history of ADHD. He sees a line of continuity between the late nineteenth century (and, by modern standards, politically incorrect) medical term *imbecility* and the mid-century classification *hyperkinesis. Hyperkinesis* was the term in use when Ritalin was first pre-scribed to pacify unmanageable children in the 1960s. At this point, the underlying condition was still thought to be relatively rare and to be caused by minimal brain damage.[27] Before they became classified under the heading ADHD, the troublesome behaviors that Ritalin could "cure" were referred to as hyperactivity. This term was still in medical vogue when the dominant sociological approach based on the medicalization of deviance was inaugurated. The combination of hyperactivity and deviance conjures up images of antisocial behavior, with boys out-numbering girls by more than ten to one. It is not difficult to imagine why hyperactivity then might have been associated with lower-class ra-ther than middle-class boys and why people in prosperous communities would be strongly averse to their children being singled out for treat-ment. The symptoms of ADHD would have to be significantly remor-alized before the contemporary social distribution skewed towards affluent communities could take shape. In this process, the disability rights movement and the successful claim it made for compensatory re-sources from the state has played a crucial part in making ADHD a respectable and worthy condition (see pages 156–157).

As the foregoing summary makes clear, there are only limited data available to construct a meaningful sociological account of the trend and social distribution of ADHD. Sociologists have been curiously unin-terested in the social parameters of ADHD, and they have not been active in pressing for the establishment of a nationwide apparatus for its mea-surement as a feature of relations of socialization. From a biomedical perspective, the evidence of ADHD is constructed as a series of personal traits exhibited by the individual patient. Sociologists can make some inferences from these data, but to understand when and how Ritalin is employed as a tool of primary socialization we need much better data on the nexus of social relationships that opens the pathway to an ADHD identity for the dependent child.[28] The evidence examined in this chapter allows us to piece together the major social parameters of the ADHD epidemic as it developed during the 1990s. Some of the best clues come from treating ADHD as a social fact and comparing communities with high and low rates, and by using these data we can confirm one further interesting feature of the social settings where ADHD symptoms flourish.

## The Gender Gap in Education and the "Run on Ritalin"

The most distinctive trend that has occurred during the period that methylphenidate emerged as a teaching aid in American elementary schools is a reversal of the gender gap in educational attainment.

Between 1970 and the end of the millennium, girls caught up with and then overtook boys in overall educational attainment. The biggest differences are recorded in reading and writing. A U.S. Department of Education study reports a reading achievement gap favoring secondary school girls widening from ten points in 1992 to sixteen points in 2002. In practical terms what this means is that an eleventh-grade boy performs at the level of an eighth-grade girl. The differential for mathematics and science still tends to favors boys, although the gap varies year by year and is not always statistically significant. As Figure 6.4 shows, the trend of girls outperforming boys is not confined to the United States but is found in all modern societies, and everywhere the scale of the literacy differential is much bigger internationally than is the uneven pattern of differentials for math and science.

The evidence of Figure 6.4 suggests that a very fundamental shift is occurring in the balance of human capital between the sexes in developed societies at the end of the millennium. In the United States this interpretation is supported by further evidence of change in gender differences in ambition for, entry to, and completion of higher education. In 1980 there was virtually no difference between boys and girls in their aspirations for higher education: 36 percent of boys and 34 percent of girls. By 1995, 49 percent of boys and 60 percent of girls expressed the same goals. Trends in social ambition and social action go hand in hand. In 1972, boys were more likely than girls to enroll in a two- or four-year college (53 percent versus 46 percent). By 1997, the gap was reversed with 64 percent of boys compared to 70 percent of girls enrolling in degree programs. As a result, females now constitute the majority of the undergraduate population (56 percent in 1996, up from 42 percent in 1970) and, once enrolled, are more committed and successful (among students enrolled in college in 1990, 50 percent of females compared to 41 percent of males had earned a degree by 1994).

The gender gap at the end of the educational career appears to begin in the preschool years. Little girls aged three to five years are reputedly more literate and much better at "small motor skills" such as holding pens and pencils, so that when they get to school, they are already better

---

**Figure 6-4.**   International differences in average scores for reading, math, and science literacy among fifteen-year-olds

*Source*: Organization for Economic Cooperation and Development, Program for International Student Assessment (PISA) 2000.

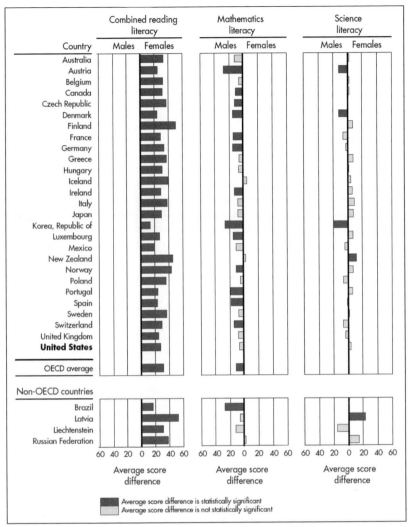

NOTE: Each bar above represents the average score difference between males and females on combined reading, mathematics or science literacy. Some of these differences are statistically significant and indicated by darker bars. For instance, the United States has a 29 point score difference favoring females in combined reading literacy, which is statistically significant. The score differences between U.S. males and females in mathematics literacy and science literacy are 7 points and 5 points, respectively, but neither is a statistically significant difference. Average score difference is calculated by subtracting scores of males from scores of females. Detail may not sum to totals due to rounding. Although the Netherlands participated in the Program for International Student Assessment (PISA) in 2000, technical problems with its sample prevent its results from being discussed here. For information on the results for the Netherlands, see OECD (2001). The OECD average is the average of the national averages of 27 OECD countries. Because PISA is principally an OECD study, the results for non-OECD countries are displayed separately from those of the OECD countries and not included in the OECD average.

equipped for the learning process. In consequence, it is not surprising that boys are almost twice as likely as girls to be required to repeat kindergarten or first grade. These sorts of differences have been linked with sex or gender differences in sociability, and there is evidence that girls are more relational, more oriented to other people, and more engaged from an earlier age in learning to interpret and manipulate social symbols and develop skills of social interaction, including what Goffman (1959) famously termed impression management. As noted, the female's relational disposition has been seen as a liability in feminist psychoanalytic writing because it appeared to hold back a girl's developing sense of individuality and, by implication, her ambition to succeed in the male occupational world (Chodorow 1978). The widening gender gap in educational achievement so vividly revealed in Figure 6.4 is a significant challenge to any argument that the more socially connected female is at a systematic disadvantage when it comes to succeeding in the public sphere where children are prepared for competition the labor market. During the last quarter of the twentieth century, girls became more ambitious than boys and made more effective use of educational opportunities to garner the credentials that could make their ambitions reality.

Could this sea change in the gender distribution of human capital be an important factor in the emergence of the idea that a sizeable proportion of the male population of the United States is literally learning disabled? And, if there is a connection, why do we only see it manifested in North America? This last question is reserved for the final section of this chapter.

We can attempt to answer the first of these questions by comparing regional variations in the rate of identifying and medicating children for ADHD with variations in the gender gap in education. We have already seen (see Figure 6.2) that students in high-use states have higher levels of educational achievement. Drawing once again on data from the United States' Drug Enforcement Administration ARCOS database,[29] we can ask a related question: do the same states that distinguish high and low use of Ritalin also exhibit distinctive patterns of gender inequality in educational attainment?

Figure 6.5 displays the results for the gender gap among students at each level of achievement in the statistics generated by the "No Child Left Behind" act. The gender gap varies with the level of educational attainment. In states where the rates of psychostimulant use are at their lowest level, the gender gap is actually a little higher among students who achieve only the basic level or who fail to do so. More telling is the gender gap among students who score above the basic level, that is, at the proficient or advanced level. Here we can see that high-use states

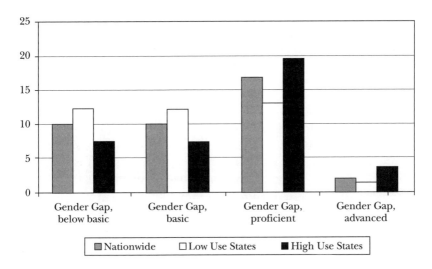

**Figure 6-5.**   The Gender Gap in Grade Four: High and Low Use States 2002 (female % minus male % at each level of attainment)

*Sources*:  U.S. Drug Enforcement Administration ARCOS database, 2000 for identifying high- and low-use states. U.S. Department of Education, Institute of Education Sciences, National Center for Education Statistics, National Assessment of Educational Progress, 2002 Writing Assessments, for testing results.

display a wider gender gap. In real terms (see Figure 6.A1 p. 163), 45 percent of fourth-grade girls in high-use states attain a proficient level compared to 25 percent of boys, a gap of 20 percent. In low-use states by contrast, only 30 percent and 16 percent of girls and boys respectively attain proficiency, and the gap falls to 14 percent. This reinforces the pattern seen earlier in Figure 6.2. Children of both sexes perform above the national average in high-use states where per capita expenditure on education is above the national norm. More generous expenditure may be paying off in the above-average performance of students, but the high priority accorded to education may simultaneously increase the anxiety of parents witnessing male children perform at a significantly lower rate than girls. Of course, this is not to suggest that parents are aware of the statistics of gender inequality exhibited in Figure 6.5. All they know is that their son is not ranked as high as they would like. The aggregate effect of many parents experiencing relative disappointment is what constitutes the collective phenomenon for which Emile Durkheim coined the term *social fact* (1938).

The ecological data used in this chapter to investigate who gets labeled ADHD paints a picture with broad brushstrokes on a large canvas highlighting the sociological characteristics of the kinds of communities (states and counties) where ADHD is most prevalent. The pattern we see does not sit easily with representations of ADHD as a congenital abnormality or a disorder brought on by modern culture in the form of junk food or rapid-fire communication and the accelerated pace of daily life. We need much better systematic evidence documenting the family settings where ADHD flourishes to fully comprehend the sociological meaning of ADHD. The evidence reviewed in this chapter is consistent with what we have called a socialization hypothesis—that the resort to medication as a child-rearing tool is best understood as an indicator of changes in social norms and relations centered on the social division of labor.

Though the pressure toward medication emanating from changes in social life are felt throughout the population, they appear to be concentrated in settings where parents have high expectations for their children's education and where the gap in attainment between boys and girls is at its widest. Boys are not the only victims of this contemporary learning disability whose symptoms are broad enough to encompass many different manifestations of inattentive childish behavior, but boys outnumber girls by a wide margin, and the ADHD criteria are skewed towards puerile masculine traits that would have been tolerated by earlier generations. In the remainder of this chapter, we attempt to identify the contemporary social forces that create pressures toward the use of medication in child rearing, and we consider whether medicalization is an appropriate metaphor for what is going on.

## Social Forces and the Medicalization of Boyhood

The hypothesis developed in this chapter is that the mushrooming rate of ADHD represents the substitution of technology for human labor in the process of child socialization both at home and in the elementary classroom. This is why adult females—mothers and the feminized profession of elementary school teachers—are the principal agents supervising the pathway into medication. These are the two primary agents of child socialization; they confront firsthand the problems of "hard to socialize" children. Methylphenidate offers a highly effective biochemical solution to the problems faced by time-challenged parents and in particular by the triple-shift adult woman charged with earning her livelihood while simultaneously creating a home and caring for her offspring. Modern mores of socialization pose significant limits on the exercise of parental power, and in certain contexts Ritalin has emerged as a vital resource for salving the maternal conscience as well as propping up the child who is falling behind his peers. Though the stakes are lower for the average teacher, Ritalin is nevertheless an invaluable resource for controlling and quieting unruly students, especially little boys who are on average less mature, slower to learn, or, at least, less motivated to engage peaceably in the "give and take" of social interaction in the modern classroom. In the group learning situation which today dominates primary education, the will to self-regulate behavior is at a premium, and little girls appear far more disposed to conform to the demands of interactive learning.

The use of powerful narcotics as a child-care aid is not new. Before opium became a regulated substance in the early twentieth century, it was liberally dispensed as an infant cordial, used by eighteenth- and nineteenth-century mothers to pacify distressed and sleepless infants.[30] The resort to methylphenidate today breaks new ground because it is used to discipline older children, even teens, in place of conventional labor-intensive modes of socialization. The socialization hypothesis emerges in view of the contemporary scale and social distribution of the practice. As we have seen, in some places up to 20 percent of boys aged seven to eleven years are routinely receiving medication to help them cope with the learning environment and to help their teachers cope with them. Their lack of self-discipline is also so deeply troubling to their parents that the drug regime is continued in the home environment, increasing the possibility than a significant minority of children, especially boys, will require lifelong medication to cope successfully in social interaction. This is a truly "stunning" sociological phenomenon—its analysis cannot be confined within the orthodox labeling perspective. In this penultimate section, we will ask what forces of change have brought about this extraordinary state of affairs. By approaching ADHD as a social fact in the Durkheimian sense, we can use what limited knowledge exists of the unusual social distribution of Ritalin consumption in the United States to uncover the contingencies that shape the unfolding pattern of psycho-pharmacological socialization. Several factors shape the chance that a family will turn to Ritalin as a tool of socialization.

One important backdrop to the emerging trend is the widespread acceptance of modernist childcare ideologies that encourage free expression while curtailing the full range of parental techniques available to control and shape the psyche of the growing child.[31] Forceful discipline in all of its manifestations has been virtually criminalized, and even slapping[32] is now condemned as a form of child abuse. Parents are led to believe that any show of righteous anger is a personal failing and that all children can be tamed without resort to physical coercion of any kind. As the cultural discourse has it, the task of the parent is to create a fully rational social being, and this cannot be achieved by inducing fear of punishment or a fatalistic orientation (Sagan 1989). Similar sentiments underlie the shift towards informality and group learning in the modern classroom. Learning to think for oneself calls for less top-down discipline and a more unstructured learning environment. There is some evidence that girls benefit more from informal settings such as these, and the recently observed widening gender gap in educational achievement might confirm this. This is one of the conclusions of feminist critic Christina Hoff Sommers in her book *The War against Boys* (Hoff Sommers 2000). Going even further, Sommers argues that the gender equity movement, with its attack on the values of traditional masculinity, has been so successful in the United States that it has tipped the balance the other way and made the average classroom a hostile and alienating learning environment for little boys.

Training the rational, emotionally flexible yet secure and intellectually creative self is a highly labor-intensive activity. As any parent knows, it is also a labor of love, calling for eons of patience and the willingness to invest plenty of interaction time with the preschool child.[33] To the extent that families embrace the Enlightenment paradigm of child raising, knowingly or otherwise, they experience the pressure to invest significant energy and emotion in the care of their children. The big problem here is the acceptance of the normative script of modern socialization alongside the disappearance of the motivation and/or the time to perform this labor-intensive task.

The modern nuclear family regime was built on a sexual division of labor that facilitated a female labor–intensive mode of early child socialization. Where the homemaker was herself highly educated, this created a stimulating home environment for children of both sexes and facilitated the early acquisition of literacy. During the second half of the twentieth century, women of all social classes increasingly withdrew their labor from the domestic sphere, and at the same time the cohesion of the modern nuclear family began to come apart. These processes had important implications for early child socialization. Little girls especially encountered new adult female role models that shifted their own developing identities and produced greater incentives to engage in education as a preparation for their own future adult selves. The opposite effect may have been felt by little boys. As the male breadwinner model receded in their practical experience, the pressure to succeed at school must have lessened.

The widening gender gap in the elementary classroom reflects these various processes. Children enter school less prepared, and any gender differences in early educability are exacerbated. This is the context in which "mature" girls begin to outstrip "immature" boys. The rising rate of economic participation among women with preschool children has simply removed the space for modern mothering from the average adult woman's time budget. Working mothers no longer feel they can afford to take time off to carefully supervise the early psychosocial development of their children. There was never any chance that fathers would take their place in an unpaid activity that adult males have never been disposed to consider a proper vocation. As a result, the private sphere is no longer a "haven in a heartless world" (Lasch 1977). In most cases, there is now nobody at home to bring up the baby, to perform what Talcott Parsons conceptualized as the emotional labor of family life.[34]

The sexual division of labor (or increasingly the lack of it) in the postmodern family has significantly lowered the age of entry to the public sphere, bringing forward the moment when the small child is expected to demonstrate the rudimentary skills of impression management. This is why entry to school or kindergarten invariably coincides with the discovery of ADHD. The strain of this moment is felt more acutely in the middle class because of its ideological commitments to "enlightened childrearing," and more particularly female parents experience it as normative guilt if and when their children fail to make the grade or to behave in a self-disciplined, that is, rational way in public settings. As Singh (2004) puts it, in a culture of "mother blame," this is one of the forces that unwittingly propels the mother to turn to Ritalin to prove that she can "put her house in order." These pressures are the primary reason why adult women in middle class families are at the forefront of the medicalization of boyhood taking the agonized initiative, one by one, to have their immature and under-socialized sons declared learning disabled and subjected to medication.

A related and equally important reason for turning to Ritalin as a child-care tool is the increased burden felt by the elementary school teacher as her contribution to primary socialization increases. In the golden age of the male breadwinner/female homemaker, the middle-class family shouldered a larger responsibility for the education of its children. Mothers had the time and opportunity to encourage habits of self-discipline and to teach the basic educational skills that give children a head start in their preschool years. The diminution of intensive private mothering must mean that many middle-class children now come to school less well prepared both socially and educationally than they used to be. This increases the workload while simultaneously making the elementary school teacher a more important agent of early training and educational progress. Research showing that the teacher is numerically the most likely person to make the first recommendation that a child be evaluated for ADHD must reflect increasing problems of maintaining order in the classroom (Sax and Kautz 2003).

The situation is not helped by the accounting requirements that emerged from the politics of educational reform in recent years that place more pressure on teachers to prove their and their schools' effectiveness by periodic testing of student progress. The same developments produce a stream of "accounts" of how individual children perform, making parents continuously aware of where their child ranks in the hierarchy of talent. As we have seen, this national accounting of educational achievement reveals a widening gap favoring girls, with boys slipping down the ranks in the basic skills of reading and writing, the prerequisites of personal success in the modern labor market. Though parents may be unaware of the aggregate statistics, individually they get their message that their son is not doing as well as his sister or the neighbor's daughter. This can explain why ADHD emerges more strongly in contexts where education is highly valued and where the gender gap is wider.

During the last quarter of the twentieth century, obtaining decent educational credentials became a much more important priority than it had been before 1950 (Collins 1979; Dore 1976). This happened partly because a changing occupational structure significantly eroded traditional well-paid blue-collar opportunities formerly monopolized by men (Matthaei 1982; Stearns 1979). These were jobs that little boys could look forward to no matter how they did at school. The decline of manual employment as an avenue for rewarding work made parents increasingly aware that their children would need to demonstrate mental acuity to operate effectively in labor markets made more competitive by the entry of the entire birth cohort—male and female alike. In 1950, the male breadwinner norm focused the little male mind and at the same time gave assurance that the best jobs were reserved for him. To a very significant degree, all this changed after 1975, and the ramifications have continued to percolate throughout society, all the way down to kindergarten. To compete in the postindustrial labor market, the high school diploma is now a must for everyone, and the pressure thereby aroused is felt before children enter their teens. If children are to succeed they need to acquire good work habits well before they enter high school.

The final factor predisposing the middle classes to consider ADHD as a solution to a child's perceived developmental problems is the normalization of disability. The disability rights movement scored notable gains in the last quarter of the twentieth century. Building on the example set by the civil rights movement, it successfully lobbied the state for legislation to level the playing field for people of all aptitudes and capacities. In effect this movement challenged the moral division between normal and abnormal by securing legislation that requires that all public facilities be designed to be freely usable by every citizen, no matter what their somatic or psychic abilities or disabilities. The effect on the learning environment has been immense. Learning disability became a respectable basis for mounting a claim for compensatory treatment.

Predictably, the more prosperous middle classes were the first to exploit this expansion of equality of opportunity in education.[35] The primary reason for the escalation in the numbers of families resorting to Ritalin as a tool of socialization was the incorporation of ADHD as an "eligible condition" under IDEA. This happened in 1991, and it meant that a diagnosis of ADHD would trigger the right to receive special educational services including "modifications and accommodations" in the educational program.[36]

Though "eligible condition" and "modifications and accommodations" are not defined, they include special provisions to level the playing field without lowering standards. They also protected officially diagnosed students in some cases from disciplinary action, such as a school suspension for serious breaches of rules. In practice a typical provision for an eligible student might be lengthening time for exams or providing a special environment and assistance in taking them. If parents can prove that their children are afflicted with ADHD, they can make demands at their children's schools for special treatment, and schools may also benefit from federal funds designed to ensure equality of opportunity for disabled children. However, the funds coming from the federal government are not nearly enough to compensate for the increased expenditure arising from the explosion in the numbers of disabled students that occurred after passage of the 1991 act. In New York in the early 1990s, students receiving special education constituted 13 percent of the school population but received 25 percent of school resources. This added up to $18,700 per capita expenditure on the average special education student, leaving less than $5,000 per student in regular classes.

In the period since ADHD became an eligible condition under IDEA, the numbers of "disabled" children in U.S. schools has increased at an unprecedented rate, but we do not know how this affected the socioeconomic and race/ethnicity distribution of the afflicted population.[37] The NCHS evidence reported above covers the period since 1997 and reveals that ADHD is skewed towards more prosperous, white, middle-class families. Whether this is a specific effect of the legislation or merely a continuation of preexisting trends is an important topic for further research.

The social parameters of the ADHD epidemic reveal that the risks of the disorder are inversely related to social and economic disadvantage. Families who seek to qualify their children as learning disabled are disproportionately white, medically insured, economically secure, and living in places with above-average public resources for education. It should not go unmentioned that this is the segment of the population that would be expected to produce the lowest incidence of congenital anomalies. "At-risk" families are also disproportionately headed by single female parents, though the published official statistics do not tell us whether the general socioeconomic and race profile persists within this group.

Unfortunately, the available evidence of the social distribution of ADHD does not tell us how the rate of medication varies according to the sexual division of labor at home and the number of hours worked by parents. This is an important area for sociological research. The socialization hypothesis advanced in this chapter predicts that the rate of medication will vary directly with a family's budget for "quality time." However, even if they are not more time challenged than average, the fact that parents are more likely attuned to modernist child raising philosophies means that they lack access to the full range of punitive sanctions for disciplining children. By rejecting the philosophy of "spare the rod, spoil the child," they are more vulnerable when a medical solution to their child's misbehavior is proposed. Since they are also likely to be more anxious about education and more concerned with monitoring progress, they face an additional inducement to accept medication when it promises to help their children "make the grade."

With some notable exceptions, the pediatric profession has undoubtedly also played an important part in encouraging the use of psychostimulant drugs as a routine aid to socialization. During the last decade, it has confidently presided over an epidemic that has spread up and down the age spectrum (Conrad and Potter 2000). An out-of-control epidemic is usually a disastrous blow to the reputation of a profession charged with safeguarding the development of the next generation. In the case of ADHD, this does not seem to apply. The profession's leading experts enthusiastically predict that those who have fallen victim to this learning disorder are a fraction of the afflicted population and that many more children, who are at present undiagnosed, could benefit from systematic medication. This prospect has periodically raised public and political concern and occasioned the setting up of White House–style conferences and congressional inquiries with a call to halt the increasing practice of administering powerful psychoactive drugs to small children. Paradoxically, these occasions, dominated by the nation's experts on child development who are the very source of the epidemic, have always turned out to be opportunities for the strengthening the legitimacy of ADHD as an authentic biomedical disability.

This happens because of the profession's hegemonic power over the ADHD discourse. Virtually all the research on ADHD is carried out under the auspices of pediatric psychiatry, and much of it is sponsored by the same pharmaceutical companies that profit from drugs like Ritalin. The questions addressed by this research do not disturb the biomedical reality of the disorder. The findings tell us virtually nothing about the social epidemiology of ADHD and the social settings in which its symptoms flourish. In fact, causal questions take a back seat to cost-benefit research to measure the relative efficiency of biochemically oriented child training. The findings typically show that using Ritalin to pacify unruly children is much quicker and cheaper than traditional therapies that seek to improve parenting skills (MTA Cooperative Group 1999, 2004).[38] These observations leave us in no doubt that drug companies and the pediatric professionals associated with them have definite interests in the spreading practice of drug-assisted parenting, but even so the evidence examined in this chapter does not lay the exclusive responsibility for the ADHD epidemic at the door of the family physician. As we have seen, the doctor's role is more accurately described as enabling rather than initiating the process of medication. Mothers and teachers—the adults most directly involved with cultivating good behavior—mostly supervise the pathway into treatment, though the scale of the epidemic in the United States reflects what Lynn Payer (1988) characterized as the country's interventionist culture of medicine. We return to this in the concluding section of the chapter.

The medicalization of boyhood involves defining childish traits more prominently displayed by boys than girls as congenital abnormalities. This involves cultural reform of a fundamental kind. The same is true of the administration of powerful narcotic drugs to children. These transformations could not occur through promotional campaigns by medical corporations. There had to be some fundamental social changes, in this case centered on gender norms and relationships, to create the conditions for Ritalin to emerge as a legitimate tool of child socialization.[39] Ritalin is a wonder medicine, a panacea for all the travails of postmodern parenthood. Taken three times a day at four-hour intervals, Ritalin can transform a distracted, disorganized, and disobedient child into a paragon of youthful bourgeois virtue—disciplined, diligent, and docile. For the time-challenged mother negotiating the impossible triple shift of parent, homemaker, and wage worker, Ritalin may be a bitter pill to swallow, but in many cases it is just too valuable to resist.

## Why Medicalization Is an Appropriate Conceptual Metaphor for the Trend Toward Psychopharmacological Socialization

We conclude with a discussion of why medicalization is an appropriate conceptual metaphor for capturing the fundamental social developments laid out in this chapter. This enables us to return to the question of why the ADHD epidemic is a U.S. phenomenon even though the gender gap in education is a universal feature of developed societies. What is gained in depicting the increasing resort to amphetamine drugs in child socialization as a process of medicalization? Are the root causes of the increased reliance on medication to be found in the medical sector of the economy and culture? In particular, how far is our understanding improved by focusing on the interests of the pediatric psychiatry profession and pharmaceutical companies in promoting the practice? Is the epidemic occurring primarily because it is profitable for the drug manufacturers or because it enhances the power, prestige, or resources of the pediatric profession?

Some of the evidence points strongly towards an affirmative answer to the last question. The extraordinary bravado of the profession's leading ADHD experts as they predict the continuing spread of the epidemic and the confident assertion that too little rather than too much Ritalin is currently being dispensed certainly leads to the conclusion that the profession takes pride in the capacity to offer a quick fix to the parents of "hard to socialize" children. It is also obvious that the drug manufacturers have a strong interest in promoting the practice. Ritalin is already one of the most profitable pharmaceutical commodities ever marketed, and the profits to be made from further escalation in the numbers of children identified as learning disabled are immense. Novartis, Ritalin's patent holder, has been actively promoting its product in medical publications and via its support for self-help groups that embrace a medical ideology of problematic child development. Yet, as we have seen, there are also signs that the primary force of medicalization comes from outside the political economy of medicine.

The most important of these signs is the knowledge of the primary role played by parents, in particular mothers, and elementary school teachers initiating the diagnostic and treatment regime for individual children. This is a classic case of the patients bringing the affliction to physicians' notice and persuading doctors to use their authority to rubber-stamp their own convictions that something is pathologically wrong with the children in their care. The case notes in Laurence

Diller's (1998) *Running on Ritalin* give an almost graphic image of how this is accomplished, revealing the pressure to which even a highly skeptical professional can be exposed. This causes us to pause and think carefully about the meaning of the observation by Conrad and Schneider (1992) that the routine work of medicalization is often accomplished by nonmedical personnel. The wording here is not sufficient to indicate the powerful interest behind the social action of the nonmedical personnel, since it conveys the false impression that they are mindlessly acting to further medical hegemony. This impression may actually be the opposite of reality. In the case of ADHD, nonmedical personnel may in fact be running the show, and to this extent professional bravado about the scale and course of the epidemic must be seen as a defense mechanism warding off criticism of professional negligence.

And there is every reason for pediatricians to be defensive about prescribing Ritalin to vulnerable infants. Ritalin and other amphetamine medications "designed" for children have never been tested on infants below school age. In consequence, there is no FDA mandate for their use at these ages, and the manufacturers' own instructions make it clear that the drugs should not be used with children aged less than five. Yet there are many reports of children as young as three or four being diagnosed with ADHD and prescribed Ritalin. In this context it is important to bear in mind the impossibility of diagnosing ADHD in a three-year-old child. That this is occurring under medical supervision is prima facie evidence of professional negligence, and the NCHS data suggests that it may be happening on a significant scale—it records that 1 percent of children aged three to four have ADHD.

These observations are sociologically significant. From a perspective of professional integrity there are strong reasons to doubt that the "out of control" force of the ADHD epidemic serves the interests of the medical profession as a whole. Frequent reports that a diagnosis of ADHD and a prescription for Ritalin are sanctioned with minimal professional supervision, sometimes even over the telephone and without a rigorous clinical evaluation, send a strong message of unprofessional conduct, that the epidemic is racing out of control because organized medicine has dropped the ball. This possibility is not lost on the general public, a large portion of which views the ADHD epidemic with great skepticism. There may be long-term consequences here for the integrity of the profession, and the sociologist must inevitably ask whether the casual way in which Ritalin prescriptions are accommodated is further evidence of the erosion of medical authority, in this case reflected in physicians' ceding their clinical monopoly over the dispensing of regulated substances to patients or their guardians.

So where does this leave our opening question on the appropriateness of the medicalization thesis as a heuristic tool? There is no doubt that the pediatric profession has played a very important enabling role in the ADHD epidemic, so important in fact that medicalization is the right conceptual terminology. The legitimacy of this conclusion is proven in light of international variation in the incidence of ADHD and especially in the use of Ritalin as an educational aid. If, as this chapter has argued, the gender gap in education was an important stimulus to the escalation of ADHD in the 1990s, why did this happen only in the United States? To answer this question we must look to national variations in the culture and political economy of medicine. ADHD reached epidemic proportions in North America's more prosperous white communities during the 1990s primarily because they were amply served by physicians whose culture of medicine is more aggressively interventionist and profit oriented than anywhere else on earth. In this context, "profit oriented" includes the efficiency drive of health care providers who, not surprisingly, favor cheap biochemical substitutes for labor-intensive therapy. The same phenomenon has not occurred to anything like the same degree abroad because of cultural variations in the ethos and organization of medicine.

The United States is undoubtedly the most profitable territory for the international pharmaceutical business, and the lack of public and collective professional control over the financing of health care is an important reason why a brave new world of child socialization could take off there. The willingness to overcome traditional scruples about using amphetamine type medicines on patients whose psyches were still in the making occurred earlier and with much greater force in the United States because of the established practice of relying more heavily on technologically oriented treatment and the inclination to administer heavy doses of drugs. These tendencies are well documented and encouraged by the free medical marketplace that still dominates the delivery of health care. Since drugs are the cheapest form of psychiatric therapy, they appealed to cost-conscious health insurers and managers of health management organizations. As Lynn Payer (1988) pointed out nearly two decades ago, U.S. medicine is more adventurous, and more profit driven, more extravagant in its use of resources (including size of the dose), and more pioneering in its embrace of new technologies, especially those biochemically engineered for the management of mind and body. This distinctive medical tradition is the most powerful enabling factor in the runaway use of drugs in child socialization.

We should also remember another enabling factor emanating from the biomedical model itself that applies more generally: the assumption of generic normality. This is the understanding that the human body and psyche come in a standard form and that deviation from the normal (i.e., dis-ease) represents a sound factual basis for chemical intervention. This assumption is particularly problematic in the context of child development because of the highly variable character of psychosomatic and psychosocial maturation and its sensitivity to social relations.

All of the foregoing have acted as strong enabling and even encouraging factors in the routine use of medicine to shape a child's disposition to cooperate in social interaction, but they could not succeed in the absence of major changes in social relationships, in particular, the organization and sexual division of labor in family life and in the gender relations that underpin and flow from it. This is what makes the ADHD epidemic an extremely important contemporary social fact.

## Appendix

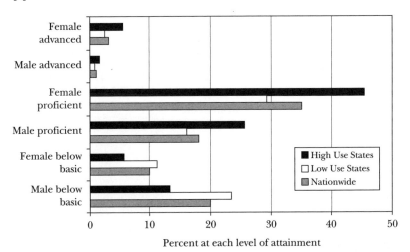

**Figure 6-A1.**   Writing achievement levels by gender in high and low use states: grade 4, 2002

*Sources*:  U.S. Drug Enforcement Administration ARCOS database, 2000 for identifying high- and low-use states. U.S. Department of Education, Institute of Education Sciences, National Center for Education Statistics, National Assessment of Educational Progress, 2002 Writing Assessments, for testing results.

Table 6-A1. Writing achievement levels by gender for fourth graders, 2002

| | Nation-wide | Low ADHD | High ADHD | Hawaii | New York | Nevada | California | New Mexico | Delaware | Rhode Island | Vermont | Massachusetts |
|---|---|---|---|---|---|---|---|---|---|---|---|---|
| Male below basic | 20% | 23.4% | 13.25% | 23% | 12% | 26% | 27% | 29% | 12% | 15% | 18% | 8% |
| Female below basic | 10 | 11.2 | 5.75 | 10 | 6 | 11 | 13 | 16 | 5 | 7 | 7 | 4 |
| Gap below basic | -10 | -12.2 | -7.5 | -13 | -6 | -15 | -14 | -13 | -7 | -8 | -11 | -4 |
| Male basic | 80 | 76.6 | 86.75 | 77 | 88 | 74 | 73 | 71 | 88 | 85 | 82 | 92 |
| Female basic | 90 | 88.8 | 94.25 | 90 | 94 | 89 | 87 | 84 | 95 | 93 | 93 | 96 |
| Gap basic | 10 | 12.2 | 7.5 | 13 | 6 | 15 | 14 | 13 | 7 | 8 | 11 | 4 |
| Male proficient | 18 | 16 | 25.5 | 15 | 30 | 10 | 14 | 11 | 25 | 22 | 21 | 34 |
| Female proficient | 35 | 29.2 | 45.25 | 21 | 44 | 25 | 32 | 24 | 46 | 39 | 42 | 54 |
| Gap proficient | 17 | 13.2 | 19.75 | 6 | 14 | 15 | 18 | 13 | 21 | 17 | 21 | 20 |
| Male advanced | 1 | 0.8 | 1.5 | 1 | 2 | 0 | 1 | 0 | 1 | 1 | 2 | 2 |
| Female advanced | 3 | 2.2 | 5.25 | 2 | 4 | 1 | 3 | 1 | 5 | 4 | 5 | 7 |
| Gap advanced | 2 | 1.4 | 3.75 | 1 | 2 | 1 | 2 | 1 | 4 | 3 | 3 | 5 |

*Sources:* U.S. Drug Enforcement Administration ARCOS database, 2000 for identifying high and low use states. U.S. Department of Education, Institute of Education Sciences, National Center for Education Statistics, National Assessment of Educational Progress, 2002 Writing Assessments for testing results.

# 1

# The Sexual Savage: Race Science and the Medicalization of Black Masculinity

Ann Marie Hickey

## Introduction

The brutal physical and sexual terror that black men have faced throughout the course of their history in the United States was based on their racist—and often medically "documented"—construction as animalistic and dangerous savages. Because the Western racial paradigm is inundated with a fascination and fear of black sexuality (see Roberts 1999), this intersection between race and sexuality has proven to be continuously dangerous terrain for black men. As history reveals, racism has continuously been interwoven with physical and psychological attacks on black men's sexual identity (Stevenson 1994; D'Emilio and Freedman 1988) and with a medicalization of race in general and of black bodies and actions in particular (Saint-Aubin 2002).

According to Stevenson (1994), no issue is more volatile than the merging of sexuality and race. The connection between black men's sexual and racial identities has existed throughout American history, and one cannot examine black racial identity without acknowledging that it has also been sexualized, or vice versa. In the case of black Americans, sexuality is the "culprit" that sets the dichotomy between black and white into motion. Whereas "race" is the visible distinction between the dichotomous black and white, sexuality is its social distinction, and the blending of race, ethnicity, and sexuality forms "sexualized perimeters around ethnic, racial, and national spaces" (Nagel 2003, 1). This intersection and interaction between race, ethnicity, and sexuality is embedded in ethnosexuality, which involves a "melding [of] categories, blurring [of] borders or at least recognizing that people come in multiple varieties" (Lorber 1999, 355). In other words, ethnosexuality is a powerful way for race, ethnicity, and sexuality to be dependent on each other for meaning and power through their social construction (Nagel 2000a, 2003, 10).

Built into a system of ethnosexuality and historical abuses against black men is the medicalization of race and sexuality. Though it claims to be impartial and neutral, science has actually aided the development of racial hierarchies (Ernst 1999). Through eugenics, medical experimentation, and other scientific endeavors, medical science has perpetuated racism towards ethnic minorities in this country (Stevenson 1994), and the combination of being a racial "Other" and a sexual savage has ensured the continual medical mistreatment of black men.

In the following pages, I show that the medicalization of black men's racial and sexual identities are intertwined and have grounded this group's medical mistreatment in the most emblematic instance of the medicalization of black male sexuality: the Tuskegee, Alabama, syphilis experiment. This chapter situates this experiment as the logical outcome of the medicalization of a black male sexuality that began just prior to Reconstruction and continued well past the end of slavery. The cases of medical mistreatment based on race science assumptions—such as that of the Tuskegee syphilis experiment—illustrate how interconnected race and sexuality are for black men in the United States and how central medical science was in making (and scientizing) this connection. In my conclusion, I consider the lingering consequences of this medical construction and control of black male sexuality: a distrust of medical professionals, low participation in medical trials and organ donations, and minimal adherence to preventive measures to combat sexually transmitted diseases.

## Constructing Race and Ethnicity: Issues of Black and White

The social construction of race and ethnicity is based on a combination of politics, the economy, culture, and the historical period in which the construction takes place. While the terms *race* and *ethnicity* are used interchangeably in popular culture, "ethnicity" is usually based on language, region, culture, and religion, in addition to different physical features (Nagel 2000a), while "race" generally refers to differing physical features that are specific to certain populations (Nagel 2000a, Hacker 1995). Both ethnicity and race are socially constructed and are thus given meaning through their cultural use.

Historically speaking, ethnic boundaries in the United States emphasize the socially constructed category of race, which took on new meaning with the adoption of slavery in the seventeenth century. The distinction between different races is clearly more than a marker based on skin tone, pigmentation, and facial features and carries cultural connotations embedded in dominant ways of thinking about the social order of the races. As Hacker (1995, 7) explains:

> In its basic meaning, "White" denotes European antecedents, while "Black" stands for Africa. Since the human species began in Africa, we can say that Black people are those whose ancestors remained on that continent, while Whites descend from those who embarked on migrations to cooler climates. This has led some to the presumption that the races are at different levels of evolutionary development. For at least half a dozen centuries, and possibly longer, "White" has implied a higher civilization based on a superior inheritance.

Thus "scientific racism" (Somerville 1997; Pascoe 1997) (which has become synonymous with "biologistic" racism [Ernst 1999, 5]) grounded essentialist thinking about black bodies and sexuality. Scientific racism is based on the logic of biological determinism in which the physical body, rather than social characteristics, signifies an actor's capacities and tendencies. While science claims to be objective and culture free, the science of biological determinism—especially in the case of black men—has proven otherwise (Stevenson 1994). From the moment white colonizers set their sights on black bodies, they were basing their beliefs about a population on their visible physical characteristics versus their own. They used essentialist views, as Somerville (1997, 47) explains, to "locate discrete physiological markers of difference through which to classify and separate types of human beings." The scientific world gave racial meanings to anatomical differences between "black" and "white" (which, consequently, were also essentialist views based on skin pigmentation). These anatomical differences, such as skin, facial angle, pelvis, skull, brain mass, and genitalia, were said to predict intelligence and behavior. This biological view of race as a predictor of behavior was, of course, cited as justification for the centuries-long discrimination and exploitation of black Americans. For example, Dennis (1995) refers to the "father of the eugenics movement," Francis Galton, as a key leader in the move to discourage childbearing and race-mixing among the "unfit"—that is, people of color.[1]

While essentialism and scientific racism "proved" that racial differences existed on purely biological terms, they did not necessarily attribute social meanings to them. Though these beliefs concerning racial differences still infiltrate our thinking today, they are "simply" biology if they lack social meaning. The meanings associated with racial differences by science included sexual practices; black men's sexuality became socially constructed as hypersexual and insatiable, and the black male emerged as dangerous and inherently deviant in medical and popular discourse (as will be expanded upon later in this chapter; Saint-Aubin 2002; Wiegman 1993). Both popular and medical fascination with and moral judgment of "deviant" sexuality focused on the allegedly animalistic and dangerous sexual nature of the black man. In fact, this social construction became so embedded in our culture that it was, and continues to be, used as motivation for violence and persecution against black men (Connell 1995).

## The Sexualization of Black Male Bodies

From the beginning of their time in the United States, black men and their masculinity and sexuality were tied to fear and sexual excess (Wiegman 1993, 458). According to Collins (1990, 171), "Race and gender oppression may both revolve around the same axis of disdain for the body; both portray the sexuality of subordinate groups as animalistic and therefore deviant." Systems of gender, racial, and sexual oppression intersect on the terrain of the body, the prime war zone of many social issues. The bodies of black men were historically depicted as the opposite (the less powerful and much more undesirable body) of the desired and privileged white male bodies, with sexuality being the fundamental difference. Whereas white masculinity was (and is) constructed as the powerful and impenetrable force, the protector as well as the dominator, black masculinity is seen as an extreme exaggeration of normal masculinity (Weinberg and Williams 1988), a masculinity that is sexually animalistic, deviant, and in need of regulation. From the inception of the United States, the black male has been labeled a "savage" who is essentially primitive and inferior to the white male (Hacker 1995). Since the time of slavery, black men have been bound to traits of "rebelliousness, vigor, power, [and] athleticism," as well as to the "inferior child" and "aggressive and dangerous animal" (Wiegman 1993, 459). This portrayal of the black male as a "deviant" sexual creature not only led to an irrational fear and public distortion among white Americans, but also served as the foundation for racism in different historical periods (Stevenson 1994; West 1993; Hodes 1993).

While black women's sexuality was a focus during slavery, black male sexuality emerged as a central social threat after Emancipation. The fear of black men having sex with white women existed throughout slavery, and Emancipation brought about the fear that freed black men would seek retribution for the ills of slavery and the abuse of black women through forced sexual contact with white women (Nagel 2003; Bardaglio 1999).

The post-Emancipation white population, still holding fast to the view that black men were dangerous, animalistic, and uncontrollable, viewed sexual relations between black men and white women as undermining the institution of slavery and as a blow to the well-established racial order. The threat of the "sexually deviant" black male became a convenient excuse to continue the discrimination, segregation, and exploitation of an entire population. Demonizing black male sexuality and posing it as a real threat to white womanhood formed the basis for laws designed to preserve white dominance (Bardaglio 1999). An ethnosexual encounter between a black man and a white woman was essentially an "ethnically-loaded public act that others in the community claim the right to define and judge and punish" (Nagel 2003, 9).

The demonization of black male sexuality and the view of the sexually dangerous black male spilled over into the modern era, as did the racially and sexually specific stereotypes and myths surrounding black male's genitalia and sexual appetites. For example, black men's masculinity and sexuality were tied to the so-called "bestial excess of an overly phallicized primitivity" (Wiegman 1993, 458). They were thought to be untamed and hypersexual and to lack sexual morals thought to be inherent in white males (Jones 1993). This common theme of the "morally perverted" black male was common in scientific work of the era (Hayes 1973, 334), and became the justification for the medicalization of black men's bodies through the rise of the race sciences.

## Black Bodies, Medicalization, and Race Science

The bodies of black men were historically depicted by science as the dichotomy to white male bodies, with sexuality being the fundamental difference that was emphasized as the dichotomous foundation. Whereas white masculinity was constructed as the powerful (yet controlled) and impenetrable force, the protector as well as the dominator, black masculinity was seen as an extreme exaggeration of normal masculinity (Weinberg and Williams 1988), a masculinity that is both sexually animalistic and deviant. During the eighteenth and nineteenth centuries, science illustrated these biological differences between black men and white men through two theories, environmentalism and biological determinism (Saint-Aubin 2002). Environmentalism focused on racial characteristics such as hair texture, skin color, and skull size and shape that were thought to result from environmental forces, while biological determinism viewed race as resulting from genetics (Saint-Aubin 2002, 248). For example, the facial angle and pelvis shape (as well as penis size) of black men were used as criteria to deem them as primitive and subsequently inferior to white men (Saint-Aubin 2002).

By the late nineteenth century, physicians and scientists took the scientific theories of racial differences one step further by postulating that black men were "closer to the lower animals also when it came to sexual appetite, lack of morality, and to a certain degree sexual anatomy" (Saint-Aubin 2002, 264). The so-called "moral perversion" of black men (Hayes 1973, 334) and portrayal of the black man as a "deviant" sexual creature not only led to irrational fears among white Americans but also served as the foundation for scientific racism and the medicalization of black men's sexuality (West 1993; Hodes 1993), as I will now explain in the following section.

## The Medicalization of Black Men

While the application of medical labels to previously nonmedical issues has occurred for centuries, it was not until the late twentieth century that research on medicalization first appeared. First published in 1972, Zola's (1997) work on medicalization (the attachment of medical labels to behavior considered socially undesirable) has long been considered as groundbreaking by researchers who have studied medical social control (Conrad 1979; Fox 1979; Levin and Idler 1981; Armstrong 2000). According to Conrad (1996, 210), Zola's inspiration for his examination of medicalization was grounded in a combination of Parsons's (1951) "sick role," labeling theory, and the then-emerging field of social constructionism. Medicalization has historically been applied in two ways. First, research in the area of medicalization of everyday life, based on Zola's (1997) work, focused on medicine's expansion of control over what is deemed relevant to the "good practice of life" (Zola 1997, 409). The daily health-related activity list is ever growing, and medicine—through the process of medicalization of normal life processes—has gained control over these activities (Zola 1997). Second, Conrad and Schneider's (1980) work on the medicalization of deviance focused on how medicine functions to "secure adherence to social norms . . . by using medical means to minimize, eliminate, or normalize deviant behavior" (Conrad 1979, 1).

Sexuality has not escaped the throngs of medicalization. Through the medicalization of sexuality—defining and labeling various issues associated with sexuality in such a way that they fall under the control of medical authority—physicians have been able to inspect their patients bodies' (and sexual behavior and performance) for faults and make specific changes—through the prescribing of medication, use of medical technologies, or surgeries—that will return patients to "normal" or functional sexual states. The medicalization of sexuality can encompass both the medicalization of everyday life (Zola 1997) and the medicalization of deviance (Conrad and Schneider 1980; Conrad 1996).

Sexuality serves as a strong and socially loaded metaphor for a system of domination (Stoler 1997). As Collins (1990) states, "controlling sexuality harnesses that power for the needs of larger, hierarchical systems by controlling the body" (179). By the nineteenth century, the system of domination of black men's bodies exhibited by medical officials and scientists had its premise in sexual and racial stereotypes. Medical science began to go to great lengths to affirm that black men and white men differed in terms of sexual morals and behaviors (Saint-Aubin 2002), and the primary way in which black men and white men were dichotomized was through the medicalization of black male sexuality.

Conrad and Schneider's (1980) theory of medicalization—how medicine functions to "secure adherence to social norms...by using medical means to minimize, eliminate, or normalize deviant behavior" (Conrad 1979, 1)—provides a good explanation on how and why medicine and science were able to control black male sexuality. Science and medicine in the nineteenth century (and on into the twentieth century) were able to use the umbrella of "medical necessity" as a means to control black male sexuality. Saint-Aubin (2002), for example, found that physicians and scientists viewed black men as "by their very nature criminals and sexual perverts," and therefore recommended castration as both a punishment and preventive measure for the greater good of society (263). In the following section, I explore another example of the medicalization of black men's sexuality: the Tuskegee syphilis experiment, where the moral judgment of black sexuality by medical science took place on a long-term and grand scale.

## The Tuskegee Syphilis Experiment

The Tuskegee syphilis experiment is arguably one of the most extreme examples of the medicalization of race and sexuality. In 1929, a grant jointly sponsored by the Julius Rosenwald Fund and the United States

Public Health Service (USPHS) was approved by the Surgeon General to study the prevalence of syphilis among rural blacks in the South (Brandt 1997, 394). The intended goal of the USPHS study was to explore mass treatment for a disease that ran rampant among poor Southern blacks. Out of six counties surveyed, Macon County, Alabama, (a county that was 82 percent African American) was found to have the highest syphilis rate at 398 cases per 1,000 people (Gray 1998, 41). The town of Tuskegee was an ideal site for the all-white medical team assembled by the USPHS because the inaccessibility of health care meant that only a handful of the African American participants had ever seen a doctor; thus the study would not be tainted by previous medical intervention.

The original study was intended to last between six and eight months, just enough time to take blood from the participants, perform spinal taps, give examinations, and send them on their way. The experiment (which officially began in 1932) was instituted as a nontherapeutic medical experiment aimed at compiling race-specific data on the evolution of syphilis in poor black males.[2] In exchange for transportation to and from the hospital, free lunches, free medicine for any disease other than syphilis,[3] and free burial (contingent on the performance of an autopsy), six hundred black men were recruited for a medical study by an overwhelmingly all-white medical team (Caplan 1992, 30):

> Subjects were recruited with misleading promises of 'special free treatment' (actually spinal taps done without anesthesia to study the neurological effects of syphilis), and were enrolled without their informed consent. (Caplan 1992, 29)

Told simply that they had "bad blood," (Gray 1995, 283) the men in fact had syphilis, a sexually transmitted disease that was rampant—36 percent of the county residents carried the syphilis virus (Jones 1993, 74)—in Macon County, Alabama, in the early part of the twentieth century. Because these men were both poor and uneducated, those in charge of the experiment assumed that they had no way of knowing that the medical staff of the government-funded program viewed them, as Jones (1996, 396) argues, as an expendable "experimental resource." These Tuskegee study participants would be kept in the dark about their involvement in the experiment until 1972, when an investigative reporter in Washington, D.C., broke the story to the general public. Federal hearings followed, yet no formal apology was given until 1997.[4]

What followed the discovery of the Tuskegee syphilis experiment was the unearthing of forty years of medical social control, white privilege, and deeply rooted racism and sexual stereotypes. The history of the

Tuskegee syphilis experiment laid the foundation for a legacy of distrust of the white medical establishment that still exists today (Thomas and Quinn 2000). However, medical experimentation on black men's bodies and abuse had a long history, most notably in the South.

## Before Tuskegee: Black Bodies and Medical Experimentation

The need to keep the black male in his "place" during the post-Reconstruction era came in the form of lynching, which sent a powerful statement to the black community about the continuing control that the white community held over the black male body. It is precisely this white power and privilege over the black male body that served as a justification for the Tuskegee syphilis experiment. But it was not only the fact that it was physically a black body that enticed the white doctors to use black men in the experiment; it was also that it was a *sexual* black body that was carrying a sexually transmitted disease. The centuries-old fear of the sexually aggressive black male (Saint-Aubin 2002; Nagel 2000a; Wiegman 1993) conjured up images of a diseased black man who would somehow infiltrate the surrounding white areas and spread a sexual disease, quite possibly to the detriment of white womanhood. Using racial and sexual stereotypes and fears of black men, the doctors and officials of Tuskegee were able to conduct experiments without fear of retribution. The medical social control and regulation of black male bodies were justified as furthering medical science; black men's so-called deviant sexual behavior was regulated and controlled by medicine to protect society as a whole. However, this regulation and control could not take place without science to back up claims of racial differences.

The early nineteenth century saw the rise of "race sciences," with an emphasis on the physical attributes of different groups of people (McGregor 1998, 11). The concept of "scientific racism" was based on a logic of biological determinism in which the physical body, rather than social characteristics, carried meaning (Somerville 1997; Pascoe 1999). Science and medicine based their beliefs about a population on their physical characteristics versus their own (Somerville 1997). The scientific world gave racial meanings to different anatomical differences between "black" and "white"—which, consequently, were also essentialist views based on skin pigmentation. These anatomical differences, such as skin, facial angle, pelvis, skull, brain mass, and genitalia, were said to predict intelligence and behavior (Somerville 1997). This biological view of race as a predictor of behavior, of course, was used by the science and medicine to discriminate and exploit black Americans, as was the case in the Tuskegee syphilis experiment.

Laboratory medicine was emphasized as "real science," while depleting or heroic therapies based on mind and body alignment were cast aside (McGregor 1998). White men were elevated to a privileged status in medicine due to the fact that the race sciences placed white men at the top of the racial hierarchy (and furthermore, medicine was an overwhelmingly white male profession, which also allowed for the privileged status). Medicine began to adhere to what McGregor (1998, 13) explains was a "stratified social order by excluding women and groups designated by race, particularly Blacks, from medical school." However, as medical subjects, racial minorities, particularly African Americans, were central to the medical and scientific enterprises.

The enslavement of blacks provided greater leeway for Southern white medical educators and researchers to use slaves for various medical purposes. As Savitt (1982, 341) argues, "When new techniques or treatments required experimentation doctors tested them on readily available and legally silent slave or free Black patients." The implementation of medical experiments over blacks quickly took on the characteristics of social control: the slave was seen as a "host or donor" in whom the "scene" of disease progression would take place, allowing for the "agents or actors" (doctors) to passively observe (Solomon 1985, 238–239).

Even if there were no active disease of the body, blacks were still used as experimental subjects. Dr. Marion Sims, a white male physician known as the "father of gynecology," used slave women to develop certain gynecological procedures during the mid-nineteenth century. These procedures, some of which forced slave women to undergo as many as thirty operations without the use of anesthesia, included vesico-vaginal fistula surgeries and Caesarean operations (Savitt 1982, 345). Sims discovered that "Caucasian patients often failed to persevere as well as Negroes during the painful and uncomfortable procedure" (Savitt 1982, 345), which supported the growing opinion of the medical community that there was an inherent physical and medical difference between the races (Savitt 1978).

Physical distinctions between black slaves and whites led physicians to suggest that members of different races must respond to disease and treatments in different ways, and that these differences were biological in nature (Worboys 1999; Savitt 1988). Cruel and unsafe experiments took place, based on the notion that there were inherent physical differences between the races that placed whites above blacks in the steadfast and ever-increasing racial hierarchy. For example, a slave was ordered into a "makeshift open-pit oven" in order to "discover the best remedies for sunstroke" (Savitt 1978, 293). Another experiment involving the bleeding of a slave every other day over a period of three weeks and the intentional blistering of the slave's skin to "ascertain how deep [his] black skin was" (Savitt 1982, 344).

Blacks were used for medical research not only while they were alive but also when they were dead. They became specimens on which autopsies were performed to determine the natural progression of the disease that killed them. Despite public opposition to dissections and autopsies in the early part of the nineteenth century, they did take place with the help of medical students and grave robbers, who would dig up black bodies for dissection (King 1998, 95). This use of blacks as human subjects carried a heavy price. As Solomon (1985, 241–242) explains, "the consequence is dehumanization and a process of division (as opposed to identification) between patients and the scientific community." The use of blacks in research and experimentation, while important to the growth of medical science, not only dehumanized its participants but produced and reproduced distinct and crippling divisions between blacks and whites.

Medical experimentation based on prevailing images of blacks as sexually deviant, promiscuous, and lacking self-control rose in frequency during the nineteenth century, when white doctors would use slave men and women who suffered from sexually transmitted diseases as experimental subjects. Gonorrhea, syphilis, "yaws" (a "cousin" of syphilis), and donovanosis ran rampant among slaves during the mid-nineteenth century, and all were associated with blacks' supposed sexual promiscuity, lack of sexual morals, and dark skin (Hammar 1997). However, Savitt (1978, 79) explains, "venereal diseases may have been more common among slaves than among whites because of promiscuity engendered by the slave system." Therefore, slave women who were raped by their white male masters passed on these sexually transmitted diseases to their male slave partners.

Because these sexually transmitted diseases reached epidemic proportions among slaves, the view of blacks as sexually promiscuous and diseased became interwoven throughout American culture. This construction of black bodies as "diseased" and sexually deviant paved the way for the implementation of more dangerous and obtrusive medical experiments in the twentieth century and subsequently led to an increase in the medicalization of black masculinity. The reliance of white Southern doctors on the use of black bodies for medical research was especially important in understanding the "effects of disease on the human body" (Savitt 1982, 332). Medical experimentation was justified because of the ethnosexual stereotypes about blacks that permeated society for centuries; these ethnosexual stereotypes, in fact, laid the foundation for what would become the Tuskegee Syphilis experiment.

## Ethnosexual Boundaries and Tuskegee

According to Lorber (1999, 355), ethnosexual boundaries, or the "melding [of] categories, blurring [of] borders or at least recognizing that people come in multiple varieties," are based on the intersections of socially constructed views of race/ethnicity and sexuality (Nagel 2000a). The racial and sexual boundaries of the Tuskegee syphilis experiment cast the black male in the category of the sexual and racial "Other" (with whites as the powerful "norm") that, according to the current medical discourse, justified the medical experimentations that followed. The sexual implications of Tuskegee have their roots in the long-standing tradition of viewing the black man as "a sexual predator, a threat to White southern womanhood and White male sexual hegemony" (Nagel 2000b, 12). This view paved the way for increasing medical control over the deviant sexual behavior of black men.

Already historically treated as disposable because of their racial identity, the black men of Macon County (Tuskegee), Alabama, were viewed by their doctors as a "notoriously syphilis-soaked race" (Jones 1993, 29). This junction between disease and race led to the medical inference that a sexually transmitted disease was a symptom of socially deviant behaviors (Worth 1990, 112; and sexuality thus became medicalized, so that deviant social behavior fell under the guise of science and medicine), as if bacteria could determine whether or not the body it would enter "deserved" a disease due to the behavior of the carrier. Those in charge of the Tuskegee syphilis experiment chose to forgo the use of medical technology to treat the syphilis epidemic among black men because they believed that, as sexual predators harboring destructive character flaws, these men would not benefit from being cured of the disease.

The "medical gaze" (Foucault 1995) extended to both the physical body and the sexual lifestyle of the subject. The black sexual lifestyle of the nineteenth century was thought to be different (untamed and hypersexual) than that of the white American sexual lifestyle of the time, and in need of medical control and regulation. As Jones (1993, 17) explains, "medical discourses on the peculiarities of Blacks offered, among other things, a pseudoscientific rationale for keeping Blacks in their places."

Sexuality serves as a strong and socially loaded metaphor for a system of domination (Stoler 1997). Though the case of the Tuskegee syphilis experiment exhibited this system of domination through medical social control, it was a system whose premise resided in sexual and racial stereotypes. Quite simply, these were poor black men who harbored a sexual disease; if these men acted upon their "animalistic" and "deviant" sexual instincts, who knows how many white women would be affected by (and infected with) syphilis? How many white men would contract this disease from their white women? After all, it did not matter if black men passed this sexually transmitted disease on to their black female partners; black women were considered to be just as sexually degenerate as their black male counterparts. As one doctor associated with the study stated,

> Morality among these people [blacks] is almost a joke, and only assumed as a matter of convenience or when there is a lack of desire and opportunity for indulgence. *A Negro man will not abstain from sexual intercourse if there is the opportunity and no mechanical obstruction, for his sexual powers are those of a specialist in a chosen field.* (Quoted in Jones 1993, 24; emphasis added)

The "low moral standards" of black women, though not emphasized in the actual study, was also thought to contribute to the spread of syphilis among blacks. "Syphilis was so prevalent among the men," according to one doctor, that "one can imagine what it was among the women, who had no virtue or chastity to protect them" (Jones 1993, 25). When three physicians discovered that they had more cases of syphilis among their female patients than their male patients, they claimed that it was a result of "the extremely immoral relationship between the sexes of this people, as is also borne out by the admission of sexual indulgence from practically all of the unmarried women" (Jones 1993, 25), which resonates with the construction of black women as equally as sexually licentious as black men (Roberts 1999). While it would seem logical that a man or woman could pass syphilis to their monogamous partner, the medical agents in charge of the experiment blamed the spread of syphilis on the untamed and wild sexual prowess of black men and women. As one doctor stated, "The Negro men love to frolic with the women; and the women love to frolic with the men; so they frolic" (Jones 1993, 25).

The social hygiene movement of the late nineteenth and early twentieth centuries was organized to treat and educate those who suffered from these and other sexually deviant afflictions (Jones 1993). While the social hygienists were willing to search for a cure for those suffering from "syphilis of the innocent"—essentially white men and women who may have contracted this disease through sex with an undesirable, or black, partner—they were unwilling to help find a cure for black syphilis unless blacks would learn to "refrain from sexual promiscuity" (Jones 1993, 47–48). White physicians, however, were pessimistic that the "black libido" could be tamed:

> 'From our knowledge of the Negro,' wrote Dr. Louis Wender, 'we should be inclined to the opinion that a chance for an education or even its acquisition does not materially influence his well known sexual promiscuity.' Other physicians concurred. 'The prophylaxis of syphilis in the Negro is especially difficult,' Dr. H.H. Hazen explained, 'for it is impossible to persuade the poor variety of Negro that sexual gratification is wrong, even when he is in the actively infectious stage [of syphilis].' (Jones 1993, 27)

## Medical Surveillance and Tuskegee

It is important to note that the Tuskegee syphilis experiment required more than a series of racist and medicalized presuppositions to proceed. In fact, many of its suppositions and practices were generic to modern medicine. The role of the white male physician as the assessor and regulator of the depraved and sexually immoral black male is deeply embedded in issues of power and medical social control (à la Foucauldian theory) that intersect ethnosexual boundaries. The first point of resonance is that black male bodies were subjected to a new, modern type of (medical) control and surveillance. Medical surveillance began in the late eighteenth century when "medical men started to subject their patients to physical examination" (Armstrong 1983, 2). Human beings, according to Staples (1997, 18), and their bodies, minds, and behaviors, were becoming the "subject of scientific inquiry and the object of its passions." Foucauldian theory describes the modern human body as something that is broken down, explored, and rearranged to suit the needs of those in power (Foucault 1995); it is through acts of coercions and manipulations on the body that its elements, gestures, and behaviors are changed to become more suitable to those in power. The modern human body was becoming something to be analyzed or monitored: bodies had to be inspected in order to judge their status, analyzed to find their deficits or diseases, and closely monitored to evaluate and judge their functioning ability (Armstrong 1983, 3). Thus, the body entered the realm of medical surveillance, becoming an "object and target of power" (Foucault 1995, 136). The medical examination, for example, became a tool to judge and observe patients. According to Foucault (1995), medical exams became so commonplace that they were considered normal, thus legitimizing the power doctors have over their patients:

> The examination combines the techniques of an observing hierarchy and those of an observing hierarchy and those of a normalizing judgment. It is

a normalizing gaze, a surveillance that makes it possible to qualify, to classify and to punish. It establishes over individuals a visibility through which one differentiates them and judges them. (184)

This emergence of the medical examination of patients, writes Foucault (1995), makes each individual a "case":

A case which at one and the same time constitutes an object for a branch of knowledge and a hold for a branch of power. The case is no longer, as in casuistry or jurisprudence, a set of circumstances defining an act and capable of modifying the application of a rule; it is the individual as he may be described, judged, measured, compared with others, in his very individuality; and it is also the individual who has to be trained or corrected, classified, normalized, excluded, etc. (191)

By treating the patient as a "case," doctors are able to observe and monitor the patient without treating the patient as an actual human being. In the case of the Tuskegee syphilis experiment, one of the central issues of the study was that of the property of the body, as Roy (1995, 56) explains: "As in slavery, the generative ability of the body made the Tuskegee subjects real property and gave untreated syphilis and the era of the Tuskegee subjects immense commercial value."

Just as the old Hippocratic ethic, according to Veatch (1987, 4), saw the patient as "a weak, debilitated, childlike victim, incapable of functioning as a real moral agent," the doctors of the study viewed the Tuskegee participants as simply bodies over which the doctor had power. This form of power increased during the routine physical examinations the men endured: the men became "cases" that the Tuskegee medical staff could monitor and observe. Once this form of social authority was constructed—the white male doctors became the "authority"—the study reached far beyond the business of actually treating the disease (Connell 1987); it became a system of treating the observed body as the "Other." Thus, the bodies of the men involved in the Tuskegee syphilis experiment became bodies that were to be broken down during autopsies and studied for their "Otherness." This connection between scientific knowledge and ethnosexually "Other" bodies, of course, is at the foundation of the Tuskegee syphilis experiment; what is missing—or rather what were crossed—were the moral boundaries that should have made human experimentation taboo.

The second point of resonance is the experiment's explicitly sexual focus. According to Foucault (1990, 116), whereas sex and sexuality were once relegated to the private sphere of the bedroom, "pedagogy, medicine, and economics . . . made sex not only a secular concern but a concern of the state as well; to be more exact, sex became a matter that required the social body as a whole, and virtually all of its individuals, to place themselves under surveillance." Clearly, the Tuskegee syphilis experiment is an instance of medicine's role in perpetuating state control of sexuality in general and of the sexuality of allegedly danger-ous populations in particular.

As a "state"-funded investigation, the Tuskegee syphilis experiment enabled white male physicians to analyze, inspect, and critique these black bodies with impunity. The state encouraged this surveillance be-cause it was viewed as a legitimate medical experiment that would fur-ther scientific knowledge. Medical surveillance was arguably the most dangerous form of medical social control that occurred in the Tuskegee syphilis experiment because of its part in the construction of the "Other." Put simply, those in power are able to survey those without power, and thus the "Other" (someone who is observed but is not the observer) is constructed. However, in the case of Tuskegee, it was not just any body that was broken down and analyzed for deficiencies but the black male body that was socially constructed as "Other" and that could be used to further scientific knowledge.

The fact that the study continued for forty years, seemingly unaf-fected by the invention of an effective treatment for the disease and the post–World War II human experimentation regulations is not a surprise. These were not simply men who had syphilis; they were black men who carried with them all the historical preconceptions of what a black male body signified in society: sexual danger, a lack of sexual morals, and hypersexual in nature (Saint-Aubin 2002; Wiegman 1993). Science and medicine used these historical preconceptions to medicalize and sub-sequently eliminate or at least retain control over black men's "deviant" sexuality for the greater good of society. By performing medical exper-imentation and other scientific endeavors on black men, medical sci-ence has perpetuated racism towards ethnic minorities in this country (Stevenson 1994), and the combination of being a racial "Other" and a sexual savage has ensured the continual medical mistreatment and medicalization of black men and their sexuality. The lingering effects of the Tuskegee syphilis experiment exemplify the pervasiveness of the medicalization of black masculinity.

## Conclusion

According to Stevenson (1994, 66), "Bad science cannot be undone. It takes too much time to reverse its effects." The Tuskegee syphilis ex-periment did more than just damage the reputation of the medical community; it left behind a legacy of deceit, conspiracy, and negligence that has permanently scarred race relations in the United States. Though the Tuskegee syphilis experiment was exposed and subsequently terminated over thirty years ago, the consequences of this experiment still shape medical research today. A federal committee was formed in 1973 to investigate the Tuskegee case; the end result was the passage of the National Research Act of 1974. This act "mandated formal protections for human subjects," which included written consent and institutional review boards, to evaluate and critique proposals involving experiments on human beings (Lederer 1995, 142). While the guidelines have been modified, the basic premise of the act remains intact.

The second long-term consequence of the Tuskegee syphilis experiment is the legacy of mistrust of the medical profession within the black community. Current black Americans' fears about exploitation by medical professionals date back to the use of slaves as subjects for medical experimentation (Gamble 2000). A legacy of scientific racism based on the logic of biological determinism in which the physical body, rather than social characteristics, signifies an actor's capacities and tendencies have also influenced the quality of medical treatment black men experience. Research reveals that blacks have continued to experience more difficulty in obtaining and benefiting from medical services than whites (Pearson 1994). Furthermore, an overall distrust of medical professionals has become almost epidemic in the black community. A full quarter of the blacks in the Alabama area mistrust all doctors (Levine 1997, 1), and a survey of black church members in New York revealed that over a third of its population believed that AIDS—another sexually transmitted disease—was a form of governmental genocide aimed at wiping out the black population (Jones 1993, 38). This belief in a governmental genocide plot against black Americans continues to emerge in current research on AIDS (Lichtenstein 2004; Thomas and Quinn 2000; Stevenson 1994).[5]

The legacy of Tuskegee may also be a significant factor in the extremely low participation of blacks in medical clinical trials, preventive health care, and, most importantly, organ donation efforts. "Organ bank workers say that fear is common, especially among blacks, who often distrust the medical system—largely because of the federal government's secret Tuskegee syphilis experiments on black men" (Reinert 1997, 1). There is also the lingering fear that birth control is a "plot" to "prevent the multiplication of bad stocks" (Gamble 2000; Stevenson 1994), a fear that has been increased by the continuing mistrust of the medical community.

Finally, the Tuskegee syphilis experiment produced lingering stereotypes of a specific race. As a result of the Tuskegee study, "researchers have been reluctant to explore associations between race and disease" (King 1992, 37). Though this association could be medically beneficial to the specific racial group being studied, it can also marginalize, stigmatize, and medicalize a group of people who are already on the fringe of society. By associating a virus with a particular race, ethnicity, or sexuality, the medical community is opening the door to value judgments, social regulation, and the medicalization of particular diseases. As Tiefer (1996, 271) explains, "The medical model has many moral elements, and medicalization is deeply connected to social regulation of right and wrong." Furthermore, the junction between disease and race led to the medical inference that a sexually transmitted disease was a symptom of socially deviant behaviors (Worth 1990, 112).

However, Tuskegee not only had severe consequences for today's black male but exemplifies how masculinities and epidemiological research pathologize and problematize masculinity as a health risk (men engage in higher risk-taking behavior than do women, deny pain and illness, etc.) This is, as Rosenfeld and Faircloth note in the Introduction to this volume, nothing new in the study of masculinity. But how does this fit explicitly into the medicalization of black masculinity and an overall thesis of the medicalization of masculinity in Western culture today?

By pointing to race as a factor in the medicalization of masculinity, I have added to its recent recognition by social scientists, who have tended to focus on sexual technologies such as Viagra. The Tuskegee experiment alerts us to the social control of the black male body and the need for medicalization to control this "savage" body, a project at which other societal structures were seen as failing, or were being phased out due to public pressure. The medicalization of this "social problem" was considered the next step in its control and regulation. While the medicalization of race on the one hand and the medicalization of femininity (and, increasingly, of masculinity) on the other have been recognized, the medicalization of the intersection of these has been largely ignored. Just as the medicalization of masculinity has emerged as a topic late in the game, so has the medicalization of *racialized* femininities and masculinities. This chapter, I suggest, points to a need for an appreciation of such intersections in the medicalization literature.

# 8

# Reconstructing the War Veteran in PTSD Therapy

Marisa M. Smith

## Introduction: Gender and Mental Health

M ental illness has historically been called the "female malady" (Showalter 1985), but, even in the modern era, women are still more likely than men to be diagnosed and treated for depression (Gold 1998; National Institute of Mental Health [NIMH] 2001). Women are also twice as likely to suffer from most anxiety disorders, including panic disorder, generalized anxiety disorder, and agoraphobia (NIMH 2001). The overwhelming predominance of eating disorders among girls and young women is particularly well documented (Bordo 1993; NIMH 2001). Only diagnoses of substance abuse and attention deficit–hyperactivity disorders are significantly more prevalent among men (Substance Abuse and Mental Health Services Administration 2003).

Both conventional wisdom and the bulk of social scientific research have asserted that at least part of the explanation for the overrepresentation of mental disorders among females is that women suffer greater emotional strains due to inadequate social support (Gold 1998), competing family and occupational demands (Barnett and Baruch 1987; Welner et al. 1979), and the overall subordinate position of women in society (Gold 1998; Ussher 1992). Feminist scholars have also argued that clinical assumptions about normal adult behavior are predicated on male behavior; consequently, women's behavior is more likely to be seen as abnormal and hence pathological.

In other words, women are more likely to be labeled mentally ill because the norm for adult behavior more closely approximates that of stereotypical male behaviors (Broverman et al. 1981). Joan Busfield (1996) asserts that gender is actually "embedded" in the official constructions of mental disorders. She contends that since so many mental disorders are characterized by "fear, anxiety, and sadness" and these are considered more socially acceptable behaviors in women, it is not surprising that more women than men fall within the diagnostic parameters of mental illness.

However, if women's cultural identities and societal expectations put them at higher risk of certain illnesses or medicalization of social and personal troubles, so, increasingly, do those of men. As Rosenfeld and Faircloth demonstrate in the Introduction to this volume, numerous feminist, epidemiological studies, and masculinities studies have medicalized masculinity (see Sabo and Gordon 1995; Harrison, Chin, and Ficarrotto 1989; Helgeson 1995). Masculinity studies in particular assert that, in Western society, the traditional masculine archetype, often referred to as hegemonic masculinity, is physically tough, emotionally stoic, aggressive, competitive, and self-reliant (Cheng 1999; Donaldson 1993). In this literature, hegemonic masculinity is both shaped by and a reflection of other divisions and hierarchies within a society, including race, socioeconomic status, age, and sexual orientation (Connell 1995; Connell 2000); hegemonic masculinity emphasizes competence, achievement, success, and proscribes introspection and emotion expression. Unfortunately, this body of work claims, demonstrating hegemonic masculinity frequently necessitates acting in ways detrimental to men's health (Courtenay 2000; Stillion 1995; for a thorough review of this literature, see Riska 2004): men, in their attempt to emulate the hegemonic form, drive too fast, drink too much, and work too hard. The alleged results are the numerous and often-repeated statistics concerning the excess male mortality from ischemic heart disease, cancer, homicide, and motor vehicle accidents (Waldron 1990), as well as men's overall shorter life expectancy (Cameron and Bernardes 1998).

Much research into men's health also claims that cultural expectations concerning appropriate masculine behavior pose particular obstacles to the treatment of illness among men (Cameron and Bernardes 1998; Courtenay 2000) and mental disorders in particular. Specifically, men are frequently reluctant to disclose personal and health problems, even to medical providers (Cameron and Bernardes 1998; Forrester 1986), and psychotherapy "requires the male to perform 'womanly' activities: giving up power and control, acknowledging weaknesses and vulnerabilities, asking for support, and being noncompetitive" (Eisenhart and Silversmith 1994, 131). As a result of this construction, clinicians must challenge male beliefs that mental disorders are a "sign of weakness, failure, femininity, or self-indulgence" (Warren 1983, 155) to engage men in the therapeutic process.

In this chapter, I focus on masculinity as both the subject of identity construction and the discursive framework for group therapy in a Veterans Affairs (VA) mental health clinic specializing in combat-related posttraumatic stress disorder (PTSD). Many institutions, such as schools (Foley 1990; Gilbert and Gilbert 1998; Willis 1981), the family (Chodorow 1978; Ochs and Taylor 1995), and the workplace (Barrett 2001; Kanter 1977; Messerschmidt 1996; Wright 1996), impart often very explicit rules and models for the production of masculine selves and also provide daily opportunities for individuals to "practice" socially validated male performances. Therapeutic institutions, designed explicitly for the purpose of identity work, also provide extensive resources to facilitate the construction of alternative masculinities, specifically a language and vocabulary for framing and understanding past behavior and constructing a new self (Loseke 2001; Pollner and Stein 2001; Weinberg 2001). Although the stated objectives of the different therapy groups for PTSD observed for this study are to help veterans manage the symptoms of traumatic stress and mitigate some of the guilt they still carry from their participation in the Vietnam War, an active and explicit renegotiation of masculine identity emerges as a key therapeutic goal as well. By participating in the different groups offered by the VA for the treatment of PTSD, veterans are exhorted to explore new ways of thinking and behaving that conflict with much of what they have associated with "manliness" from their childhood, the military, and the larger culture. In short, they are asked to participate in the medicalization of their own, pre-PTSD masculinity to achieve mental health.

Following a brief discussion of methods, I show how interaction in PTSD group therapy initially replicates many of the features of traditional male discourse and hegemonic masculinity; symptomatic behaviors are at first associated with military training and then linked to traditional male socialization. I also illustrate how, in the early stages of group therapy, traditional constructions of masculinity become a resource to further the objectives of therapy; clinicians focus on emotion management while appealing to traditionally male attributes, such as self-control, logic, and rationality. I then demonstrate how group therapy works to create an alternative masculine identity through the appropriation of military, religious, and scientific discourses. I conclude by illustrating how the final sessions of group therapy retroactively medicalize traditional male attributes to reinforce a new, posttraumatic masculinity emphasizing self-disclosure, empathy, and emotional expression.

## Data and Methods

I spent two and a half years conducting ethnographic fieldwork in a West Coast VA outpatient clinic specializing in combat-related PTSD, focusing on the experience and treatment of PTSD. A faculty advisor, who held a joint appointment at the VA, facilitated clinic access. Subsequently, I observed four therapy groups attended primarily by Vietnam combat veterans: the Orientation Group, Anger Management, the Grief Group, and the Spiritual Recovery Group. Because I was not permitted to tape-record discussions in group therapy, this study is not a formal discourse analysis. However, in keeping with ethnographic methods, I did take notes and recreated group discussion as thoroughly as possible at the end of each session. From my field notes, I identified some broad language patterns and uses, which form the basis of my analytical framework.

Because the VA medical center is a major teaching institution and patients were familiar with and generally tolerant of residents and interns, my presence in the clinic as a student learning about PTSD and Vietnam veterans was met with few objections. I was pleasantly surprised to learn that most patients were flattered that someone was interested in their experiences and often stated they hoped their story would help other veterans or at least educate civilians about Vietnam and PTSD. A university institutional review board approved this study, and all participants gave written consent. Names and identifying information have been changed to protect confidentiality.

## PTSD and the Posttraumatic Stress Disorder Clinical Team

In 1980, the American Psychiatric Association (APA) included the diagnosis of PTSD in the *Diagnostic and Statistical Manual of Mental Disorders* (*DSM*) in response to the growing number of Vietnam veterans exhibiting a perplexing penumbra of behavioral problems (Scott 1993). In the fourth edition of the *DSM* (1994), symptoms are listed under four main criteria. The first criterion states that the person must have been exposed to a traumatic event to which he or she responded with fear, helplessness, or horror; the second criterion specifies that the individual relives or reexperiences the trauma in some way, usually as dreams or intrusive thoughts; the third criterion refers to avoidance behaviors through which the person attempts to avoid any memories or triggers of the traumatic event; and the fourth criterion describes arousal symptoms associated with the trauma such as insomnia, anger and irritability, and difficulty concentrating.

The VA clinic that specializes in the diagnosis and treatment of PTSD is known as the Posttraumatic Stress Disorder Clinical Team or simply PCT. The racial distribution of the clinic population is predominantly white. Almost all patients had graduated from high school and a few had attended college. Most veterans had served in the Army or Marine Corps and a smaller number had served in the Navy. Their years of active-duty military service ranged from two to twenty years and from one to six tours in Vietnam. Some had gone to Vietnam as early as 1963 and others as late as 1972. Almost all were eighteen or nineteen years of age when they joined the military and most had volunteered for the draft. Only one patient had been an officer. Patients were generally unemployed, retired, disabled, or working sporadically and could therefore access the clinic services without charge. Veterans who were found by a VA compensation and pension panel to be service-connected for PTSD could also receive therapy at no cost, regardless of income.

Vietnam veterans participate in group therapy for several months by attending four generally sequential psychotherapy groups, each having between five and twelve members. Each group meets once a week for twelve weeks and is offered four times per year. Patients may also choose to continue group therapy indefinitely through so-called "alumni" groups. Participation in these groups comprise the steps leading from a precombat masculinity to an emotionally expressive and insightful one that enables these veterans to handle the trauma of their war experiences and to achieve mental health.

Most patients newly diagnosed with PTSD begin group therapy with the Orientation Group, which meets for one hour each week. The stated objectives of the group are to teach the veterans about PTSD, to help them develop coping skills to deal with their symptoms, and to introduce them to the dynamics of group therapy. Joseph Everett, a VA chaplain and Vietnam veteran, is the primary therapist assigned to the Orientation Group. Dr. Joshua Kleinman, a clinical psychologist and director of the PCT, occasionally substitutes for Chaplain Everett. Following completion of the Orientation Group, most patients attend Anger Management, which is facilitated by Ramon Garcia, who is a Vietnam veteran and a licensed clinical social worker. Anger Management meets for one hour and fifteen minutes and focuses on, as the title would suggest, strategies for controlling aggressive and/or violent behavior.

Concurrent with Anger Management, most veterans also participate in Chaplain Everett's Spiritual Recovery Group, modeled after Alcoholics Anonymous's (AA) Twelve-Step Program.[1] Not coincidentally, there are twelve steps to spiritual recovery, which patients are encouraged to read and contemplate; however, unlike AA, there are no "sponsors," and there is considerably less pressure to actively "work the steps." There is discussion in the group about the meaning of each of the steps, but patients do not give the equivalent of "sobriety stories" and "drunkalogues" that depict the benefits of the spiritual lifestyle in contrast to their agnostic or atheistic past. The Spiritual Recovery program is premised on the assumption that a fundamental consequence of combat is a loss of faith in God: exposed to wanton violence and horrendous destruction of land and people with no visible benefit to any one, least of all the dead, soldiers question why God would permit such a tragedy. In this program, the twelve steps address the morality of war and killing.

The final group in the sequence offered by the PCT is the Grief Group, also led by Mr. Garcia. Initial sessions are two hours in length but are extended to three hours for the final weeks. The Grief Group is organized around the theme of grief and loss over the life span. This is the only group where patients are allowed, and in fact required, to discuss their experiences in combat in any depth.

## Gender, Language, and PTSD Group Therapy

Language is a particularly important tool in the making of gendered identities (Coates 2003; Tannen 1990). Kira Hall (1995), for example, shows how telephone sex workers—not all of whom are heterosexual females—use stereotypically feminine language to construct themselves as sexy, available women. In contrast, Bonnie McElhinny (1995) demonstrates how female police officers appropriate traditionally masculine discourse to portray themselves as law enforcement professionals in a historically blue-collar, male occupation. In a male-dominated university engineering program, female students alternately adopt feminine and masculine linguistic behaviors, frequently shifting between cooperative and competitive roles (Bergvall 1996). Even in the relatively mundane context of family dinnertime conversation, mothers are typically introducers of narratives whereas fathers generally assume the role of primary recipient and problematizer of children's and especially mothers' narratives (Ochs and Taylor 1995), thereby creating a gendered power hierarchy evident in many other cross-gender communications (DeFrancisco 1998; Fishman 1993).

Tracy Karner (1995) has argued that the very language used to describe PTSD evokes masculinity: "The context of combat and Vietnam allow[s] these men to enter into the therapeutic discourse and discuss symptomology while still maintaining self-identities as virile men" (Karner 1995, 45). She notes that the therapeutic discourse changes symptoms of anxiety to "hypervigilance," and panic attacks become "exaggerated startle response" learned under fire. In the groups I observed, however, the masculine language of PTSD extends beyond the mere characterization of symptoms. The narrative structure and style of discourse used in early sessions of group therapy replicate the typical patterns of male talk. Deborah Tannen (1990) has characterized male talk as "report talk," which consists largely of giving advice and information, the objective of which is to establish expertise and hierarchy. In contrast, she describes female talk as "rapport talk" through which women share feelings and provide emotional support. The goal of conversation for women is thus intimacy and cooperation. Masculine discourse frequently involves an overarching concern with status and competition (Johnstone 1993). Jennifer Coates (2003) has further identified four distinguishing characteristics of men's stories. First, topics are impersonal, focusing on stereotypically male activities, such as drinking, fighting, or technology and machinery. Second, the characters in the stories are almost exclusively male. Third, a great deal of attention is paid to details in men's stories. Finally, vulgar, profane, or "taboo" language is commonplace. These four characteristics serve to keep the story impersonal and to portray the speaker as the expert or hero of the tale (Coates 1997, 2003; Holmes 1997; Johnstone 1993).

Many of the characteristics of male talk identified by Coates (2003) can be seen in the early group therapy sessions at the VA—again, designed to teach veterans about PTSD and how to cope with it. In the following excerpt from the Orientation Group, Ruben, Billy, Kirk, Larry, and Albert, all of whom are Vietnam combat veterans, discuss their behavior with Dr. Kleinman.

RUBEN: I drive my wife crazy. I go around the house closing windows and doors. I asked her if the garage was secured. She said, "yes." I went and checked, and it wasn't.

BILLY: I keep a weapon under my bed.

KIRK: I won't have a weapon. It wouldn't be to fight. It'd be to kill.

DR. KLEINMAN: Hyperarousal was adaptive in combat, but it takes a toll on body and mind. You've heard of cholesterol? Well, there is another substance that the body produces called cortisol, which is a predecessor to adrenaline. It "revs" you up, so you start looking for danger. The other behavior that some of you have mentioned is isolation and avoidance so that you won't get triggered.

LARRY: My supervisor, she gets in my face, just inches from my nose. . . . "Get out of my face. If you want to act like a man, then I'll treat you like a man. And I'll kick your ass." She goes screaming that I said I was going to kick her ass.

DR. KLEINMAN: Sounds like you're talking about boundary issues and personal space. If someone's that close to you, you're either going to make love or make war. So you learn to numb those feelings. Any other way you typically numb emotions?

BILLY: Drugs and alcohol.

RUBEN: I guess I was a gang-banger as a kid but that helped me survive in Vietnam.

DR. KLEINMAN: How many people misused drugs or alcohol when they got back? [all hands] Then it's unanimous. Now you don't have anything to hide behind. That's why we give our guys meds. We substitute our meds for your meds. Ours, we can regulate the dosage.

Hegemonic masculinity is clearly being enacted through this interaction. Not only do these brief statements from the Orientation Group rely on the norms of conventional male discourse (impersonal, stereotypical male topics, almost exclusively male characters, attention to detail, and profanity), but they also reinforce typically masculine norms of violence and aggression. The veterans do not mention any particularly personal issues or concerns and discuss no emotions; however, they do mention fighting and excessive use of alcohol. Ruben's concern about "securing" his house immediately suggests military action rather than unreasonable paranoia. Moreover, Ruben frames his presence in therapy as his wife's problem: he has driven his wife "crazy" but only because of her oversight: presumably, he would not need to check all the doors and windows if his wife had remembered to lock the garage.

The veterans' discussion also reveals a concern with status and competition. Kirk's statement that he will not keep a gun because he would kill someone implies a contest with Billy over who is more dangerous. Larry's recounting of his altercation with his supervisor is the most overt discussion of masculinity in that his female supervisor's assertive position is taken to mean that she wants to be a man (apparently because "real" women cannot be aggressive). His stated desire to "kick her ass" further reproduces stereotypically masculine traits by evoking and legitimating the threat of violence and fairly explicit misogyny (Coates 2003).

The psychologist is also an active participant in this presentation of masculinity. Consistent with Karner's (1985) analysis, Dr. Kleinman names aggressive behavior "hyperarousal" as a category of PTSD symptoms associated with combat, clearly reinforcing its masculine rather than strictly pathological quality. Later in the session, when Ruben remarks that he questions his own survival when so many in his unit were killed, Dr. Kleinman frames that admission as guilt, as well as a reason for numbing emotions with drugs and alcohol. Thus he initiates two other common features of male discourse—emotional restraint and the topic of drinking or drugs—which enable the veterans to demonstrate the hegemonic male attributes of fearlessness and risk taking.

I should point out that, even from the beginning of group therapy, some veterans voice an alternative masculinity, which is usually dismissed by the clinicians in the early stages of therapy. For example, the following excerpt from the Orientation Group with Chaplain Everett demonstrates how certain behaviors are made consistent with the clinical narrative, which explains the genesis of PTSD symptoms in combat and reinforces the norms of hegemonic masculinity.

CHAPLAIN EVERETT: There are some things that we experience that overwhelm us: rape, combat, genocide. For two thousand years they've always known that war causes problems. . . . But after World War II, if you could walk, then you were okay. It wasn't until Vietnam that people really started to take this seriously. . . . In combat, let's say you lost your best friend. What do you do?
KIRK: Cry.
CHAPLAIN EVERETT: You cry but for how long? You can cry but not go through the emotional process. You stuff it. What is the one emotion that works in combat?
BILLY: Anger.
CHAPLAIN EVERETT: Combat is institutionalized, ruthless violence, and you express some emotions while repressing others. You may try drinking and drugging to blot it out, but when you stop the memories come back.

Kirk obviously gives an answer that is inconsistent with hegemonic masculinity or with the PTSD clinical narrative, which associates problematic behavior with military training and combat. Billy, however, answers "correctly" by stating that grief is turned into anger, a more stereotypically masculine response. By the time they have completed the Orientation Group, veterans need little coaxing in adopting the PTSD narrative.

DR. KLEINMAN: Now we talked about veterans isolating, which means staying where you feel comfortable and safe, usually in your homes. You tend to think that the outside world is dangerous and hostile. Why is that?
BILLY: Combat.
GREG: Possible confrontation.
DR. KLEINMAN: Most veterans avoid and isolate because it feels like combat.

Beliefs consistent with hegemonic masculinity are also given voice in a therapeutic exercise referred to as the "Three-Way Mirror." The exercise focuses on asking the veteran to look back at particular stages or "panels" in his development (specifically childhood, Vietnam, and post-Vietnam) in order to identify how the experience of combat affected his emotional expressiveness, attitudes, and relationships with other people.

Integral to the Three-Way Mirror is the assumption that emotional practices are learned, and men learn to repress most emotions, especially pain and sadness. In the introduction to the first panel of the Three-Way Mirror in Anger Management, the social worker, Mr. Garcia, asks: "What pissed you off as a child? How were you taught to express emotions? What experiences molded how you expressed emotions? We all grew up in the fifties and boys didn't cry; [we watched] John Wayne movies, and he certainly never cried." In the following excerpt from the Anger Management Group, Julio, a Mexican-American Army veteran, describes how he learned that being a man means repressing emotions.

MR. GARCIA: What forms of anger expression did you learn? What did those experiences teach you about anger?

JULIO: That it helped me. Sometimes I feel bad about the way he [my father] treated me. . . . I remember one time he sent me to go buy this type of alcohol. On the way home I tripped and fell. I broke the bottle. My father kicked my ass.

MR. GARCIA: How old were you?

JULIO: Nine or ten.

MR. GARCIA: What did you learn from that?

JULIO: I don't know.

MR. GARCIA: You learned to stuff it and take the beating?

JULIO: I had no choice. He'd hit my face.

MR. GARCIA: How do you feel?

JULIO: Good but sad.

MR. GARCIA: I keep asking about anger expression. What did you learn?

JULIO: Men never cry. He'd hurt me but then tell me, "Men don't cry."

MR. GARCIA: So what did that teach you? Men are supposed to stuff their emotions.

Even veterans with less obviously abusive upbringings acknowledge the importance of early socialization to beliefs about masculinity. Below is an excerpt from an Anger Management therapy session in which the narrator, Peter, a white Army veteran, describes a rather unproblematic childhood, which nonetheless encouraged him to embrace a stereotypically masculine affect. John Wayne is an obvious masculine icon, and Peter clearly articulates many of the key features of stereotypically appropriate masculine affect that Wayne represents. Despite the fact that Peter does not actually admit to behaving in a manner entirely consistent with hegemonic masculinity, both patient and clinician acknowledge that emotional restriction, violence, and domination are important components of it.

PETER: I had a pretty normal childhood. . . . I was born right after the Japanese surrender and grew up on John Wayne movies. In any of his movies—Indian, war, whatever—the only way to resolve a conflict was talk and then punch or shoot them if they didn't go along. I try to use verbal skills, and then I get physical if people don't see the flawless logic of my argument [speaking facetiously]. No violence, no poverty, no racism, no sexual abuse.

MR. GARCIA: You win the "Ozzie and Harriet" award for most idyllic childhood. What did you learn about anger expression?

PETER: Yelling.

MR. GARCIA: So you were allowed to express your anger?

PETER: Not much. I didn't get into trouble very often.

In contrast to the early sessions of group therapy, PTSD symptoms are not explicitly named during the Three-Way Mirror exercises. However, by linking behaviors, which frequently overlap with PTSD symptoms, to male socialization, masculinity as much as experiences in combat becomes intertwined with the therapeutic process. Although the Three-Way Mirror ostensibly reinforces traditional male behavior, it also demonstrates that masculinity is an active, not passive, subject. In the next stage of therapy, masculinity also becomes a resource to facilitate changes in problematic behavior.

## Making Emotions Manly

Several early therapeutic exercises are structured in such a way that they do not conflict with the norms of traditional masculinity: Emotions are objectified and the focus of the sessions is emotional management, not emotional expression. In so doing, clinicians appeal to particular "male" virtues, reason, rationality, and self-control. Masculinity thus facilitates rather than impedes the objectives of therapy: control of anger and aggression. Mr. Garcia, the clinical social worker, begins Anger Management sessions by asking each of the participants to rate their current emotional state using a numerical scale, zero to ten, called the "Subjective Unit of Distress Scale" (SUDS). He explains, "This is a check of how I am feeling. Am I feeling calm? Calm is how you feel when you finish meditation, or how you feel when you're soaking in a bathtub or how you feel after waking up from a nice nap. That's a zero. If you're feeling anxious, then that's a seven. Anger is an eight. They put fear at nine." The SUDS is a way to quantify and objectify an essentially unquantifiable and highly subjective phenomenon, namely individual feeling. Although the measure is not meant to objectively compare levels of agitation across patients, it does provide a vocabulary through which patients can discuss and monitor their own emotional states. The number then becomes an abstract, distancing way of talking about emotions without having to relate any deeply personal information, retaining typically masculine modes of expression.

In addition to the SUDS, early therapy sessions focus on problem solving, self-control, and rational thought processes. Although Arlie Hochschild (1983) has argued that emotional self-control is increasingly a component of the service economy and thus closely associated with women, Peter Stearns (1990) suggests that emotional management has been an aspect of white, middle-class, managerial masculinity for at least the last century. According to Stearns (1990), by the middle of the nineteenth century middle-class men were being "urged to restrain or channel all excessive emotion, including ... misplaced anger" (Stearns 1990, 128). Self-control, it was thought, enabled men to harness "the intense passions attributed to male nature" and acquire the "disciplined focus necessary for success" in the business world (Stearns 1990, 128).

Emotional self-control is an explicit objective in Anger Management. One example of this focus on self-control is a therapeutic exercise known as the "cognitive loop." On a flip board, Mr. Garcia draws a series of arrows making up a circle with four links or steps. The first step is labeled an event or anger trigger, the second the thought that occurs after the event, and the third the emotional response that leads to a reaction (step four). The goal of the exercise is to demonstrate that emotional responses are not random occurrences but are actually the result of a cognitive process, which can be diagramed and analyzed.

In group therapy, veterans take turns practicing the cognitive loop using recent events in their daily lives. Elliot, one of the veterans participating in Anger Management, relates an argument he had with his daughter after she had wrecked her car. Although he admitted that he should have been relieved, her several previous auto accidents caused him to become angry. Mr. Garcia responds to Elliot's story by demonstrating the cognitive loop. The precipitating event was the car accident. Elliot's thought was that his daughter was being careless because she had been in previous accidents. The emotion was anger. Mr. Garcia then asks Elliot what his reaction would have been had his daughter suffered a serious injury. Elliot replies that he would have been more understanding. Thus, the exercise focuses on thinking about his daughter's safety, not about her perceived irresponsible behavior; the appropriate emotional response is then concern, not anger. Exercises such as the cognitive loop make emotions and therapy more masculine because feelings are constructed as rational and controllable, desirable male attributes.

## Reinterpreting Masculinity

Although clinicians often rely on typically middle-class male values of reason and rationality to facilitate therapeutic goals such as moderating anger and aggression, they also begin to challenge traditional conceptions of masculinity. Using scientific, religious, and military discourses, traits such as empathy, sensitivity, and cooperation become reinterpreted as specifically masculine qualities rather than as feminine, weak, or pathological ones. Emotional expression, compassion, and empathy, the objectives of therapy, are reconstructed as masculine.

Biology has often been used to objectify the differences between men and women as well as to normalize male behavior such as aggression and to pathologize female behavior such as emotionality (Lutz 1990). In PTSD group therapy, however, biomedical idioms are used to normalize the expression of emotions in men. In the Grief Group, Mr. Garcia suggests that as men reach middle age, they experience "machopause." Machopause is not, of course, an accepted medical condition, but is assumed to be analogous to menopause: just as menopause refers to the cessation of the female menstrual cycle, machopause refers to the end of machismo with its associated aggression, belligerence, and emotional immaturity. As a consequence of a normal "change of life," then, veterans should embrace tears and emotions as part of an inevitable biological process. Like menopause, machopause is linked to hormones. Mr. Garcia explains: "There's a hormone called prolactin. It is the hormone that allows women to produce milk but also to produce tears. Up until the age of seven, boys and girls have the same amount, but, after that, boys produce less. Once men enter middle age, their prolactin levels increase." Crying, although presumably not lactation, thus becomes a normal part of a more mature masculinity rather than a sign of weakness or femininity. Here, stoicism is likened to an inappropriate attempt to retain a youthful masculinity rather than an attempt to embrace a more mature and more emotionally responsive masculine self.

Whereas the social worker appropriates scientific language, the chaplain utilizes both religious imagery and military metaphors to challenge the traditional meanings of masculinity. The religious imagery used here is heavily gendered, embedded in a long-standing association between Christian virtues and femininity. Virtue, morality, purity, and piety have been the professed attributes of (white) women for most of the nation's history.[2] Breaking with this tradition in the Spiritual Recovery Group, Chaplain Everett subtly suggests that it is the male combat veteran who possesses superior moral insight, even if not moral superiority, as a result of taking human life, rather than the woman who remain at home. The Spiritual Recovery Guide, written by Chaplain Everett for combat veterans, states that "combat destroys expectations and assumptions about life in ways nothing else does. The shallow images of God[,] which our culture thrusts upon us[,] are demolished in battle. God's power is truly awesome and beyond our ability to understand. It takes little true faith to believe in God when surrounded by plenty" (p. 24). According to this guide, faith is a much more severe test when it is challenged by pain, suffering, and deprivation, and, because of their combat experiences, veterans, like early mystics and saints, come to recognize the vast chasm that separates humans and God. Although most people are aware of the darkness within themselves (inclinations towards violence, greed, lust, and pride, which are the roots of human misery), however, combat veterans have a much deeper understanding of the human capacity for evil.

In one Spiritual Recovery Group session, a veteran asks how he can forgive those who protested the Vietnam War and spat on the returning soldiers. Chaplain Everett responds by couching the challenges veterans face in spiritual terms: "Let's look at the self-righteous group that believed you were responsible for atrocities or whatever and did the spitting. They looked at you and said 'I would never do such a thing' when the truth is they are fully capable given the circumstances. They are ignorant. You may still take a high moral ground and forgive them." For male combat veterans, the traditionally feminine language of piety and humility becomes empowering and redemptive, while the traditional male language of vengeance and pride becomes a source of moral and psychological weakness.

Chaplain Everett also uses military metaphors to lay the foundation for an alternative to hegemonic masculinity. He describes spiritual recovery as a "spiritual boot camp," which includes "spiritual push-ups" as intellectual and moral exercises. Stereotypically feminine virtues such as forgiveness and tenderness become masculine in the context of military language and images. For example, step seven of the Spiritual Recovery program requires that the veteran forgive himself and others. The program guide states reassuringly "forgiveness is not a 'touchy-feely' activity. It is 'hard core'" (p. 16). To forgive, veterans must give up hatreds and resentments: "This is impossible at first, just do it anyway. Do it until it becomes only difficult. . . . Remember the statement that someone once told me represents the spirit of the Marine Corps: 'The impossible takes us a little while to accomplish, the difficult we do immediately.' Okay, Marines, go to it. Soldiers, sailors, and airmen, are you going to let these Marines get ahead of you in this little exercise?" (p. 19). Here, forgiveness becomes not a sign of weakness, as it would within the context of a traditional masculinity, but a demanding activity requiring strength and perseverance.

Similarly, step nine states that veterans must develop a "discipline of trust" by learning to trust others and to trust that God will return to them the ability to love themselves and others. Discipline is generally a term associated with hard work, not love or compassion. Trust, however, is generally understood as emanating from innocence or naiveté rather than from determination and fortitude. Love and trust become the ultimate objectives of an arduous, but also liberating mission.

Thus, the man envisioned by the Spiritual Recovery Group is not weak or soft but rather a warrior on a mission. As the program guide explains, "where before you may have performed search and destroy or search and rescue missions, you are now engaged in a search and bring peace mission" (p. 26). Veterans are counseled to undertake a "recon mission" into the territory of love and friendship (p. 23). Ultimately, the "final mission of a combat soldier" is to become a bringer of "peace, prayerfulness, happiness and rejoicing." He will infiltrate "enemy lines" and, as a "warrior of peace," use the "weapons of peace, mercy, and kindness" to overcome greed, hate, and selfishness (p. 1). Borrowing military and religious language, masculinity is now constructed to embody compassion and benevolence.

## Narrating Posttraumatic Masculinities

The Grief Group concludes with the veterans narrating their combat and postcombat experiences with the Three-Way Mirror. The second and third panels of the Three-Way Mirror represent a fairly clear departure from the earlier sessions of group therapy and even from the precombat narratives.[3] Whereas the first panel emphasizes that men learn to repress most emotions, especially pain and sadness, the focus of these later stages of therapy is on admitting to personal losses or failures in addition to giving and receiving emotional support.

The third panel is an important opportunity to practice a key component of this new, posttraumatic masculinity because it allows for the public disclosure of failure. Previous social scientific research on self-disclosure has documented that, in most circumstances, men self-disclose less frequently than women. Although this difference is partially due to opportunity (men, especially husbands with children, have fewer social ties than women—see Cohen 1995), men are also reluctant to self-disclose, even when given the chance, because of the possibility of appearing weak or vulnerable before other men (Reid and Fine 1992) or conceding power in a relationship (Sattel 1983).

Group participants are encouraged to admit to personal failures in their adult life, a clear deviation from the typical norms of male story-telling that favor the expression of strength and conquest. Most of the group participants have been unemployed for long periods of time, and many have lost wives and children. Some have also been in prison. By revealing failures before other men, the veterans are clearly breaking with these norms. Ricardo, a Latino Army veteran, experienced considerable estrangement from family and friends after his return from Vietnam.

RICARDO: I roamed around for about seven years. I got jobs here and there. I was in jail. I never had a record before I went to Vietnam. At twenty-seven, I got married. I had two kids in seven years. Then I went to jail, and my wife divorced me. I've never been remarried. I never hear from my family. I was in a veterans' parade in 1989. ...Protesters were calling us "baby killers." One of my friends went after him. A few months later, he died: he choked on his own vomit. He drank himself to death. Three other friends have died since then, one in my own living room.... It's time to get a grip on things before I end up like my buddies who never talked about Vietnam. My military experience was pretty traumatic, and I still feel like I'm in full combat mode: I'll just take you out.

MR. GARCIA: So is that why you were in jail? Because of violence?

RICARDO: Yeah. I assaulted a guy. I shot a guy in the kneecaps.... [There is] this three strikes law so if I go to jail again, they'll put me away for life. I've been cruising along seeing counselors for a few years. Then I get this letter from the state saying that I owe...back child support, which is bullshit. My ex-wife is remarried.... I've left her alone, and she has not made it easy for me to see my kids. She lives way up north, so it's not like I can just get in a car, drive up, and see them. Basically I just fucked off the last thirty years of my life.

MR. GARCIA: I know it's not easy to share some of these things, but you're doing important grief work here.

Ricardo does not attempt to excuse or minimize his situation, although he makes a point of stating that his problems began only after returning from Vietnam in "full combat mode." Nevertheless, his narrative is quite striking in its admission of job loss, estrangement from family, imprisonment, and drug use. The experience of masculinity presented here can be contrasted to the initial sessions of group therapy: in the Orientation Group, veterans referred to interpersonal violence and marital discord, but during the Grief Group they must describe their experiences as personal losses rather than as affronts to their masculinity.

In the concluding weeks of the Grief Group, the combat panel of the Three-Way Mirror provides a final opportunity for veterans to enact a new, post-traumatic masculinity. Veterans are required to respond to the experiences of others. Introducing the combat panel, Mr. Garcia explains:

> In the military, we were trained to take any feelings related to grief and turn them into anger and revenge. Anger and revenge help people to function in combat. So I want you to give specifics: How did it work for you? Pick one or two significant losses. This is an opportunity to debrief, to share the details of events prior, during, and after the loss. I'm asking you to pick a traumatic loss that caused you to "stuff it" or get angry. One purpose is to honor those that we have lost, to say their name, to help you to do grief work, to talk about what that loss meant, to get if off your chest, to get the support of the group, and help you make sense of what happened.

The exercise presumes that the veterans reacted to their combat trauma by using stereotypically male coping mechanisms: anger or emotional repression. Nevertheless, the objective of the exercise is to psychologically relive the event, this time allowing for the attendant emotions to be expressed. Moreover, other group participants should break with the standards of traditional male discourse by acknowledging the speaker's and their own emotions. Unlike the previous groups, where participants' comments or "cross-talk" are discouraged,[4] there is an explicit expectation that the other group members will now empathize with the feelings of others and offer them support. Although Mr. Garcia usually offers the initial comments following a veteran's narrative, he then calls on other group members to contribute. Below is an excerpt from a session of the Grief Group. Arthur and Duane are Army veterans. Ruben is a Marine Corps veteran. Arthur has just described how he and Jefferson, another member of his squad, were caught in a firefight.

ARTHUR: Any time we moved, there would be more fire. I was carrying the radio, and Jefferson was carrying the battery pack. I was getting tired, so we switched. Right after that, Jefferson took a round in the gut. I couldn't go anywhere. I couldn't do anything other than try to help him keep his guts in.

MR. GARCIA: Were you talking to him? Was he conscious?

ARTHUR: Yeah. But he wasn't making much sense. He was in pain, and I think he was hallucinating.

MR. GARCIA: How were you feeling?

ARTHUR: Scared. Pissed off. Looking for somebody to blame. Frustration. There was nothing I could do. . . . Why him and not me? He made it through the whole night. They found us a half hour after he died.

MR. GARCIA: What are you feeling now?

ARTHUR: Like I'd rather not be sitting here.

MR. GARCIA: Anger? Sadness?

ARTHUR: Sad, angry, guilty . . . I don't spend a lot of time talking about this shit. After that, I quit feeling. It was like I had a switch that I turned off. But that's not me. I have too much caring and too much affection for people.

Arthur acknowledges his feelings but also admits to repressing them. Significantly, he states that it is his "real" self that has emotions—having embraced a new, emotive masculinity, his authentic self emerges as a deeply emotional one. Other group members then begin to participate in the discussion.

DUANE: As you were talking, I just realized something. You feel relief that someone's no longer suffering. When my mom died, I felt guilty. But she had asthma and emphysema. She was suffering. It's okay to give up the guilt. Thank you.

ARTHUR: I went to a class at the hospital for depression, and one thing they taught me is, instead of feeling guilty, feel sad. It has worked. It's better to feel sad than guilty.

MR. GARCIA: Sadness is more manageable than guilt. That's a grief move. Guilt is anger directed towards yourself. Sadness is grieving. It's honoring the relationship. Guilt is selfish or self-centered. . . . Any feedback for Arthur on feelings?

RUBEN: You never want to be around new guys [in combat]. They may not be there tomorrow. They always got point [lead position] or rear guard because you wouldn't want to waste an experienced person on some minor patrol. It was a common experience. And the radio was always a target. Radio means artillery. It means reinforcements. They're going to cap [shoot] his ass.

MR. GARCIA: Can you relate to the feelings? You're talking about tactics.

RUBEN: I can relate to the denial of the reality of death.

In some respects, Arthur's narrative could be interpreted as the quintessential war story—Arthur is the protagonist who relates a harrowing escape from the battlefield. However, Arthur focuses more on Jefferson's suffering and death, as well as his inability to save him, than he does on his own heroism. Mr. Garcia does not ask about the specific details of Jefferson's death or even about the coping skills in combat that would be associated with PTSD. Rather, he repeatedly asks Arthur to identify his feelings as he narrates his story. He prompts Arthur by naming specific emotions (anger, grief, guilt) and then praises him for his efforts to articulate them in the group. He then asks the other participants to offer support. Duane voluntarily mentions his own recognition, inspired by his own mother's death, that relief over the end of a loved one's suffering can replace guilt. Ruben responds more directly to Arthur's narrative, but as he makes a rational assessment—radiomen made easy targets in Vietnam, and, therefore, it was not Arthur's fault that Jefferson died—rather than an emotional response, Mr. Garcia tries to redirect his comments from realization to emotions.

As the preceding excerpt demonstrates, by the end of the Grief Group the standards for participation in group therapy have changed. The objective of the Grief Group is not to strategize methods for avoiding or resolving conflicts but to share deeply personal information and actively emote the concordant feelings. In the process, a new masculinity is enacted. Rather than competing with each other over who can be more aggressive or more fearsome, veterans now share their pain and fears. Rather than demonstrating their stoicism and rationality, they display their empathy and compassion.

## Conclusion

Most studies of women and psychiatry criticize the medical profession for obfuscating the legitimate personal, political, and social problems facing women under the guise of treating mental illness (Ehrenreich and English 1978; Showalter 1985; Smith-Rosenberg 1985; Ussher 1992). However, as I have tried to demonstrate, in the group therapy sessions for men diagnosed with combat-related PTSD that I observed, the limitations of much of hegemonic or traditional masculinity are articulated. Although the "voice of medicine" (Mishler 1984) is sometimes evoked to explain "pathological" behavior, neither biology nor culture is viewed as impervious to individual agency. Despite the fact that neither the politics of the Cold War nor American imperialism is debated in therapy, the role of the military and the broader culture in creating a problematic and potentially self-destructive male identity is a theme that emerges in the therapeutic process. PTSD group therapy implicitly or explicitly posits the responses to stressors (e.g., combat trauma) as at least partially conditioned by societal expectations for creating the masculine self. Significantly, in therapy, masculinity is both a source of "troubles" and a resource to overcome them. Some exercises, such as the Three-Way Mirror, allow veterans to explore their beliefs about masculinity and how those beliefs affect the ways in which they express emotion. Other exercises, for example the cognitive loop, appeal to traditionally male virtues, such as reason, logic, and self-control, to manage allegedly traditional male vices, such as rage and violence. Under the therapeutic gaze, masculinity thus emerges as both an obstacle to mental health and a malleable subject.

In *The Remasculinization of America*, Susan Jeffords (1989) argues that in the decades after Vietnam, veterans of that particular war were actually reconstructed as hypermasculine in popular culture, the "Rambo" films being the most obvious example. In the therapy groups I observed, however, the reconstruction of Vietnam veterans took a different trajectory— rather than being reconfigured into alienated vigilantes, these veterans were encouraged to reconstruct themselves as compassionate "warriors for peace." Initially, group therapy closely adheres to the norms of male discourse (little personal information is shared, no feelings are expressed, and only experiences with drugs, alcohol, and violence are shared). Likewise, emotions are constructed as objects to be managed and controlled. However, the values of hegemonic masculinity are slowly pathologized and supplanted by an alternative construction of masculinity; qualities once labeled "feminine" become masculinized. Language appropriated from medicine, the military, and even religion is evoked to frame empathy, kindness, and trust as legitimately masculine characteristics. At the conclusion of PTSD group therapy, veterans talk about the war and combat, the paradigmatic masculine discourse, but they are also able to articulate emotions such as guilt, sorrow, and regret. Veterans thus enact an alternative, posttraumatic masculinity, one that incorporates strength and resilience with emotional expression and compassion.

# Notes

## Introduction

1. See Lee 2004; Conrad and Schneider 1992; Grubb 1990.

2. See Wertz and Wertz 1989; Barker 2003; Marshall and Woollett 2000; Fox and Worts 1999.

3. See Conrad 1975; Conrad and Potter 2000; Rafalovich 2001; Erchak and Rosenfeld 1989; Malacrida 2002.

4. See Hansen 1997; Chauncey 1994; Minton 1996; Allen 1997; Epstein 2003.

5. See Aspinall 1998; Carey 1998; Schoen 2001; Santiago-Irazarry 2001; Kaw 2003.

6. See Azzarto 1986; Arluke and Petersen; Lyman 1989; Binney, Estes, and Ingman 1990; Estes and Binney 1989.

7. It is telling that the African American gay community has faulted its churches for failing to bring safe-sex messages to their congregations.

8. As with feminism in general, a split emerged between liberal feminists, who "tend to view women's access to preventive services in the area of reproductive health as an equal-rights issue," and radical feminists, who "tend to interpret preventive measures as a form of medical surveillance and part of the larger social control of women in a society guided by the interest of men and the profit motive of corporate medicine" (Riska 2003, 67).

9. According to Hartley 2003, the American Psychiatric Association only stopped classifying hysteria as a disease in 1952.

10. Such an attempt to keep both structure and action at the center is reminiscent of Anthony Giddens and Pierre Bourdieu to a degree, though Connell has rejected comparison with at least the latter.

11. Much of the criticism of hegemonic masculinity as a concept comes from profeminist male academics, not from antifeminists. An early critical essay by Mike Donaldson (1993) claims that the concept is unclear, may be internally contradictory, and raises problems about the interrelation of gender inequality and class inequality. (Connell's most extended statement follows Donaldson's concern.) Clatterbaugh (1998) suggests that the term is being used in a far wider range of ways than Connell intended, with the net result

being that the term becomes highly problematic. Demetriou (2001) claims that Connell has problematically simplified the relation of gay men and gay masculinity to hegemonic masculinity, while Hearn (2004) echoes Clatterbaugh and suggests a switch in focus from "hegemonic masculinity" to "the hegemony of men." These authors in some cases also suggest that the terms "masculinity" and "masculinities" are of increasingly less value, and that attention should be returned to "men."

12. The explicitly feminist approach of this research is evident not only in its political agenda but in its wholesale pathologizing of masculine actions and processes, including male rejection of feminist goals. Consider Whitehead and Barrett's (2001, 7) judgmental statement that "despite the evident multiplicity of masculine expression, traditional masculinities and associated values still prevail in most cultural settings. Countless numbers of men still act dominant and 'hard,' deny their emotions, resort to violence as a means of self-expression, and seek to validate their masculinity in the public world of work rather than the private world of family and relationships."

13. There is, of course, a growing body of work that criticizes masculinity studies for, *inter alia*, its reliance on the essentialist sex/gender binary, ahistorical take on masculinity, assumption that gender differences are innate, focus on diversity to the exclusion of issues of power, failure to reflectively assess the theoretical concepts on which it relies, and exaggeration of the differences between men and women (see MacInnes 1998; Petersen 2003). Interestingly, while Alan Petersen rightly exhorts masculinity scholars to incorporate a Foucauldian, historical/discursive perspective, which he writes would help "reveal the ways in which the male body has been posited as both object and site for the exercise of power and to explore the implications of this for the subjectivities of men" (2003, 65), he focuses on scientific representations rather than the medicalization of men's bodies and behaviors. For a critique of the "demonizing and pathologizing" of masculinity, see Heartfield 2002.

14. Riska (2003) implies that the medicalization of masculinity began in the 1950s with the invention of the type A man as an explanatory framework for men's higher mortality rates from CHD. In the mid-1950s, the dominant explanation for the cause of CHD in men was emotional factors. The type A argument was that a certain personality type (type A), characterized by "the relentless striving of the middle-class entrepreneur became in the eyes of medicine a major risk factor for coronary heart disease" (Riska 2003, 72)—in short, the "moral aspects of heterosexual masculinity" (devotion to earning wages to support the middle-class family)—were medicalized as "risk factors" for heart disease. By the mid-1980s, however, this paradigm fell out of favor, as it was proved to be useless in explaining mortality rates (although it survived in popular culture and in profeminist works on male health—see Helgeson 1995). In the late 1970s, stress researchers introduced the concept of the "hardy man," who, by virtue of his commitment to work, his tendency to see change as a challenge rather than a danger, and his self-perception as someone who controlled his life, could weather the stresses of the workplace and of modern life *and* sustain "the traditional

qualities associated with white middle-class masculinity" (Riska 2003, 73). This demedicalized masculinity—rather than being a liability to health, masculinity assured it, and it was the absence of these masculine traits that placed men at risk.

## Chapter 1

1. This chapter is based on research previously published in Loe 2004.

2. Viagra is a popular yet expensive oral treatment for "erectile dysfunction," marketed by Pfizer Pharmaceuticals in the United States, which sends blood to the genitals when a person is physically aroused. Viagra was intended for use by mature males with erectile dysfunction exacerbated by prostate cancer, diabetes, or other medical situations. In its first year, Viagra became the fastest selling drug in history, generating over a billion dollars in sales.

3. Pfizer was among the first to perfect the "help-seeking ad," which, according to FDA regulations, does not require a list of potential side effects and warnings associated with a product if the drug is not named in the ad. Many of Pfizer's Viagra ads (including the initial Bob Dole ads) mention the condition, erectile dysfunction, and flash "Pfizer" at the end of the commercial, but do not list warnings and side effects. It is due to successful branding and brand awareness that ED and Pfizer have become largely synonymous with Viagra in the public imagination.

4. For more on this, see Loe 2004.

5. For more on how diverse social groups, including women, experts, critics, and marketers make sense of the Viagra phenomenon, please see Loe 2004.

6. The term "apparatus," later technology, names the connection between discursive practices, institutional relations, and material effects that, working together, produce a meaning or "truth effect" for the human body (Basalmo 1996, 21).

7. For a history of the ways in which the poor were marked as disease carriers and controlled by the medical establishment, see, for example, Brandt 1997. For a discussion of adolescent sexuality as a social problem, see Nathanson 1991. For a discussion of AIDS as conflated with homosexuality, see Terry 1995. Medicine has also been a tool of power and control in colonial contexts, where third-world women (for the most part) have been concurrently sexualized, surveyed, disciplined, and experimented upon. Scholars have shown that in the colonial era, technology, medicine, and science assisted in the control and surveillance of the Other. The exoticized female Other became a dehumanized object of scientific inquiry and a marker of exciting and dangerous sexual primitiveness. (See Morsy's discussion of Sarah Bartmann, a South African indentured servant in the 1800s who was an object of scientific observation and dissection due to her markers of "sexual primitiveness." In America, people of color have either been ignored by the medical establishment, stigmatized as dirty and diseased, sterilized, or studied and used for medical trials and experiments (see Jones 1993 and Roberts 1999).

8. The pharmacology of sex comes out of a context of medical hegemony in the late twentieth century, during which pharmaceutical companies exercised increasing authority over areas of life, such as sexuality, not previously requiring prescription drugs.

9. Drawing on Foucault, many feminists who write about the body see technology as a cultural apparatus working with social, historical, and cultural forces to produce the body as a "sign of culture" (Basalmo 1996, 3; DeLauretis 1987). We live in a world in which "bionic bodies" or cyborg bodies—bodies that mix the organic with the technological, the natural with the cultural—are commonplace (Basalmo 1996, 5; Haraway 1991).

10. This fix-it paradigm grew and developed in the twentieth century with the help of the war machine, impelling the development of plastic surgical technique which has won its place as a recognized surgical specialty (Hausman 1996, 49). Reconstructive plastic surgery was used around wartime to "reconfigure the body" through consistently redefining the normal body and its reparable deviations, much like endocrinology's approach to menopausal women (Hausman 1995, 50). Such findings provided medicine with the tools to enforce sexual essentialism. Both endocrinology and plastic surgery are medical technologies that some have argued can (and should) be used to regulate human behavior through the production and maintenance of a physical "normality" that will lead to psychological "normality" and health. It is precisely the production and instillation of this discursive network . . . that sets the stage for the emergence of transsexualism in the 1950s (Hausman 1996, 62–63).

11. De Lauretis (1987) argues that while gender and sexuality may appear hegemonic, different constructions of each exist in the margins of hegemonic discourses, inscribed in micropolitical practices and local levels of resistance.

12. *Phallocentrism* refers to the phallus, a male organ that symbolizes power and control. Susan Bordo (2000) explores the link between masculinity and the phallus throughout Western history, from Roman phallic gods, to St. Augustine's "lustful member," to John Bobbit's detachable penis, to Bill Clinton's not-so-private parts. Bordo argues that for long as we can remember the phallus has embodied our cultural imagination, symbolic of power, permission, defiance, and performance. Annie Potts adds that medicine and sexology produce and perpetuate the idea that an erect penis signifies "healthy" male sexuality—a destructive form of hegemonic masculinity that "ignores the diversity of penile pleasures" (2000, 89).

13. Interestingly, several of the men I spoke with, primarily those who had undergone prostate surgery, felt more of a stigma associated with incontinence than impotence. This is yet another area where millions of men suffer in silence.

14. Shame is a theme that came up quite a bit in my interviews with Viagra users. The shame of admitting erectile difficulties to oneself, one's partner, and one's doctor was a common theme. Several men also mentioned the stigma involved in being seen as a Viagra user by the outside world. For example, Thom said, "One of the hardest things is going to pharmacies and asking for

these things. Because it is hard not to feel that when you get a young clerk that they are not making some judgments about you. That you are some kind of sex nut or something trying to buy this stuff." The stigma associated with Viagra use, at least in the early years of this product's availability, has led many of my informants to be extremely private about their Viagra use, sometimes not even sharing this information with romantic partners.

15. Potts argues that we need an expansive view of male sexuality that need not rely on phallic ambitions. This would require a rethinking of penis-power and "a relinquishment of this organ's executive position in sex" to "embrace of a variety of penile styles: flaccid, erect, and semiflaccid/semierect." This way, male bodies might become differently inscribed and coded for diverse pleasures (Potts 2000, 100).

16. Relationship experts have described this "delicate dance" that couples do when they are dealing with situations like sexual dysfunction. Without open communication between partners, the fear of "failure" can lead to avoidance and alienation, which can only exacerbate the problem.

17. See any of Goldstein's coauthored reports in the *International Journal of Impotence Research*, volumes 10, 11, 12, and 15. A November 1997 cover story on impotence in *Newsweek* quoted Goldstein as describing erectile functioning as "all hydraulics" and suggesting that dysfunction required "rebuilding the male machine."

18. Interestingly, Nora Jacobson (2000) found this to be the case in her research on women and breast implants.

19. Previous treatments for ED included a liquid injected directly into the penis that would produce an erection for several hours (Caverject). Viagra is constructed as a superior treatment due to its simple delivery (as a pill) and its production of a penis that will wait to become erect until the user is ready.

20. I have Michael Kimmel to thank for helping me come up with the term *corporate corporealities.*

## Chapter 2

1. Until 2003, Viagra's patent protection prohibited FDA approval for similar pharmaceutical products.

2. As Leonore Tiefer (1994) explains, the medical profession implicitly defines a normal erection "as 'hard enough for penetration' and lasting 'until ejaculation,' informally, that means a few minutes. Anything less is 'impotence'" (372).

3. Already available in Europe, these drugs have taken significant market share from Viagra. In Germany, for example, Cialis has taken a 27 percent share, while Levitra has 14 percent of the market (Teather 2003).

4. Due to federal changes in the regulation of pharmaceutical advertising, drug companies can now advertise their products directly to consumers through mainstream magazines and television commercials. Previously, pharmaceutical advertising campaigns were limited primarily to physician- and health care provider–oriented journals, or to physicians directly through promotional

information, drug samples, and gifts. Today, the majority of pharmaceutical advertising money has shifted to "direct" advertising to consumers themselves (Mamo and Fishman 2001, 17).

5. The history of impotence is similar to the history of (male) homosexuality (see Foucault 1977, 1978; Weeks 1977), in that "the impotent man" as a type of *person* or as a matter of identity was literally invented in scientific discourse only in the late nineteenth century: "The word impotent is used to describe the man who does not get an erection, not just his penis. When a man is told by his doctor that he is impotent or when the man turns to his partner and says he is impotent: they [*sic*] are saying a lot more than that the penis cannot become erect" (quoted in Tiefer 1987, 165).

6. In other words, the phenomenon marked as "impotence" may in fact be a universal experience, even if it may not always be marked as such, if marked at all. But coupling the phenomenon marked as "impotence" with identity (and pathology) is historically specific, socially constructed, and a relatively recent occurrence.

7. Administered orally, the drug takes effect between forty to sixty minutes after ingestion and remains effective for two to four hours.

8. The term *phallocentrism* refers to penis- or phallic-centered sexuality in which intercourse, vaginal or anal, is the objective of the sexual encounter (Potts 2000).

9. Lifestyle drugs treat life-limiting rather than life-threatening conditions. Examples of these conditions include hair loss, memory loss, skin problems, and mild allergies. Such drugs generally promise to make life better in some way (Mamo and Fishman 2001).

10. Articles from the following periodicals were selected for in-depth analysis: *The Age* (Melbourne) (1 article), *Boston Globe* (2), *Boston Herald* (2), *Brand Strategy* (1 article), *Business Week* (1), *Chicago Sun-Times* (1), *Daily Telegraph* (London) (1), *Daily Telegraph* (Sydney) (1), *Financial Times* (London) (1), *The Gazette* (Montreal) (1), *The Guardian* (4), *The Independent* (London) (2), *Los Angeles Times* (1), *The Mirror* (1), *Newsday* (New York) (1), *New York Times* (4), *The Observer* (1), *Ottawa Citizen* (2), *Pharmacy New* (Australia) (1), *Philadelphia Magazine* (1), *Pittsburgh Post-Gazette* (2), *Seattle Times* (5), *Straits Times* (Singapore) (1), *Sunday Telegraph* (London) (1), *Sunday Times* (London) (2), *The Times* (London) (1), *Toronto Star* (1), *USA Today* (2), *Washington Post* (1).

11. According to Adele Clarke and her colleagues (2003), the use of randomized clinical trials has become the "gold standard" for the legitimization of biomedical claims.

12. Interestingly, some sex therapists see Viagra's delayed effect as a potential benefit, in the belief that it promotes anticipation and foreplay (Marshall 2002, 150–51).

13. Cialis's makers have made no plans to hire a sports celebrity, preferring instead to emphasize the pill's longer duration.

14. Rather than raising questions about the direction of impotence treatment marketing, most media accounts seem so superficial and uncritical that

they appear to condone it. One exception, an article entitled "Sex enhancers' competition gives rise to ridicule," was published in the *Boston Herald*. After illustrating how the campaigns for the new drugs promise "optimal performance...enhancement...that extra edge," the author writes "And so billions are about to be made off male 'edge' insecurity" (Eagan 2002).

## Chapter 3

*Acknowledgments*: We would like to thank Dana Rosenfeld, Christopher Faircloth, Matthew Schmidt, Monica Casper, Robyn Mierzwa, and Andy Walters for their helpful comments.

1. One of the unintended consequences of using DNA evidence for conviction is the fact that DNA evidence has also been used for exoneration. According to Liptak (2003), more than 120 people have been exonerated by DNA evidence. As Peter Neufeld of the Cardozo Law School Innocence Project said, "It's kind of a truth machine. But any machine when it gets in the hands of human beings can be manipulated or abused" (quoted in Liptak 2003).

2. As a "silent witness," sperm does not need to endlessly and inconsistently recount events but can rather be culled for specific scientific information. Seminal fluid contains DNA, which, in the scientific gaze, is rational and objective proof of male presence and activity at a particular scene, thus replacing the untrustworthiness of women's experiences, bodies, testimony, and (in)ability to fend off attack with more reliable evidence. In both criminal and entertainment worlds, women are generally portrayed as the passive recipients of sperm (indeed, on many crime shows, women are passive in the extreme, that is, dead). The rise of DNA forensics as practice and entertainment has recast women as an inert staging ground into which sperm is deposited; female victims (or their bodies) become crime scenes from which the "real" evidence—the seminal samples—is swabbed. This representation of women as a passive repository evokes the world of straight porn: where women are simply holes for things to poke or spill into. Might the DNA sample be the forensic equivalent of a cum shot? Women are props for male and seminal action: raping, ejaculating, policing, collecting, testing, prosecuting, examining, and proving.

3. Despite all the hype and use of sex crimes as a hook to get citizens to vote for tough crime laws and violation of privacy, in reality many rape kits are not processed due to expense and backlog of cases. This use of rape and sex crimes to sway voters is an effective ploy to gain more access to individuals, thus potentially violating civil rights.

4. Certainly the role of paternity testing is another use of DNA forensics highly linked to tropes of masculinity. However, since DNA testing for paternity cases is after sperm and semen have been implicated (the seed has been spilled), it is not useful to our analysis to look at these tests, which rely on blood testing technologies. See Daemmrich 1998 for an analysis of the actor network created through paternity testing.

5. Due to the unique biological properties of sperm cells, DNA testing of semen samples uses slightly different protocols from testing other biological materials such as saliva or blood. In 1980 David Botstein and coworkers were the first to exploit these variations found between people, the type of variation they used is called restriction fragment length polymorphism or RFLP (Rudin and Inman 2002a, 21). RFLP identifies a specific restriction enzyme that reveals a pattern difference between the DNA fragment sizes in individual organisms. In 1983 Alec Jeffreys, a professor at the University of Leicester, found that these repeated sequences contain "core" sequences. This opened the way for the development of probes containing the core sequences (Amirani 1995).

6. Currently there are two procedures used in forensics for conducting DNA testing, RFLP and PCR. PCR is a process mediated by an enzyme that synthesizes new DNA from an existing template that can yield millions of copies of a desired DNA sequence (Rudin and Inman 2002a, 211). PCR is the standard in the field, preferred because smaller and more degraded samples can be tested and it is more cost effective.

7. Transcripts from Department of Justice news conference on March 11, 2003, with Attorney General John Ashcroft include testimony from Kellie Greene, founder and director of Speaking out About Rape, Inc., with the aim of garnering support for President Bush's DNA Initiative. "I was raped in 1994, and in April of 1997, I was called by the detective who was working my case down to the police station. She showed me a picture of the rapist and I asked how did she know. She said, 'DNA tells us.' To this day, the only reason I know what the rapist looks like is because DNA tells me. . . . Since then, I have become a huge crusader of DNA. I love DNA—it is our friend. Because DNA can do so much. It identifies the bad guy, it tells us who is committing these crimes."

8. *C.S.I.* is now broadcast in 175 countries, making it the most-watched television program in the world, according to Peter Sussman, chief executive of Alliance Atlantis, a Canadian production studio that co-owns the series with CBS (Carter 2003).

9. From "One Hit Wonder" (season 3, episode 14), NICK: Hey, Grissom. Got what looks like a semen stain. It's crusted, it's not fresh," and "From Primum Non Nocere" (season 2, episode 16), GRISSOM investigating the bedroom of a victim, "Well, Jane may play hockey, but her sheets are distinctly female." SARA, using a UV light says, "There are semen stains everywhere. Not very Victoria Secret.")

10. From Checkmate's Web site, www.getcheckmate.com.

11. One company, GenuServe (www.genuserve.com), offers home fidelity kits as well as laboratory services with the following price tags:

Sperm detection—to determine if a stain or fluid is semen with or w/o sperm

Acid Phosphatase Microscopic inspection—the substance is wet mounted and examined under a high power microscope for the presence of semen, P30 semen detection for vascectomized and azopermatic $165.00–225.00

DNA extraction—Will test sperm contained in condom, jar, plastic bottles, Kleenex or other sterile container—Works best if sent in quickly but they have extracted sperm several years old. $300.00

Sperm Comparison—(Differential Lysis) If there is more than one persons DNA on the sample area $700.00

Sperm Determination—If you want to know sperm on article matches the buccal swab you provide. $580.00.

Condom Matching—If cells outside of the condom match a DNA sample you provide. There is only a 50% chance of DNA being extracted from the outside of the condom. $580.00.

DNA Comparison—Have a DNA comparison if you would like to have a DNA profile found within a stained area $130.00

## Chapter 4

1. Indeed, this understanding is gaining recognition in the literature: Elianne Riska, writing two decades after Reissman, highlights the gendered nature of the medicalization thesis by examining type A behavioral patterns as risk factors for heart disease. She writes that "the original theory on Type A personality pointed indirectly to traditional masculinity as a risk factor" (2003, 75), suggesting that certain male-specific traits have come under medical jurisdiction.

2. The efficacy of testosterone replacement therapy is not well known, although a few small studies suggest some benefit for various age-related conditions. One study suggests that testosterone decreases LDL cholesterol in older men and may improve the quality of life in men with angina, or chronic chest pain (Morley and Perry 2003). One of the main health concerns among the aging population is frailty, caused by sarcopenia, or a deterioration of lean muscle mass. Bodily frailty leaves the elderly population more prone to falls and broken bones. There is evidence that testosterone replacement therapy has the potential to increase lean muscle mass if accompanied by rehabilitation. As Morley and Perry (2003, 371) write, "well designed large clinical trials in sarcopenia and/or frail men are essential to determine whether this potential is a reality or merely a modern urban myth." While a small amount of clinical data suggests that testosterone therapy may have some benefit in terms of various bodily conditions later in life, it does not appear as if testosterone replacement therapy has the potential to completely reinvigorate aging male bodies. In short, testosterone replacement therapy has not yet demonstrated efficacy in reversing or correcting signs of the aging process (Wespes and Schulman 2002).

3. Klinefelter's syndrome is one of the more common developmental disorders of the reproductive tract in which a male has a chromosomal abnormality (XXY), undeveloped testes and gynecomastia, which is excessive development of the mammary glands in the male. Testosterone supplementation is often prescribed to individuals who have Klinefelter's syndrome.

4. As a topical solution, Rogaine is applied to the scalp twice a day. In clinical trials, Rogaine was moderately effective, although it could only be used in men with hair loss of a certain severity.

## Chapter 5

1. SciArt refers to creative collaborations between scientists and artists, producing artistic works that have scientific content or meanings and metaphors, and so on. Collaborations are often presented as important not only in terms of the work produced but also of the process of sharing artistic and scientific ideas and interests and the new knowledge that may be generated by it.

2. The Visible Human Project refers to the digital, three-dimensional recording of real human bodies undertaken by the United States National Library of Medicine at Bethesda. Bodies have been dissected, photographed, and then converted into digital files, which are then made accessible to medical researchers via the Web (see Waldby 2000).

3. Biobanking refers to the storing or "banking" of human organs or tissues to be used in pioneering medical treatments and research.

4. Harold Shipman, a U.K. general practitioner, was convicted of murdering fifteen of his elderly patients and forging a will. The case caused scandal in the United Kingdom and outrage that Shipman had succeeded in killing his patients with impunity in a way that suggested that there were serious flaws in the medical systems that should protect patients from unscrupulous doctors.

## Chapter 6

1. This report is attributed to Gretchen Feussner, a government pharmacologist (Drug Enforcement Administration) giving evidence to a National institutes of Health conference on the diagnosis and treatment of ADHD in November 1998. She reported that the United States' production of methylphenidate increased from 1,768 kilograms in 1990 to 14,442 kilograms in 1998 (Breggin 2001, 13)

2. Deserving of special protection and compensation in the educational system—see pages 00 of this chapter.

3. Singh 2003 observes that mothers often take the initiative in evaluating their children for ADHD without prior consultation with the father.

4. This is Weber's definition of object of sociological analysis—social action meaning action oriented in the course of its direction by social meanings.

5. An alternative hypothesis of course is that children's behavior is getting worse. This interpretation underlies explanations that attribute ADHD symptoms to junk food or to "rapid-fire culture." These explanations sidestep the gender differential. The distinctive social composition of the population at high risk does not lend itself to an explanation based on deteriorating behavioral standards in any absolute sense.

6. Reference here to Surgeon General's web site http://www.surgeongen eral.gov/library/mentalhealth/chapter3/sec4.html.

7. This began to happen during the late sixties, several decades after it was realized that amphetamines produced different psychoactive effects when administered to children as opposed to adults. Instead of stimulating the nervous system, amphetamines exert a calming effect on children. This had been established in the 1930s through the experimental amphetamine treatment of children with behavioral disorders, but the findings did not immediately establish a legitimate basis for their routine application among children.

8. The object in this version of object relations theory is the penis. Male babies quickly learn that they are separate and different because they have one and their mothers do not. Little girls take longer to develop a clear ego boundary because they strongly identify with the carer who shares identical body parts.

9. New drugs for ADHD can overcome this limitation.

10. According to Illona Singh, pediatricians in Britain are more likely to insist that children are put under continuous medication (I. Singh, personal communication).

11. The reference here is Shorter's (1975) "modern" family with its characteristic sexual division of labor and its capacity to provide intensive childcare. See Sagan (1989) for a strong endorsement of the health-generating power of the modern family.

12. This is the sort of range quoted by the American Psychiatric Association (1994, 2000). However, it also appears in Conrad (1976), and it is hard to imagine that the same range applied in the both periods. Rowland, Lesesne, and Abramowitz (2002) propose that the 3- to 7-percent estimate derives not from empirical studies at all but from the distributional cutoffs for clinical significance in two of the most widely used behavior or symptom checklists used to assess ADHD, the Child Behavior Checklist and the Conners Parent and Teacher ratings scales. These scales have defined clinically important cut points at the extremes of a bell curve—typically 1.5 to 2 standard deviations above the mean, or about 93 to 98 percent of the distribution. While the authors criticize the circularity of this method for its potential to underestimate the "natural" rate of ADHD in the population, such an approach also ignores the question of the rates of actual diagnoses in the population based on these diagnostic criteria.

13. Physicians are legally obliged to report cases of some diseases to public authorities. Typically, these involve infective diseases with an epidemic potential such as smallpox. Where this requirement exists, the accuracy of statistical estimates improves exponentially.

14. Given the lack of official evidence, researchers have used four primary means to attempt to measure the prevalence of ADHD diagnosis and treatment in the general population: self-report of diagnosis or treatment among samples of the population, examination of clinical or pharmaceutical records, examination of school records and surveys among school nurses, and an examination of production quotas of methylphenidate and other drugs used in the treatment of the condition.

15. For the true incidence, we are here referring to medically sanctified cases.

16. An increase of similar scope is reported by Robinson and colleagues (1999), who used the National Ambulatory Medical Care Survey to discern trends in the prevalence of doctors' office-based visits among children aged 5 to 18 years resulting in a diagnosis of ADHD between 1990 and 1995. They report a 2.3 percent increase from 1.1 percent to 2.8 percent between 1990 and 1995 for office-based visits resulting in a diagnosis of ADHD. A larger increase comes from Olfson et al. (2003), who reported trends in outpatient treatment of ADHD children rising from 0.9 percent of children in 1987 to 3.4 percent of children in 1997.

17. The NCHS record rates of ADHD in female-headed single-parent households that are nearly twice the rate of those headed by two parents or by a male single parent in 2002. While these findings are suggestive, few studies currently collect comprehensive data on household composition and dynamics to assess wider patterns of ADHD across diverse family types.

18. Studies based on school records usually also exclude students enrolled in private schools or those receiving schooling at home. They obviously depend on the accuracy of the school records. Bearing in mind these limitations, which tend to under- rather than overestimate the rate of medication, it is striking that studies conducted using this strategy do reveal rates of treatment for ADHD are well in excess of national estimates published by the Centers for Disease Control and Prevention on the basis of the National Health Interview Survey.

19. LeFever, Dawson, and Morrow (1999) found that children of military families were significantly more likely than children with civilian parents to take ADHD medication during school hours.

20. An additional and substantial body of studies has attempted to determine the ADHD prevalence in the population by evaluating samples of youth against *DSM*-based diagnostic criteria (e.g., Nolan, Gadow, and Sprafkin 2001; Baumgaertel, Wolraich, and Dietrich 1995; Carlson, Tamm, and Gaub 1997; DuPaul et al. 1997; Gaub and Carlson 1997; Wolraich et al. 1996, 1998). These studies typically report higher prevalence rates—anywhere from 8 to 25 percent. These higher rates are largely a function of the fact that the researchers are including among ADHD cases anyone who scores high on their diagnostic measures and therefore include more youth than simply those with an official clinical diagnosis. The goal of these studies is to uncover the "natural" rate of ADHD within the population. It is interesting to note that these studies do report consistent gender differences in ADHD rates, with boys anywhere from three to five times more likely to exhibit diagnostic criteria of ADHD, depending upon age and ADHD subtype (i.e., inattention versus hyperactivity).

21. The same impression of large geographical variations at the county level is conveyed in some studies based on medical records. Rappley et al. (1995) analyzed a population-based data set of all prescriptions filled in the state of Michigan during February and March 1992 to determine the point prevalence of methylphenidate use among children aged zero to nineteen. The authors find that the rate of treatment varied considerably, with the rate of

methylphenidate use among all children ranging from 2.5 per 1,000 to 28 per 1,000 across various counties. The authors claim that this wide range in the number of children using methylphenidate is not explained by rural versus urban makeup, socioeconomic composition, ethnic makeup, number of physicians per capita, proximity to tertiary care centers, or proportion of the county population younger than twenty years old. Additionally, Safer and Malever (2000) examined the results of a statewide survey of public school nurses in Maryland conducted in April 1998 to determine the point prevalence of drug treatment for ADHD among school-aged children in the state. The authors report that school district rates of methylphenidate treatment varied five-fold geographically, from a low of 1.18 percent to a high of 6.02 percent. The authors find that race/ethnicity demographics were not to account for these disparities; they do suggest that the presence of specialty clinics for treating ADHD children might have been to blame for the high rates of treatment in three of the four highest counties in the state.

22. This included 1,515 low-consumption counties (1,796 grams) and 1,515 high-consumption counties (4,923 grams). See Bokhari, Mayes, and Scheffler (2004).

23. Confirming the iatrogenic character of ADHD, these authors also show that high-use counties have a greater percentage of specialist physicians— pediatricians, psychiatrists, and neurologists. Overall, in places where the ratio of young to old physicians is higher, children are more likely to end up on the Ritalin regime.

24. Source: United States Drug Enforcement Administration ARCOS Database, 2000. This data does not separate Ritalin from other drugs used to treat ADHD.

25. In their study of a single county in North Carolina, Rowland, Lesesne, and Abramowitz (2002) report that 8 percent of white elementary school children were being treated for ADHD with medication compared to 5 percent of African American children and 2 percent of Hispanic children.

26. See http://www.nces.ed.gov/nationsreportcard/writing/results2002/item mapgrade4.asp for a fuller explanation of each level and its score threshold.

27. MBD meant minimal brain damage in the early twentieth century. By the 1980s, with still no progress in identifying any autonomous biomedical signs of the ADHD, the term minimal brain dysfunction has replaced the definitive original acronym.

28. Laurence Diller (1998) makes a number of observations on the absence of a social epidemiology of ADHD. As he puts it: "Remarkably, no study exists to my knowledge that has tried to correlate referrals for ADD evaluations of children under five to those who attended structured day care as opposed to those who stayed at home. If such a study were to demonstrate fewer problems for the children looked after at home or in home day care, parents might have greater psychological or political support for those choices." Op cit. P. 81. and again on p. 90. "Amazingly, there are no studies that address the relationship of class size to the incidence of ADHD."

29. This data does not separate Ritalin from other drugs used to treat ADHD.

30. See Virginia Berridge (1999). A parallel text for the United States is *Dark Paradise: Opiate Addiction before 1940* by David T. Courtwright 1982. Cambridge: Harvard University Press.

31. Leonard Sagan (1989), in his *Health of Nations,* makes the bold claim that the Enlightenment-sponsored mode of socialization referred to here is the fundamental cause of the rise of modern longevity.

32. The appropriate term is *smacking* in the United Kingdom.

33. These facts tended to be downplayed in some second-wave feminist discourse, which represented private mothering as a wasteful, even antisocial form of female labor and child socialization as a virtually natural self-directed process—see Barrett and McIntosh, *The Anti-social Family.*

34. Talcott Parsons and Robert Bales (1964) identified socialization and the "stabilization of the adult personality" as the key functions of the modern nuclear family. Their functionalist theory stressed the importance of the home as a refuge from the competitive public sphere, where irrational love and the principles of substantive rather than formal rationality prevail—particularism over universalism, affective partiality over neutrality, and so on.

35. Julian LeGrand (1982) in his *Strategy of Equality* documents how welfare state policies designed to increase equality in practice bring advantages to those who know how to exploit them. He shows for Britain how middle-class people, rather than the poor, gained more from the National Health Service, from free university education, from housing subsidies, and so on. National spending on education in the United States increased 28 percent between 1991 and 1998, but most of the increase went on special education—leaving this aside, the average increase per student was only 0.7 percent. This means that the diversion of revenue towards students with learning disabilities represents a massive redistribution of public resources. What we know of the social distribution of ADHD indicates that prosperous families benefited disproportionately from the change.

36. See Diller (1998) op cit. 151–153 for detail on the special accommodations and the political lobbying that went on to get ADD classified under IDEA. In the first instance, ADD was excluded from the list of eligible conditions, and it was only after a massive letter writing campaign orchestrated by Children and Adults with Attention Deficit/Hyperactivity Disorder (CHADD) that the new legislation was amended to include it.

37. Diller (1998) op cit., 150 notes that when the IDEA came up for congressional "reauthorization" in 1997, "the number of children classified as disabled had grown to an 'eye-opening' 10% of the school population."

38. In Ritzer's terms, this is equivalent to the McDonaldization of socialization.

39. The same conclusion may be drawn about women and cigarettes. Though it is often assumed that the cigarette corporations engineered a reform of gender ideologies about women and smoking, the chronological evidence indicates that it was only when women themselves breached the cultural barriers that the big tobacco cashed in (see Scudson 1990).

## Chapter 7

1. This is just one of the many examples (see McGregor [1998] and Hammar [1997]) of how biology was associated with behavior and morality.

2. Only one other known experiment that dealt with untreated syphilis existed prior to the Tuskegee study. Known as the "Oslo (Norway) Study," nearly two thousand syphilis patients were examined at an Oslo clinic between 1891 and 1910. However, unlike the Tuskegee study, this study predated penicillin and other remedies, was a retrospective study, and did not appear to be specific to one race or based on sexual stereotypes (Jones 1993).

3. The families of the men who died from syphilis were given a fifty-dollar burial stipend in exchange for permission to perform an autopsy (Jones 1993). The irony, of course, is that this burial stipend, touted as a generous act, would have been unnecessary if the men had been treated with penicillin in the first place.

4. The "punishment" for the Tuskegee syphilis experiment was a revamping of human experimentation regulations, a cash settlement ($37,500 for living syphilitics; $15,000 to the heirs of the deceased syphilitics; $16,000 to the living controls; and $5,000 to the heirs of the deceased controls) and a formal apology from President Bill Clinton in 1997 (Gray 1998, 98; Jones 1993).

5. Blacks continue to have misconceptions about modes of transmission of HIV/AIDS as well as lack of sufficient information concerning treatment for HIV/AIDS (Pearson 1994). This is especially dangerous for the black population because AIDS has hit this already racially stigmatized and marginalized group at a markedly higher death and sickness rate than whites. Research shows that sexually transmitted diseases, such as syphilis and HIV/AIDS, have risen dramatically among minorities, while rates have stabilized among the white community (Williams and Collins 1995). Further research reveals that black men with AIDS often refuse treatment because they continue to hold fears that they will be used as guinea pigs similar to how subjects in the Tuskegee syphilis experiment were used (Gamble 2000, 432).

## Chapter 8

1. See D. R. Rudy's *Becoming Alcoholic* for a detailed discussion of the Twelve Steps program.

2. With declining male membership during the eighteenth century, American churches increasingly contributed to the development of women's virtuous character in order to appeal their increasing female parish (Riley 1986, 52). Ministers condemned "those forces antithetical to women's interests—materialism, immorality, intemperance, and licentiousness. They helped to formulate a new definition of female character. Christian virtues, such as humility, submission, piety, and charity, were now, they suggested, primarily female virtues. Most important, ministers confirmed female moral superiority" (Woloch 1984, 120).

3. The third panel of the Three-Way Mirror in the Grief Group is actually completed second in the sequence of narratives and addresses marital and family losses, through death or divorce, employment losses, lack of a home-coming, and other problems dealing with the stigma of having served in Viet-nam. Mr. Garcia explained that participants narrate the second panel last because the losses from Vietnam are often the most traumatic and hence dif-ficult for them to articulate. The third panel is not narrated orally in Anger Management, in part because of time constraints, and, in part because current experiences with anger are addressed in other exercises.

4. References to specific combat experiences can "trigger" symptoms of PTSD. Clinicians, therefore, limit such discussions until later in therapy when veterans are presumably more capable of processing traumatic memories.

# References

## Web Sites

Lilly ICOS. *Cialis.* http://www.cialis.com.
Bayer Pharmaceuticals Corporation. *Levitra.* http://www.Levitra.com.
ISCID (International Society for Complexity Information and Design) Encyclopedia of Science and Philosophy BETA "RFLP." http://www.iscid.org/encyclopedia (accessed May 16 2003).

## Infidelity Kit Sources

1. http://infidelitycheck.us/dna_infidelity_test.html (last accessed 9/2/03)
2. www.infidelitykit.com (last accessed 6/3/03 and 9/3/03)
3. www.dnatestingcentre.com (last accessed 9/2/03)
4. www.cluefinder.tripod (last accessed 6/3/03 and 9/3/03)
5. www.genuserve.com (last accessed 6/3/03 and 9/3/03)
6. www.checktive.com (last accessed 9/2/03)
7. www.spermdetection.com (last accessed 9/2/03)
8. www.sementest.com—(last accessed 11/21/03)
9. www.milleniumdivorce.com—(last accessed 9/2003)
10. www.dnatestingplace.com (last accessed 10/30/03)
11. www.getcheckmate.com (last accessed 9/2/03)
12. www.semenstainedpanties.com (last accessed 9/25/03)

## Books and Articles

Abel, Emily E. 2000. "A Historical Perspective on Care." Pp. 8–14 in *Care Work: Gender, Class, and the Welfare State*, edited by M. H. Meyer. New York: Routledge.
Allen, Garland E. 1997. "The Double Edged Sword of Genetic Determinism: Social and Political Agendas in Genetic Studies of Homosexuality, 1940–1994." Pp. 242–270 in *Science and Homosexualities*, edited by V. A. Rosario. New York: Routledge.

219

Allen, Jane. September 1, 2003. "For Men, Choices Beyond Viagra." *Los Angeles Times,* pg. F.1.

American Association of Clinical Endocrinologists. 2002. "Medical Guidelines for Clinical Practice for the Evaluation and Treatment of Hypogonadism in Adult Male Patients." *Endocrine Practice* 8: 439–456.

American Psychiatric Association. 1994. *The Diagnostic and Statistical Manual of Mental Disorders,* 4th ed. Text Revision. Washington, DC: American Psychiatric Association.

American Psychiatric Association. 2000. "Attention-deficit and Disruptive Behavior Disorders." Pages 78–85 in *Diagnostic and Statistical Manual of Mental Disorders, Fourth Edition (DSM-IV).* Text Revision. Washington, DC. American Psychiatric Association.

Amirani, Amir. 1995. "Sir Alec Jeffreys on DNA Profiling and Minisatellites." ISI ScienceWatch Interviews. http://www.sciencewatch.com/interviews/sir_alec_jeffreys.html (accessed May 7, 2003).

Archer, John, and Barbara Lloyd. 1982. *Sex and Gender.* Harmondsworth, UK: Penguin.

Arluke, Arnold, and John Peterson. 1981. "The Accidental Medicalization of Old Age and its Social Control Implications." Pp. 271–284 in *Dimensions: Aging, Culture and Health,* edited by C. Fry. New York: Praeger.

Armstrong, David. 1983. *Political Anatomy of the Body.* Cambridge: Cambridge University Press.

Armstrong, David. 2000. "Social Theorizing about Health and Illness." Pp. 24–35 in *Handbook of Social Studies in Health and Medicine,* edited by G. Albrecht, R. Fitzpatrick, and S. Scrimshaw. Thousand Oaks, CA: Sage Publications.

Arndt, Michael. 2003. "Is Viagra Vulnerable?" *Business Week,* October 27. http://businessweek.com/index.html (accessed November 9, 2003).

Aspinall, Peter J. 1998. "Describing the 'White' Ethnic Group and its Composition in Medical Research." *Social Science and Medicine* 47(11): 1797–1808.

Ayers, Robert. 1999. "Serene and Happy and Distant: An Interview with Orlan." Pp. 171–184 in *Body Modification,* edited by M. Featherstone. London: Sage Publications.

Azzarto, Jacqueline. 1986. "Medicalization of Problems of the Elderly." *Health and Social Work* 11(3): 189–195.

Aziz, M. Ashraf, James C. Mckenzie, James S. Wilson, Robert J. Cowie, Sylvanus A. Ayeni, and Barbara K. Dunn. 2002. "The Human Cadaver in the Age of Biomedical Informatics." *The Anatomical Record* (New Anat) 269: 20–32.

Babbie, Earl. 1989. *The Practice of Social Research,* 5th ed. Belmont, CA: Wadsworth.

Backett-Milburn, Katherine, and Linda Mckie, eds. 2001. *Constructing Gendered Bodies.* London: Palgrave.

Bardaglio, Peter. 1999. " 'Shameful Matches': The Regulation of Interracial Sex and Marriage in the South before 1900." Pp. 112–140 in *Sex, Love, Race: Crossing Boundaries in North American History,* edited by M. Hodes. New York: New York University Press.

Barker, Kristin. 1998. "A Ship Upon a Stormy Sea: The Medicalization of Pregnancy." *Social Science and Medicine* 47(8): 1067–1076.

Barker, Kristin. 2003. "Birthing and Bureaucratic Women: Needs Talk and the Definitional Legacy of the Sheppard-Towner Act." *Feminist Studies* 29(2): 333–356.

Barker-Benfield, G. J. 1976. *The Horrors of the Half-known Life: Male Attitudes Toward Women and Sexuality in the Nineteenth Century.* New York: Harper & Row.

Barkley, Russell A. 1990. *Attention-Hyperactivity Disorder: A Handbook for Diagnosis and Treatment.* New York: Guilford Press.

Barnett, Rosalind C., and Grace K. Baruch. 1987. "Social Roles, Gender, and Psychological Distress." Pp. 122–143 in *Gender and Stress*, edited by Rosalind C. Barnett, Lois Biener, and Grace K. Baruch. New York: The Free Press.

Barrett, Frank J. 2001. "The Organizational Construction of Hegemonic Masculinity: The Case of the US Navy." Pp. 77–99 in *The Masculinities Reader*, edited by Stephen M. Whitehead and Frank J. Barrett. Malden, MA: Polity Press.

Barrett, Michele, and Mary McIntosh. 1982. *The Anti-Social Family.* London: Verso.

Basalmo, Anne. 1996. *Technologies of the Gendered Body: Reading Cyborg Women.* Durham, NC: Duke University Press.

Bauchner, Howard, and Robert Vinci. 2001. "What Have We Learnt from the Alder Hey Affair?" *British Medical Journal* 322: 309–310.

Baumgaertel, Anna, Mark Wolraich, and Mary Dietrich. 1995. "Attention Deficit Disorders in a German Elementary School-Aged Sample." *Journal of the American Academy of Child and Adolescent Psychiatry* 34: 629–638.

Bayard, H. 1839. Translation of "Emploi du Microscope en Medecine Legale, Examen Microscopique du Sperme Desseche sur le Linge, sur les Tissus de Nature et de Coloration Diverses" in *Annales d'Hygiene Publique et de Medecine Legale* 22: 134–170.

BBC News Online. September 30, 2002. "University Defends 'Corpse-free Classes.'" http://news.bbc.co.uk/1/hi/health/2288631.stm.

Beck, Ulrich. 1992. *Risk Society: Towards a New Modernity.* London, Sage.

Becker, Gay, and Robert D. Nachtigall. 1992. "Eager for Medicalization: The Social Production of Infertility as a Disease." *Sociology of Health and Illness* 14(4): 456–471.

Bell, Susan E. 1987. "Changing Ideas: The Medicalization of Menopause." *Social Science and Medicine* 24(6): 535–542.

Bell, Susan E. 1990. "Sociological Perspectives on the Medicalization of Menopause." *Annals of the New York Academy of Sciences* 592: 173–178.

Berger, John. 1977. *Ways of Seeing.* New York: Penguin.

Bergvall, Victoria L. 1996. "Constructing and Enacting Gender through Discourse: Negotiating Roles as Female Engineering Students." Pp. 173–201 in *Rethinking Language and Gender Research: Theory and Practice*, edited by Victoria L. Bergvall, Janet M. Bing, and Alice F. Freed. London: Addison Wesley Longman Limited.

Berridge, Virginia. 1999. *Opium and the People: Opiate Use and Drug Control in Nineteenth and Early Twentieth Century England.* London: Free Association Books.

Binney, Elizabeth A., Carroll Estes, and Stanley R. Ingman. 1990. "Medicalization, Public Policy and the Elderly: Social Services in Jeopardy?" *Social Science and Medicine* 30(7): 761–771.

Blackwell, Marilyn S. 1999. "The Deserving Sick: Poor Women and the Medicalization of Poverty in Brattleboro, Vermont." *Journal of Women's History* 11(1): 53–74. Bloomington, IN: Indiana University Press.

Bokhari, Farasat, Rick Mayes, and Richard M. Scheffler. 2004. "An Analysis of the Significant Variation in Psychostimulant Use across the USA." *Pharmacoepidemiology and Drug Safety.* www.interscience.wiley.com.

Bordo, Susan. 1993. *Unbearable Weight: Feminism, Western Culture and the Body.* Berkeley: University of California Press.

Bordo, Susan. 2000. *The Male Body: A New Look at Men in Public and Private.* New York: Farrar, Straus and Giroux.

Boston Women's Health Collective. 1973. *Our Bodies, Ourselves: A Book by and for Women.* New York: Simon and Schuster.

Bouhanna, P., and J. C. Dardour. 2000. *Hair Replacement Surgery: Textbook and Atlas.* New York: Springer.

Brandt, Allan. 1997. "Racism and Research: The Case of the Tuskegee Syphilis Study." Pp. 312–404 in *Sickness and Health in America,* edited by J. Leavitt and R. L. Numbers. Madison, WI: University of Wisconsin Press.

Breggin, Peter R. 2001. *Talking Back to Ritalin.* Cambridge: Perseus Publishers.

Briggs, Laura. 2000. "The Race of Hysteria: 'Overcivilization' and the 'Savage' Woman in Late Nineteenth Century Obstetrics and Gynecology." *American Quarterly* 52: 246–273.

British Medical Association. 1995. *Report of the BMA Working Party on Medical Education 1995.* London: BMA.

British Medical Association. 1991. *Report of the Medical Academic Staff Working Party on the Undergraduate Curriculum.* London: BMA.

Broverman, Inge K., Donald M. Broverman, Frank E. Clarkson, Paul S. Rosenkrantz, and Susan R. Vogel. 1981. "Sex Role Stereotypes and Clinical Judgments of Mental Health." Pp. 86–97 in *Women and Mental Health,* edited by Elizabeth Howell and Marjorie Bayes. New York: Basic Books.

Brumberg, Joan Jacobs. 2001. "Anorexia Nervosa in Context." Pp. 94–108 in *The Sociology of Health and Illness: Critical Perspectives,* 6th ed., edited by P. Conrad. New York: Worth Publishers.

Bullough, Vern. 1987. "Technology for the Prevention of 'les maladies produites par la masturbation.'" *Technology and Culture* 28(4): 828–832.

Busfield, Joan. 1996. *Men, Women, and Madness: Understanding Mental Disorder.* New York: New York University Press.

Butler, Judith. 1993. *Bodies that Matter.* London: Routledge.

Cameron, Elaine, and Jon Bernardes. 1998. "Gender and Disadvantage in Health: Men's Health for a Change." *Sociology of Health and Illness* 20: 673–693.

Cancian, Francesca M. 1986. "The Feminization of Love." *Signs* 11(4): 692–709.

Caplan, Arthur. 1992. "When Evil Intrudes." *Hastings Center Report* 22(6): 29–32.

Capra, Fritjof. 1983. *The Turning Point: Science, Society and the Rising Culture.* London: Flamingo.

Carey, Allison C. 1998. "Gender and Compulsory Sterilization Programs in America: 1907–1950." *Journal of Historical Sociology* 11: 74–105.

Carlson, Caryn, Leann Tamm, and Miranda Gaub. 1997. "Gender Differences in Children with ADHD, ODD, and Co-occurring ADHD/ODD Identified in a School Population." *Journal of the American Academy of Child and Adolescent Psychiatry* 36(12): 1706–1714.

Carpiano, Richard M. 2001. "Passive Medicalization: The Case of Viagra and Erectile Dysfunction." *Sociological Spectrum* 21: 441–450.

Carrigan, Tim, Bob Connell, and John Lee. 1985. "Towards a New Sociology of Masculinity." *Theory and Society* 14(5): 551–604.

Carter, Bill. August 11, 2003. "From Creator of 'C.S.I.,' Testimonials to Himself." *New York Times.*

CBSNEWS.com. 2004. "Hard Science: Rx for Sex." Accessed January 22. (http://cbsnews.com/stories/2004/01/19/48hours/main).

Channel 4. 2001. "The Anatomists." http://www.channel4.com/science/microsites/A/anatomists/index.html (accessed 22 July 2005).

Chappell, Nina L. 1999. "Director's Perspective: Revisiting the Medicalization of Community Care." *University of Victoria Centre on Aging Bulletin* 7: 1–3.

Charmaz, Kathy. 1995. "Identity Dilemmas of Chronically Ill Men." Pp. 266–291 in *Men's Health and Illness: Gender, Power, and the Body,* edited by D. Sabo and D. F. Gordon. Thousand Oaks, CA: Sage Publications.

Chauncey, George. 1994. *Gay New York: Gender, Urban Culture, and the Making of the Gay Male World, 1890–1940.* New York: Basic Books.

Chen, Anthony S. 1999. "Lives at the Center of the Periphery, Lives at the Periphery of the Center: Chinese American Masculinities and Bargaining with Hegemony." *Gender & Society* 13(4): 584–607.

Cheng, Cliff. 1999. "Marginalized Masculinities and Hegemonic Masculinity: An Introduction." *The Journal of Men's Studies* 7: 295–315.

Chisum, W. Jerry, and Brent E. Turvey. 2000. "Evidence Dynamics: Locard's Exchange Principle & Crime Reconstruction." *Journal of Behavioral Profiling* 1(1). http://www.profiling.org/journal (accessed May 13, 2003).

Chodorow, Nancy. 1978. *The Reproduction of Mothering: Psychoanalysis and the Sociology of Gender.* Berkeley: University of California Press.

Clarke, Adele, and Joan Fujimura, eds. 1992. *The Right Tools for the Job: At Work in Twentieth Century Life Sciences.* Princeton: Princeton University Press.

Clarke, Adele E., Janet K. Shim, Laura Fosket Mamo, and Jennifer Ruth Fishman. 2003. "Biomedicalization: Technoscientific Transformations of Health, Illness, and U.S. Biomedicine." *American Sociological Review* 68(2): 161–194.

Clarke, Adele E. 1991. "Social Worlds Theory as Organization Theory." Pp. 119–158 in *Social Organization and Social Process: Essays in Honor of Anselm Strauss,* edited by David Maines. Hawthorne, NY: Aldine de Gruyter.

Clarke, Julie. 2000. "The Sacrificial Body of Orlan." Pp. 185–207 in *Body Modification,* edited by M. Featherstone. London: Sage Publications.

Clatterbaugh, Kenneth. 1998. "What is Problematic about Masculinities?" *Men and Masculinities* 1(1): 24–45.

Coates, Jennifer. 1997. "One-at-a-time: The Organization of Men's Talk." Pp. 107–129 in *Language and Masculinity*, edited by Sally Johnson and Ulrike Hanna Meinhof. Cambridge, MA: Blackwell Publishers, Inc.

Coates, Jennifer. 2003. *Men Talk*. Malden, MA: Blackwell Publishing, Ltd.

Cohen, Theodore F. 1995. "Men's Families, Men's Friends: A Structural Analysis of Constraints on Men's Social Ties." Pp. 115–131 in *Men's Friendships*, edited by Peter M. Nardi. Newbury Park, CA: Sage Publications.

Collins, Patricia Hill. 1990. *Black Feminist Thought*. New York: Routledge Press.

Collins, Randall. 1979. *The Credential Society: An Historical Sociology of Education and Stratification*. New York: Academic Press.

Connell, Robert W. 1995. *Masculinities*. Berkeley: University of California Press.

Connell, Robert W. 1987. *Gender and Power: Society, the Person, and Sexual Politics*. Stanford, CA: Stanford University Press.

Connell, Robert W. 1992. "A Very Straight Gay: Masculinity, Homosexual Experience, and the Dynamics of Gender." *American Sociological Review* 57: 735–751.

Connell, Robert W. 1995. *Masculinities*. Berkeley: University of California Press.

Connell, Robert W. 1996. "Teaching the Boys: New Research on Masculinity, and Gender Strategies for Schools." *Teachers College Record* 98(2): 206–235.

Connell, Robert W. 2000. *The Men and the Boys*. Berkeley: University of California Press.

Conrad, Peter. 1975. "The Discovery of Hyperkenesis: Notes on the Discovery of Deviant Behavior." *Social Problems* 23: 12–21.

Conrad, Peter. 1976. *Identifying Hyperactive Children: The Medicalization of Deviant Behavior*. Lexington, MA: Lexington Books.

Conrad, Peter. 1979. "Types of Medical Social Control." *Sociology of Health and Illness* 1(1): 1–11.

Conrad, Peter. 1992. "Medicalization and Social Control." *Annual Review of Sociology* 18: 209–232.

Conrad, Peter. 1996. "Medicalization and Social Control." Pp. 137–162 in *Perspectives in Medical Sociology*, edited by P. Brown. Prospect Heights, IL: Waveland Press.

Conrad, Peter. 2000. "Medicalization, Genetics, and Human Problems." Pp. 322–333 in *Handbook of Medical Sociology*, 5th ed., edited by C. Bird, P. Conrad, and A. M. Fremont. New York: Prentice Hall.

Conrad, Peter, and Allison Angell. 2004. "Homosexuality and Remedicalization." *Society* 41(5): 32–39.

Conrad, Peter, and Valerie Leiter. 2004. "Medicalization, Markets and Consumers." *Journal of Health and Social Behavior* 45(extra issue): 158–176.

Conrad, Peter, and Deborah Potter. 2000. "From Hyperactive Children to ADHD Adults: Observations on the Expansion of Medical Categories." *Social Problems* 47(4): 559–582.

Conrad, Peter, and Schneider, Joseph. 1980. *Deviance and Medicalization: From Badness to Sickness*. London: Mosby.

Conrad, Peter, and Joseph W. Schneider. 1992. *Deviance and Medicalization: From Badness to Sickness*. Philadelphia: Temple University Press.

Cooper, Wendy. 1971. *Hair: Sex, Society, Symbolism*. New York: Stein and Day.

Courtenay, Will H. 2000. "Constructions of Masculinity and Their Influence on Men's Well-Being." *Social Science and Medicine* 50: 1385–1401.

Courtwright, David T. 1982. *Dark Paradise: Opiate Addiction in America before 1940*. Cambridge: Harvard University Press.

Crawford, Robert. 1985. "A Cultural Account of 'Health': Control, Release, and the Social Body." Pp. 60–106 in *Issues in the Political Economy of Health*, edited by J. B. McKinlay. New York: Methuen-Tavistock.

Curtis, Neal. 2000. "The Body as Outlaw: Lyotard, Kafka and the Visible Human Project." Pp. 249–266 in *Body Modification*, edited by M. Featherstone. London: Sage Publications.

Daemmrich, Arthur. 1998. "The Evidence Does Not Speak for Itself: Expert Witnesses and the Organization of DNA—Typing Companies." *Social Studies of Science*. 28(5–6), 741–772.

Dangerfield, Peter H., John Bligh, Sam Leinster, and R. Griffiths. 1996. 'Curriculum reform in Britain and its effects on Anatomy.' *Clinical Anatomy*, 6: 418(abstract).

David, Deborah, and Robert Brannon. 1976. *The Forty-Nine Percent Majority*. Reading, MA: Addison-Wesley.

Davis, Angela. 1981. *Women, Race & Class*. New York: Vintage.

Davis, Kathy. 1995. *Reshaping the Female Body: The Dilemma of Cosmetic Surgery*. New York: Routledge.

Dawber, Rodney, and Dominique Van Neste, eds. 1995. *Hair and Scalp Disorders: Common Presenting Signs, Differential Diagnosis and Treatment*. London: Martin Dunitz.

de Bruxelles, Simon. September 30, 2002. "Medical School Consigns Cadavers to History." *The Times*.

DeFrancisco, Victoria Leto. 1998. "The Sounds of Silence: How Men Silence Women in Marital Relations." Pp. 176–184 in *Language and Gender: A Reader*, edited by Jennifer Coates. Malden, MA: Blackwell Publishers, Inc.

DeLauretis, Teresa. 1987. *Technologies of Gender*. Indiana: Indiana University Press.

Demetrious, Demetrakis Z. 2001. "Connell's Concept of Hegemonic Masculinity: A Critique." *Theory and Society* 30: 327–361.

D'Emilio, John, and Estelle Freedman. 1998. *Intimate Matters: A History of Sexuality in America*. Chicago: University of Chicago Press.

Dennis, Rutledge. 1995. "Social Darwinism, Scientific Racism, and the Metaphysics of Race." *The Journal of Negro Education* 64(3): 243–252.

Department of Health. 1989. *France Report: Undergraduate Medical and Dental Education 1st Report 1989*. London: HMSO.

Diller, Laurence H. 1998. *Running on Ritalin*. New York: Bantam.

Doctor's Guide Global Edition. 2000. "FDA Approves Prescription Androgel for Low Testosterone." Buffalo Grove, IL: Doctor's Guide Publishing. http://www.pslgroup.com/dg/1780fa.htm (accessed June 14, 2004).

Donaldson, Mike. 1993. "What is Hegemonic Masculinity?" *Theory and Society* 22: 643–657.

Donzelot, Jacques. 1979. *The Policing of Families.* New York: Pantheon Books.

Doonar, Joanna. 2003. "Viagra Faces Stiff Competition." *Brand Strategy,* August 11. (accessed September 24, 2003, Available: LEXIS-NEXIS).

Dore, Ron. 1976. *The Diploma Disease.* London: Allen and Unwin.

Douglas, Mary. 1966. *Purity and Danger: An Analysis of the Concepts of Pollution and Taboo.* New York: Routledge.

Dubos, Rene. 1959. *Mirage of Health: Utopias, Progress, and Biological Change.* New Brunswick, NJ: Rutgers University Press.

Dumm, Thomas. 1999. "Leaky Sovereignty: Clinton's Impeachment and the Crisis of Infantile Republicanism." *Theory and Event* 2(4).

DuPaul, George, Thomas Power, Arthur Anastopoulos, Robert Reid, Kara McGoey, and Martin Ikeda. 1997. "Teacher Ratings of Attention Deficit Hyperactivity Disorder Symptoms: Factor Structure and Normative Data." *Psychological Assessment* 9: 436–444.

Durkheim, Emile. 1938. *The Rules of Sociological Method.* London: Collier Macmillan.

Durkheim, Emile. 1960 [1912]. *The Elementary Forms of Religious Life.* London: Allen and Unwin.

Duster, Troy. 2003. *Backdoor to Eugenics.* New York: Routledge.

Dyer, George S. M., and Mary E. L. Thorndike. 2000. "Quidne Mortui Vivos Docent? The Evolving Purpose of Human Dissection in Medical Education." *Academic Medicine* 75(10): 969–979.

Eagan, Margery. 2002. "Sex Enhancers' Competition Gives Rise to Ridicule." *Boston Herald,* May 30. (accessed November 6, 2003, Available: LEXIS-NEXIS).

Ehrenreich, Barbara, Gloria Jacobs, and Elizabeth Hess. 1986. *Re-Making Love: The Feminization of Sex.* New York: Doubleday.

Ehrenreich, Barbara. 1983. "Reasons of the Heart: Cardiology Rewrites the Masculine Script." Pp. 68–87 in *The Hearts of Men: American Dreams and the Flight from Commitment.* Garden City, NY: Anchor Books.

Ehrenreich, Barbara, and Deirdre English. 1973. *Complaints and Disorders: The Sexual Politics of Sickness.* Old Westbury, NY: The Feminist Press.

Ehrenreich, Barbara, and Deirdre English. 1974. *Witches, Midwives and Nurses: A History of Women Healers.* Old Westbury, NY: The Feminist Press.

Ehrenreich, Barbara, and Deirdre English. 1978. *For Her Own Good: 150 Years of the Experts' Advice to Women.* Garden City, NY: Anchor Books.

Eisenhart, Carl E., and Daniel J. Silversmith. 1994. "The Influence of the Traditional Male Role on Alcohol Abuse and the Therapeutic Process." *The Journal of Men's Studies* 3: 127–135.

Elias, Norbert. 1978 [1939]. *The Civilizing Process: Vol. I: The History of Manners.* Oxford, UK: Basil Blackwell.

Elias, Norbert. 1982 [1939]. *The Civilizing Process: Vol. II: State Formations and Civilization.* Oxford, UK: Basil Blackwell.

Elliot, Carl. 2003. *Better than Well: American Medicine Meets the American Dream.* New York: Norton.

Engelhardt, H. Tristin. 1974. "The Disease of Masturbation: Values and the Concept of Disease." *Bulletin of the History of Medicine* 48: 234–248.

Engels, Frederich. 1987 [1845]. *The Conditions of the Working Class in England.* Harmondsworth, UK: Penguin.

Epstein, Stephen. 1988. "Moral Contagion and the Medicalization of Gay Identity: AIDS in Historical Perspective." *Research in Law, Deviance and Social Control* 9: 3–36.

Epstein, Stephen. 2003. "Sexualizing Governance and Medicalizing Identities: The Emergence of 'State-centered' LGBT Health Politics in the United States." *Sexualities* 6(2): 131–171.

Erchak, Gerald M., and Richard Rosenfeld. 1989. "Learning Disabilities, Dyslexia, and the Medicalization of the Classroom." Pp. 79–97 in *Images of Issues*, edited by J. Best. New York: Aldine de Gruyter.

Ernst, Waltraud. 1999. "Historical and Contemporary Perspectives on Race, Science and Medicine." Pp. 1–28 in *Race, Science and Medicine, 1700–1960*, edited by W. Ernst and B. Harris. New York: Routledge.

Estes, Caroll L., and Elizabeth A. Binney. 1989. "The Biomedicalisation of Aging: Dangers and Dilemmas." *The Gerontologist* 29: 587–596.

Etzioni, Amitai. 2000. "The Toughest Pill to Swallow." *The Responsive Community* 10(4): 8–10.

Faircloth, Christopher A. 2003. *Aging Bodies: Images and Everyday Experience.* Walnut Creek, CA: AltaMira Press.

Falk, Pasi. 1994. *The Consuming Body.* London: Sage Publications.

Farmer, Paul. 1988. "Bad Blood, Spoiled Milk: Bodily Fluids as Moral Barometers in Rural Haiti." *American Ethnologist* 15(1): 62–83.

Farnell, Ross. 1999. "In Dialogue with 'Posthuman' Bodies: Interview with Stelarc." Pp. 129–147 in *Body Modification,* edited by M. Featherstone. London: Sage Publications.

Farrell, Warren. 1975. *The Liberated Man.* New York: Random House.

Fasteau, Marc F. 1974. *The Male Machine.* New York: McGraw-Hill.

Fasteau, Marc Feigen. 1975. *The Male Machine.* New York: Dell.

Featherstone, Mike. 1991. *Consumer Culture and Postmodernism.* London: Sage Publications.

Figert, Anne E. 1995. "The Three Faces of PMS: The Professional, Gendered, and Scientific Structuring of a Psychiatric Disorder." *Social Problems* 42: 56–73.

Fine, Michelle, Lois Weis, Judi Addleston, and Julia Marusza. 1997. "(In) Secure Times: Constructing White Working-class Masculinities in the Late-20th Century." *Gender & Society* 11(1): 52–68.

Finkler, Kaja. 2000. *Experiencing the New Genetics: Family and Kinship on the Medical Frontier.* Philadelphia: University of Pennsylvania Press.

Finkler, Kaja. 2001. "The Kin in the Gene: The Medicalization of Family and Kinship in American Society." *Current Anthropology* 42(2): 235–263.

Finkler, Kaja, Cecile Skrzynia, and James P. Evans. 2003. "The New Genetics and its Consequences for Family, Kinship, Medicine and the Medical Genetics." *Social Science and Medicine* 57(3): 403–412.

Fischer, David. 1997. "The Bald Truth: Americans Turn to Weaves, Rugs, Plugs, and Drugs to Alleviate Hair Loss." *U.S. News & World Report* (August 4), 44.

Fishman, Pamela M. 1983. "Interaction: The Work Women Do." Pp. 89–102 in *Language, Gender and Society,* edited by Barrie Thorne, Cheris Kramarae, and Nancy Henley. Rowley, MA: Newbury House Publisher, Inc.

Florence, A. (1895). Translation of: "Du Sperme et des Taches de Sperme en Medecine Legale." In Archives d'Anthropologie Criminelle de Criminologie et de Psychologie Normale et Pathologique 10: 417–434. (1st part); 11: 37–46 and 146–165 and 249–265 (2nd part) (1896).

Foley, Douglas E. 1990. *Learning Capitalist Culture: Deep in the Heart of Tejas.* Philadelphia: University of Pennsylvania Press.

Foley, Stephen. 2002. "GlaxoSmithKline Looks to Bayer for Tonic to Pep up its Struggling Drugs Pipeline." *The Independent* (London), November 19. (accessed November 2, 2003, Available: LEXIS-NEXIS).

Forrester, David A. 1986. "Myths of Masculinity: Impact Upon Men's Health." *Nursing Clinics of North America* 21: 15–23.

Foucault, Michel. 1973. *The Birth of the Clinic, An Archaeology of Medical Perception.* New York: Vintage.

Foucault, Michel. 1977. *Discipline and Punish: The Birth of the Prison.* London: Tavistock.

Foucault, Michel. 1978. *The History of Sexuality, an Introduction.* New York: Random House.

Foucault, Michel. 1988. "Technologies of the Self." Pp. 16–49 in *Technologies of the Self: A Seminar with Michel Foucault,* edited by P. C. Hutton. London: Tavistock.

Foucault, Michel. 1990. *The History of Sexuality, an Introduction,* 2nd ed. New York: Vintage Books.

Foucault, Michel. 1995. *Discipline and Punish, The Birth of the Prison,* 2nd ed. New York: Vintage Books.

Fox, Bonnie, and Diana Worts. 1999. "Revisiting the Critique of Medicalized Childbirth: A Contribution to the Sociology of Birth." *Gender & Society* 13(3): 326–346.

Fox, Renee. 1979. *Essays in Medical Sociology.* New York: Wiley Press.

Fracher, Jeffery, and Michael Kimmel. 1995. "Hard Issues and Soft Spots: Counseling Men about Sexuality." In *Men's Lives,* edited by M. Kimmel and M. Messner. Boston: Allyn & Bacon.

Franklin, Sarah, and Ragone, Helena. 1998. *Reproducing Reproduction: Kinship, Power, and Technological Innovation.* Philadelphia: University of Pennsylvania Press.

Freiden, Betina. 2003. "The Dead Body and Organ Transplantation." Pp. 55–76 in *Aging Bodies: Images and Everyday Experience,* edited by C. Faircloth. Walnut Creek, CA: Alta Mira.

Freidson, Elliot. 1970. *Profession of Medicine.* New York: Dodd, Mead.

Friedan, Betty. 1993. "The New Menopause Brouhaha." Pp. 472–499 in *The Fountain of Age.* New York: Simon and Schuster.

Friedman, David. 2001. *A Mind of Its Own: A Cultural History of the Penis.* New York: The Free Press.

Fuhrmans, Vanessa. 2003. "The First Drugs to Challenge Viagra are Expected on U.S. Store Shelves Later This Year." *Chicago Sun-Times,* March 30. (accessed September 18, 2003, Available: LEXIS-NEXIS).

Gaensslen, Robert E. 1983. *Sourcebook in Forensic Serology, Immunology, and Biochemistry.* Washington, DC: National Institute of Justice.

Gagnon, John. 1977. *Human Sexualities.* Glenview, IL: Scott Foresman.

Gaia, A. Celeste. 2002. "Understanding Emotional Intimacy: A Review of Conceptualization, Assessment and the Role of Gender." *International Social Science Review* 77(3–4): 151–170.

Gamble, Vanessa N. 2000. "Under the Shadow of Tuskegee: African Americans and Health Care." Pp. 431–442 in *Tuskegee's Truths: Rethinking the Tuskegee Syphilis Study,* edited by S. Reverby. Chapel Hill: University of North Carolina Press.

Gannon, Joyce. 2003. "Viagra's Success Brings Competition from Two Rivals; 'Little Blue Pill' Built a $2.5 Billion Market." *Pittsburgh Post-Gazette,* May 2. (accessed November 11, 2003, Available: LEXIS-NEXIS).

Gatens, Moira. 1996. *Imaginary Bodies: Ethics, Power and Corporeality.* New York: Routledge.

Gaub, Miranda, and Caryn Carlson. 1997. "Behavioral Characteristics of *DSM-IV* ADHD Subtypes: Comparisons of Teacher Identified Children in a School-Based Population." *Journal of Abnormal Child Psychology* 25: 102–111.

General Medical Council. 1993. *Tomorrow's Doctors.* Report of the Education Committee. London: GMC.

Gerschick, Thomas J. 2000. "Toward a Theory of Disability and Gender." *Signs* 25(4): 1263–1268.

Gerschick, Thomas J., and Adam Stephen Miller. 2004. "Coming to Terms: Masculinity and Physical Disability." Pp. 349–362 in *Men's Lives,* edited by M. Kimmel and M. Messner. Boston: Pearson Education, Inc.

Giacomini, Mita, Patricia Rozée-Koker, and Fran Pepitone-Arreola-Rockwell. 1986. "Gender Bias in Human Anatomy Textbook Illustrations." *Psychology of Women Quarterly* 10: 413–420.

Giddens, Anthony. (1991). *Modernity and Self-Identity: Self and Society in the Late Modern Age.* Cambridge: Polity Press.

Gilbert, Rob, and Pam Gilbert. 1998. *Masculinity Goes to School.* New York: Routledge.

Gilman, Sander L. 2001. *Making the Body Beautiful: A Cultural History of Aesthetic Surgery.* Princeton: Princeton University Press.

Glaser, Barney, and Anselm Strauss. 1967. *Discovery of Grounded Theory: Strategies for Qualitative Research.* New York: de Gruyter.

Goffman, Erving. 1959. *The Presentation of Self in Everyday Life.* Garden City, NY: Doubleday Anchor.

Goffman, Erving. 1963a. *Stigma: Notes on the Management of Spoiled Identity.* Englewood Cliffs, NJ: Prentice-Hall.

Goffman, Erving. 1963b. *Behavior in Public Places: Notes on the Social Organization of Gatherings.* Glencoe: The Free Press.

Goffman, Erving. 1967. *Interaction Ritual: Essays on Face-to-Face Behavior.* New York: Doubleday Anchor.

Gold, Judith M. 1998. "Gender Differences in Psychiatric Illness and Treatments: A Critical Review." *The Journal of Nervous and Mental Disease* 186: 769–775.

Goldberg, Carey. 2003. "First of Two Viagra Rivals OK'd for Sale." *Boston Globe,* April 21. (accessed November 11, 2003, Available: LEXIS-NEXIS).

Goldman, Larry, Myron Genel, Rebecca Bezman, and Priscilla Slanetz. 1998. "Diagnosis and Treatment of Attention-Deficit/Hyperactivity Disorder in Children and Adolescents." *Journal of the American Medical Association* 279(14): 1100–1107.

Gooren, Louis. 2003. "Androgen Deficiency in the Aging Male: Benefits and Risks of Androgen Supplementation." *Journal of Steroid Biochemistry and Molecular Biology* 85: 349–355.

Gray, Fred. 1995. *Bus Ride to Justice.* Montgomery: Black Belt Press.

Gray, Fred. 1998. *The Tuskegee Syphilis Study.* Montgomery: Black Belt Press.

Greater London Authority. 2004. *Alison Lapper Pregnant and Hotel for the Birds Selected for 4th Plinth.* Press Release. March 15.

Gregory, S. Ryan, and Thomas R. Cole. 2002. "The Changing Role of Dissection in Medical Education." *MSJAMA,* 287: 1180–1181.

Groneman, Carol. 1994. "Nymphomania: The Historical Construction of Female Sexuality." *Signs: Journal of Women in Culture and Society* 19(2): 337–367.

Groopman, Jerome. July 29, 2002. "Hormones for Men." *The New Yorker Magazine.*

Grosz, Elizabeth. 1995. *Space, Time, and Perversion: Essays on the Politics of Bodies.* New York: Routledge.

Grove, Stephen, Mary Lafarge, Patricia Knowles, and Richard Dodder. 1989. "Sport as an Advertising Theme to Target Collegians: A Cross-Cultural Explanation." *Journal of International Consumer Marketing* 2(2): 61–74.

Grubb, Andrew. 1990. "Abortion Law in England: The Medicalization of a Crime." *Law, Medicine and Health Care* 18(1–2): 146–161.

Gubrium, Jaber F, and James Holstein. 2003. "The Everyday Visibility of the Aging Body. Pp. 205–227 in *Aging Bodies: Meanings and Perspectives,* edited by C. Faircloth. Walnut Creek, CA: Alta Mira Press.

Gullette, Margaret Morganroth. 1997. "All Together Now: The New Sexual Politics of Midlife Bodies." Pp. 221–247 in *The Male Body: Features, Destinies, Exposures*, edited by L. Goldstein. Ann Arbor, MI: University of Michigan Press.

Hacker, Andrew. 1995. *Two Nations: Black and White, Separate, Hostile, Unequal.* New York: Ballantine.

Halfon, Saul. 1998. "Collecting, Testing and Convincing: Forensic DNA Experts in Courts." *Social Studies of Science* 28(5–6): 801–828.

Hall, Kira. 1995. "Lip Service on the Fantasy Line." Pp. 183–216 in *Gender Articulated: Language and the Socially Constructed Self*, edited by Kira Hall and Mary Bucholtz. New York: Routledge.

Hall, Lesley. 1991. *Hidden Anxieties: Male Sexuality, 1900–1950.* Cambridge: Polity Press.

Halliwell, Emma, and Helga Dittmar. 2003. "A Qualitative Investigation of Women's and Men's Body Image Concerns and their Attitudes Toward Aging." *Sex Roles* 49: 675–684.

Halpern, S. A. (1990). "Medicalization as Professional Process: Postwar Trends in Paediatrics." *Journal of Health and Social Behavior* 31(1): 28–42.

Halwell, Brian. 1999. "Sperm Counts are Dropping." *World Watch* 12(2): 32–33.

Hammar, Lawrence. 1997. "The Dark Side of Donovanosis: Color, Climate, Race and Racism in American South Venereology." *The Journal of Medical Humanities* 18(1): 29–57.

Hansen, Bert. 1997. "American Physicians' 'Discovery' of Homosexuals, 1880–1900: A New Diagnosis in a Changing Society." Pp. 13–31 in *Sickness and Health in America: Readings in the History of Medicine and Public Health* (3rd ed), edited by J. W. Leavitt and R. Numbers. Madison, WI: University of Wisconsin Press.

Haraway, Donna. 1991. *Simians, Cyborgs, and Women: The Reinvention of Nature.* New York: Routledge.

Haraway, Donna. 1999. "The Virtual Speculum in the New World Order." Pp. 49–96 in *Revisioning Women, Health and Healing: Feminist, Cultural, and Technoscience Perspectives*, edited by Adele E. Clarke and Virginia L. Olesen. New York: Routledge.

Harris, Gardiner. 2003a. "After 5 Years, Rivals Emerge Ready to Give Viagra a Fight." *New York Times*, April 21. (accessed September, 26 2003, Available: LEXIS-NEXIS).

Harris, Gardiner. 2003b. "Levitra, a Rival with Ribald Ads, Gains on Viagra." *New York Times*, September 18. (accessed September, 26 2003, Available: LEXIS-NEXIS).

Harris, Robbie. 1999. *It's So Amazing: A Book about Eggs, Sperm, Birth, Babies and Families.* Cambridge, MA: Candlewick Press.

Harrison, James, James Chin, and Thomas Ficarrotto. 1989. "Warning: Masculinity May be Dangerous to Your Health." Pp. 246–309 in *Men's Lives*, edited by Michael S. Kimmel and Michael A. Messner. New York: Macmillan Publishing Co.

Harrison, James, James Chin, and Thomas Ficarrotto. 1992. "Warning: Masculinity may be Dangerous to your Health." Pp. 271–285 in *Men's Lives,* edited by M. Kimmel and M. Messner. New York: MacMillan Publishing Co.

Hartley, H. 2003. "'Big Pharma' in our Bedrooms: An Analysis of the Medicalization of Women's Sexual Problems." Pp. 89–129 in *Gender Perspectives on Health and Medicine: Key Themes. Advances in Gender Research* 7(1–9), edited by M. S. Segal and V. Demos. Oxford, UK: Elsevier Press.

Hausman, Bernice. 1995. *Changing Sex: Transsexualism, Technology, and the Idea of Gender.* Durham, NC: Duke University Press.

Hayes, James. 1973. "Sociology and Racism: An Analysis of the First Era of American Sociology." *Phylon* 34(4): 330–341.

Hearn, Jeff. 2004. "From Hegemonic Masculinity to the Hegemony of Men." *Feminist Theory* 5(1): 97–120.

Heartfield, James. 2002. "There is no Masculinity Crisis." *Genders* 35. http://www.genders.org/g35/g35_heartfield.html.

Heaton, Jeremy. 2003. "The Impact of Viagra over 5 Years: Why is it a Worldwide Phenomenon?" 2nd International Consultation on Erectile and Sexual Dysfunctions, Paris.

Helgeson, Vicki S. 1995. "Masculinity, Men's Roles, and Coronary Heart Disease." Pp. 68–104 in *Men's Health and Illness: Gender, Power, and the Body,* edited by D. Sabo and D. F. Gordon. Thousand Oaks, CA: Sage Publications.

Hempel, Carlene. September 2, 2003. "TV's Whodunit Effect..." *Boston Globe Magazine.*

Hepworth, Michael, and Mike Featherstone. 1998. "The Male Menopause: Lay Accounts and the Cultural Reconstruction of Midlife." Pp. 276–301 in *The Body in Everyday Life,* edited by S. Nettleton and J. Watson. London: Routledge.

Hislop, Jenny, and Sara Arber. 2003. "Understanding Women's Sleep Management: Beyond Medicalisation-Healthicisation." *Sociology of Health and Illness* 25(7): 815–837.

Hochschild, Arlie. 1983. *The Managed Heart: Commercialization of Human Feeling.* Berkeley: University of California Press.

Hodes, Martha. 1993. "The Sexualization of Reconstruction Politics: White Women and Black Men in the South after the Civil War." *Journal of the History of Sexuality* 3(3): 402–417.

Hoff Sommers, Christina. 2000. *The War Against Boys: How Misguided Feminism is Harming our Young Men.* New York: Simon and Schuster.

Holmes, Janet. 1997. "Story-telling in New Zealand Women's and Men's Talk." Pp. 263–93 in *Gender and Discourse,* edited by Ruth Wodak. London: Sage Publications.

Horvitz, Leslie. 1997. "Can Better Sex Come in a Pill? The Nineties Impotence Cure?" *Insight on the News,* December 15. (accessed September 26, 2003, Available: LEXIS-NEXIS).

Howard, Theresa. 2003. "Expect an Ad-stravaganza as Viagra Gets Competition." *USA Today,* August 25, www.cialis.com (accessed November 11, 2003, Available: LEXIS-NEXIS).

Hume, Mike. 2003. "Whatever Happened to RIP? This Unhealthy Obsession with Peering into Morgues." *The Times Online*, June 4. http://www.spiked-online.com/Articles/00000006DDD5htm.

Institute of Medicine. 2004. *Testosterone and Aging: Clinical Research Directions.* Washington, DC: The National Academies Press.

Irvine, Janice. 1990. *Disorders of Desire: Sex and Gender in Modern American Sexology.* Philadelphia: Temple University Press.

Jackson, Stevi, and Sue Scott. 2001. "Putting the Body's Feet on the Ground: Towards a Sociological Reconceptualization of Gendered and Sexual Embodiment." Pp. 7–24 in *Constructing Gendered Bodies*, edited by K. Backett-Milburn and L. McKie. London: Palgrave.

Jacobson, Nora. 2000. *Cleavage: Technology, Controversy and the Ironies of the Man-Made Breast.* New Brunswick, NJ: Rutgers University Press.

Jasanoff, Sheila. 1995. *Science at the Bar: Law, Science and Technology in America.* Cambridge: Harvard University Press.

Jeffords, Susan. 1989. *The Remasculinization of America: Gender and the Vietnam War.* Bloomington, IN: Indiana University Press.

Jeffreys, Alec J. 1993. "1992 William Allan Award Address." *American Journal of Human Genetics* 53(1).

Johnstone, Barbara. 1993. "Community and Contest: Midwestern Men and Women Creating their World in Conversational Storytelling." Pp. 62–80 in *Gender and Conversational Interaction*, edited by Deborah Tannen. New York: Oxford University Press.

Jones, James. 1993. *Bad Blood: The Tuskegee Syphilis Experiment.* New York: The Free Press.

Jones, James. 1996. "The Tuskegee Syphilis Experiment." Pp 386–398 in *Perspectives in Medical Sociology*, edited by P. Brown. New York: Waveland Press.

*Journal of the American Medical Association.* 1903. "Prophylaxis of Baldness." 40: 249.

Kanter, Rosabeth Moss. 1977. *Men and Women of the Corporation.* New York: Basic Books.

Karner, Tracy X. 1995. "Medicalizing Masculinity: Post Traumatic Stress Disorder in Vietnam Veterans." *Masculinities* 3: 23–65.

Katz, Jack, ed. 1988. "Ways of the Badass." Pp. 80–113 in *Seductions of Crime: Moral and Sensual Attractions in Doing Evil.* New York: Basic Books.

Katz, Jack, ed. 1988. "Of Hardmen and 'Bad Niggers': Gender and Ethnicity in the Background of Stickup." Pp. 237–273 in *Seductions of Crime: Moral and Sensual Attractions in Doing Evil.* New York: Basic Books.

Katz, Stephen, and Barbara Marshall. 2004. "New Sex for Old: Lifestyle, Consumerism, and the Ethics of Aging Well." *Journal of Aging Studies* 17: 3–16.

Kaufman, Michael. 1987. "The Construction of Masculinity and the Triad of Men's Violence." Pp. 1–29 in *Beyond Patriarchy*, edited by M. Kaufman. New York: Oxford University Press.

Kaw, Eugenia. 2003. "Medicalization of Racial Features: Asian-American Women and Cosmetic Surgery." Pp. 184–200 in *The Politics of Women's Bodies: Sexuality,*

*Appearance, and Behavior,* edited by R. Weitz. New York: Oxford University Press.

Kearns, Walter. 1939. "The Clinical Application of Testosterone." *Journal of the American Medical Association* 112: 2257.

Kempers, R. 1976. "The Tricentennial of the Discovery of Sperm." *Fertility and Sterility* 27(5): 630–705.

Kenway, Jane. 1996. "Reasserting Masculinity in Australian Schools." *Women's Studies International Forum* 19(4): 447–466.

Khan, Sajjad and Dow B. Stough. 1996. "Determination of Hairline Placement." Pp. 425–429 in *Hair Replacement: Surgical and Medical,* edited by Dow B. Stough and Robert S. Haber. St. Louis, MO: Mosby.

Kimmel, Michael. 1996. *Manhood in America: A Cultural History.* New York: The Free Press.

Kimmel, Michael, and Michael Messner. 1989. *Men's Lives.* Boston: Allyn and Bacon.

Kind, Stuart, and M. Overman. 1972. *Science Against Crime.* U.S.: Aldus Book Ltd. Doubleday.

King, Charles R. 1989. "Parallels Between Neurasthenia and Premenstrual Syndrome." *Women and Health* 15(4): 1–23.

King, Patricia A. 1992. "The Dangers of Difference." *Hastings Center Report* 22(6): 35–38.

King, Patricia A. 1998. "Race, Justice, and Research." Pp. 88–111 in *Beyond Consent,* edited by J. Kahn, A. Mastroianni, and J. Sugarman. New York: Oxford University Press.

Kinsey, Alfred. 1953. *Sexual Behavior in the Human Female.* New York: Simon and Schuster.

Kirk, Paul L. 1953. *Crime Investigation.* New York: Interscience Publishers, Inc.

Kivel, Paul. 1999. *Boys Will Be Men.* Gabriola Island, BC, Canada: New Society Publishers.

Kleinberg-Levin, David M. 1990. "The Discursive Formation of the Body in the History of Medicine." *Journal of Medicine and Philosophy* 15(5): 515–538.

Kluger, Jeffrey. October 12, 2002. "How Science Solves Crimes: From Ballistics to DNA, Forensic Scientists are Revolutionizing Police Work—on TV and in Reality. And Just in Time." *Time Magazine.*

Knorr-Cetina, Karin D., and Michael Mulkay, eds. 1983. *Science Observed: Perspectives on the Social Study of Science.* London: Sage Publications.

Kobus, Hilton J., E. Silenieks, and J. Scharnberg. 2002. "Improving the Effectiveness of Fluorescence for the Detection of Semen Stains." *Journal of Forensic Science* 47(4): 819–823.

Kolata, Gina. November 13, 2003. "Panel Recommends Studies on Testosterone Therapy." *New York Times,* Pg. A22.

Kozak, David. 1994. "Reifying the Body through the Medicalization of Violent Death." *Human Organization* 53(1): 48–54.

Krum, Sharon. 2001. "Private Investigations." *The Guardian.* November 15. Accessed September 26, 2003. (http://www.guardian.co.uk).

Lane, Megan. 2004. "The Modern-day Venus de Milo." *BBC News Online.* Wednesday March 17. http://news.bbc.co.uk/1/hi/magazine/3515560.stm.

Laqueur, Thomas W. 1990. *Making Sex: Body and Gender from the Greeks to Freud.* Cambridge, MA: Harvard University Press.

Larsen, Reed, and Joseph, Pleck. 1998. "Hidden Feelings: Emotionality in Boys and Men." In *Gender and Motivation,* edited by D. Bernstein, Volume 45 of the Nebraska Symposium on Motivation. Lincoln: University of Nebraska Press.

Lasch, Christopher. 1977. *Haven in a Heartless World: The Family Besieged.* New York: Basic Books.

Latour, Bruno. 1999. *Pandora's Hope: Essays on the Reality of Science Studies.* Cambridge, MA: Harvard University Press.

Latour, Bruno. 2000. "When Things Strike Back: A Possible Contribution of 'Science Studies' to the Social Sciences." *The British Journal of Sociology* 51(1): 107–123.

Lawrence, Susan C., and Kai Bendixen. 1992. "His and Hers: Male and Female Anatomy in Anatomy Texts for U.S. Medical Students, 1890–1989." *Social Science and Medicine* 35(7): 925–934.

Leavitt, Judith W. 1989. "The Medicalization of Childbirth in the Twentieth Century." *Transactions & Studies of the College of Physicians of Philadelphia* 5(11:4): 299–319.

Lederer, Susan E. 1995. *Subjected to Science.* Baltimore, MD: Johns Hopkins University Press.

Lee, Ellie. 2004. *Abortion, Motherhood, and Mental Health: Medicalizing Reproduction in the United States and Great Britain* (Social Problems and Social Issues). New York: Aldine de Gruyter.

LeFever, Gretchen, Keila Dawson and Ardythe Morrow. 1999. "The Extent of Drug Therapy for Attention Deficit-Hyperactivity Disorder Among Children in Public Schools." *American Journal of Public Health* 89(9): 1359–1364.

LeGrand, Julian. 1982. *The Strategy of Equality: Redistribution and the Social Services.* London: Taylor and Francis.

Levin, Lowell S., and Ellen L. Idler. 1981. *The Hidden Health Care System.* Cambridge, MA: Ballinger Publishing Co.

Levine, Jeff. 1997. "Sour Legacy of Tuskegee Syphilis Study Lingers." *CNN Online.* May 16, 1997. Accessed May 5, 2000, www.cnn.com.

Levine, Martin P. 1998. *Gay Macho: The Life and Death of the Homosexual Clone.* New York: New York University Press.

Lichtenstein, Bronwen. 2004. "Caught at the Clinic: African American Men, Stigma, and STI Treatment in the Deep South." *Gender & Society* 18(3): 369–388.

*Lifedrivemagazine.* 2002. "One Couple Looks Back at Facing Up to ED and Ahead," Lifedrivemagazine.com, accessed April 12, 2002.

Liptak, Adam. March 16, 2003. "The Nation; You Think DNA Evidence Is Foolproof? Try Again." *New York Times.*

Litt, Jacquelyn S. 2000. *Medicalized Motherhood: Perspectives from the Lives of African American and Jewish Women.* New Brunswick, NJ: Rutgers University Press.

Lloyd, Genevieve. 1984. *The Man of Reason: 'Male' and 'Female' in Western Philosophy.* London: Methuen.

Lock, Margaret. 1984. "Licorice in Leviathan: The Medicalization of the Care of the Japanese Elderly." *Culture, Medicine and Psychiatry* 8: 121–139.

Lock, Margaret. 1987. "Protests of a Good Wife and Wise Mother: The Medicalization of Distress in Japan." Pp. 130–157 in *Health, Illness and Medical Care in Japan,* edited by E. Norbeck and M. Lock. Honolulu: University of Hawaii Press.

Lock, Margaret. 1993. *Encounters with Aging: Mythologies of Menopause in Japan and North America.* Berkeley: University of California Press.

Lock, Margaret. 1998. "Anomalous Ageing: Managing the Postmenopausal Body." *Body & Society* 4(1): 35–61.

Loe, Meika. 2001. "Fixing Broken Masculinity: Viagra as a Technology for the Production of Gender and Sexuality." *Sexuality and Culture* 5(3): 97–125.

Loe, Meika. 2004. *The Rise of Viagra: How the Little Blue Pill Changed Sex in America.* New York: New York University Press.

Lorber, Judith, and Lisa Jean Moore. 2002. *Gender and the Social Construction of Illness.* Thousand Oaks, CA: Sage Publications.

Lorber, Judith. 1997. *Gender and the Social Construction of Illness.* Thousand Oaks, CA: Sage Publications.

Lorber, Judith. 1999. "Crossing Borders and Erasing Boundaries: Paradoxes of Identity Politics." *Sociological Focus* 32(4): 355–370.

Loseke, Donileen R. 2001. "Lived Realities and Formula Stories of 'Battered Women.'" Pp. 107–126 in *Institutional Selves: Troubled Identities in a Postmodern World,* edited by Jaber F. Gubrium and James A. Holstein. New York: Oxford University Press.

Luciano, Lynne. 2001. *Looking Good: Male Body Image in Modern America.* New York: Hill and Wang.

Lupton, Deborah. 1997. "Foucault and the Medicalization Critique." Pp. 94–110 in *Foucault, Health and Medicine,* edited by A. Petersen and R. Bunton. New York: Routledge.

Lupton, Deborah. 1999. "Introduction: Risk and Sociocultural Theory." Pp. 1–11 in *Risk and Sociocultural Theory: New Directions and Perspectives,* edited by D. Lupton. Cambridge: Cambridge University Press.

Lutz, Catherine A. 1990. "Engendered Emotion: Gender, Power, and the Rhetoric of Emotional Control in American Discourse." Pp. 69–91 in *Language and the Politics of Emotion,* edited by Catherine A. Lutz and Lila Abu-Lughob. Cambridge: Cambridge University Press.

Lyman, Karen A. 1989. "Bringing the Social Back in: A Critique of the Biomedicalisation of Dementia." *The Gerontologist* 29: 597–605.

Lynch, Michael. 1997. *Scientific Practice and Ordinary Action: Ethnomethodology and Social Studies of Science.* Cambridge: Cambridge University Press.

Lynch, Michael. 1998. "The Discursive Production of Uncertainty: The OJ Simpson 'Dream Team' and the Sociology of Knowledge Machine." *Social Studies of Science* 28(5–6): 829.

Maccoby, Eleanor E., and Carol Jacklin. 1987. *Psychology of Sex Differences.* Stanford, CA: Stanford University Press.

MacInnes, John. 1998. *The End of Masculinity: The Confusion of Sexual Genesis and Sexual Difference in Modern Society.* Buckingham: Open University Press.

MacPherson, Crawford B. 1962. *The Political Theory of Possessive Individualism: From Hobbes to Locke.* Oxford: Oxford University Press.

Maines, Rachel P. 1998. *Technology of Orgasm: "Hysteria," the Vibrator, and Women's Sexual Satisfaction.* Baltimore, MD: Johns Hopkins University Press.

Majors, Richard G., and Jacob U. Gordon, eds. 1994. *The American Black Male: His Present Status and His Future.* Chicago: Nelson-Hall.

Malacrida, Claudia. 2002. "Professional Legitimacy and Medicalization: Educators and AD(H)D in Canada and England." Paper presented at the International Sociological Association Conference.

Mamo, Laura, and Jennifer R. Fishman. 2001. "Potency in All the Right Places: Viagra as a Gendered Technology of the Body." *Body & Society* 7(4): 13–35.

Markens, Susan. 1996. "The Problematic of 'Experience': A Political and Cultural Critique of PMS." *Gender & Society* 10(1): 42–58.

Marks, Sandy C., Jr., Sandra L. Bertman, and June C. Penny. 1997. "Human Anatomy: A Foundation for Education about Death and Dying in Medicine." *Clinical Anatomy* 10: 118–122.

Marritt, Emanuel. 1993. "The Overwhelming Responsibility." *Hair Transplant Forum International* Special Edition: 4.

Marritt, Emanuel, and Leonard M. Dzubow. 1996. "Reassessment of Male Pattern Baldness: A Reevaluation of the Treatment." Pp. 30–41 in *Hair Replacement: Surgical and Medical,* edited by D. W. Stough and R. S. Haber. St. Louis, MO: Mosby.

Marshall, Barbara. 2002. "'Hard Science': Gendered Constructions of Sexual Dysfunction in the 'Viagra Age.'" *Sexualities* 5(2): 131–158.

Marshall, Barbara L., and Stephen Katz. 2002. "Forever Functional: Sexual Fitness and the Ageing Male Body." *Body & Society* 8: 43–70.

Marshall, Harriet, and Anne Woollett. 2000. "Fit to Reproduce? The Regulative Role of Pregnancy Texts." *Feminism & Psychology* 10(3): 351–366.

Martin, Emily. 1987. *The Woman in the Body: A Cultural Analysis of Reproduction.* Boston: Beacon Press.

Martin, Emily. 1994. *Flexible Bodies.* Boston: Beacon Press.

Marx, Karl. 1954 [1867]. *Capital, Vol. 1.* London: Lawrence and Wishart.

Matthaei, Julia. 1982. *An Economic History of Women in America: Women's Work, the Sexual Division of Labor and the Development of Capitalism.* Harvester Press: Brighton.

McCrea, Frances B. 1993. "The Politics of Menopause: The 'Discovery' of a Deficiency Disease." *Social Problems* 31(1): 111–123.

McDougall, Christopher. "Affairs: Stiff Competition." *Philadelphia Magazine,* July. (accessed September 26, 2003, Available: LEXIS-NEXIS).

McElhinny, Bonnie. 1995. "Challenging Hegemonic Masculinities: Female and Male Police Officers Handling Domestic Violence." Pp. 217–244 in *Gender*

*Articulated: Language and the Socially Constructed Self*, edited by Kira Hall and Mary Bucholtz. New York: Routledge.

McGregor, Deborah K. 1998. *From Midwives to Medicine*. New Brunswick, NJ: Rutgers University Press.

McGuffey, C. Shawn, and B. Lindsay Rich. 1999. "Playing in the Gender Transgression Zone." *Gender & Society* 13(5): 608–627.

McKinlay, John B., and Allison Gemmel. 2003. "Hormone Replacement Therapy/Policy: There's Gold in Them Thar Pills." New England Research Institutes, Watertown, MA. Unpublished manuscript.

McLachlan, John C., James F. Aiton, Susan C. Whiten, and Steven D. Smart. 1997. "3-D Modeling of Human Embryo Morphology Using QuickTime VR." Pp. 227–37 in *Molecular Genetics of Human Development*, edited by T. Strachan, S. Lindsay, D. Wilson. Oxford: Bios Scientific Publishers, Ltd.

McLachlan, John C., John Bligh, Paul Bradley, and Judy Searle. 2004. "Teaching Anatomy Without Cadavers." *Medical Education* 38(4): 418–424.

McLachlan, John C., and Sam Regan de Bere. 2004. *Anatomy is Life, Not Death: The Relevance of the Arts and Humanities to the Anatomy Curriculum*. Paper presented to the Arts and Humanities Committee. Dublin.

McLaughlin, Lisa, and Alice Park. 2000. "Are You Man Enough?" *Time* 155: 58–63.

Melick, Mary Evans, Henry J. Steadman, and Joseph J. Cocozza. 1979. "The Medicalization of Criminal Behavior among Mental Patients." *Journal of Health and Social Behavior* 20(3): 228–237.

Messerschmidt, James W. 1996. "Managing to Kill: Masculinities and the Space Shuttle *Challenger* Disaster." Pp. 29–53 in *Masculinities in Organizations*, edited by Cliff Cheng. Thousand Oaks, CA: Sage Publications.

Messner, Michael. 1992. *Power at Play: Sports and the Problem of Masculinity*. Boston: Beacon.

Messner, Michael. 1997. *The Politics of Masculinities: Men in Movements*. Thousand Oaks, CA: Sage Publications.

Meyer, Vicki F. 2001. "The Medicalization of Menopause: Critique and Consequences." *International Journal of Health Services* 31: 769–792.

Minton, H. L. 1996. "Community Empowerment and the Medicalization of Homosexuality: Constructing Sexual Identities in the 1930s." *Journal of the History of Sexuality* 6: 435–458.

Mishler, Elliot. 1984. *Discourse of Medicine: Dialectics of Medical Interviews*. Norwood, NJ: Albex Publishing Co.

Mitchell, B. S., and C. R. Stephens. May 2004. "Teaching Anatomy without Cadavers: Southampton Anatomy Tutors Reply." Letter to the Editor, *Medical Education*.

Moore, Lisa Jean. 2003. "Billy, the Sad Sperm with No Tail: Representations of Sperm in Children's Books." *Sexualities*. 6(3–4): 279–305.

Moore, Lisa Jean. 2002. "Extracting Men from Semen: Masculinity in Scientific Representations of Sperm." *Social Text* 73: 1–46.

Moore, Lisa Jean, and Adele E. Clarke. 1995. "Clitoral Conventions and Transgressions: Graphic Representations in Anatomy Texts, c1900–1991." *Feminist Studies* 21(2): 255–301.

Moore, Lisa Jean, and Adele E. Clarke. 2001. "A Traffic in Cyberanatomies: Sex/Gender/Sexualities in Local and Global Formations." *Body & Society* 7(1): 57–96.

Moore, Lisa Jean, and Matthew Schmidt. 1999. "On The Construction of Male Differences: Marketing Variations in Technosemen." *Men and Masculinities* 1(4): 339–359.

Morley, John E., and H. M. Perry III. 2003. "Androgen Treatment of Male Hypogonadism in Older Males." *Journal of Steroid Biochemistry & Molecular Biology* 85: 367–373.

Morris, Rebecca, Yaping Liu, Lee Marles, Zaixin Yang, Carol Trempus, Shulan Li, Jamie S. Lin, Janet A. Sawicki, and George Cotsarelis. 2004. "Capturing and Profiling Hair Follicle Stem Cells." *Nature Biotechnology* 22: 411–417.

Morrow, Carol Klaperman. 1982. "Sick Doctors: The Social Construction of Professional Deviance." *Social Problems* 30(1): 92–108.

MTA Cooperative Group. 1999. "A 14 Month Randomized Clinical Trial of Treatment Strategies for Attention–deficit Hyperactivity Disorder." *Archives of General Psychiatry* 56: 1073–1086.

MTA Cooperative Group. April 2004. "National Institute of Mental Health Multimodal Treatment Study of ADHD Follow-up: 24-Month Outcomes of Treatment Strategies for Attention-Deficit/Hyperactivity Disorder." *Pediatrics* 113(4): 754–761.

Muiderman, Kevin. 2001. "Hair Restoration Surgery Through Micrografting Techniques." *Plastic Surgical Nursing* 21: 141–142.

Mumford, K. 1997. "'Lost Manhood' Found: Male Sexual Impotence and Victorian Culture in the United States." Pp. 75–99 in *American Sexual Politics: Sex, Gender and Race since the Civil War*, edited by J. C. Fouts and M. S. Tantillo. Chicago: University of Chicago Press.

Mumford, Kevin. 1992. "'Lost Manhood' Found: Male Sexual Impotence and Victorian Culture in the United States." *Journal of the History of Sexuality* 3(1): 33–57.

Nagel, Joane. 2000a. "Ethnicity and Sexuality." *Annual Review of Sociology* 26: 107–133.

Nagel, Joane. 2000b. "Sexualizing the Sociological: Queering and Querying the Intimate Substructure of Social Life." *The Sociological Quarterly* 41(1): 1–17.

Nagel, Joane. 2003. *Race, Ethnicity, and Sexuality: Intimate Intersections, Forbidden Frontiers*. Oxford: Oxford University Press.

National Center for Health Statistics. 2004. *Summary Health Statistics for US Children: National Health Interview Survey, 2002*. Washington, DC: US Government Printing Office.

National Center for Education Statistics. 2001. *Outcomes of Learning Results from the 2000 Program of International Student Assessment of 15 Year Olds in Reading,*

*Mathematics and Science Literacy.* Washington, DC: US Government Printing Office.

National Institute of Mental Health. 2001. "The Numbers Count: Mental Disorders in America." Bethesda, MD: National Institute of Mental Health, National Institutes of Health, U.S. Department of Health and Human Services, NIH Publication #01–4584, New York: Routledge.

Nettleton, Sarah, and Jonathan Watson, eds. 1998. *The Body in Everyday Life.* London: Routledge.

Nickell, Joe, and John F. Fischer. 1999. *Crime Science Methods of Forensic Detection.* Lexington: University Press of Kentucky.

Nieschlag, Eberhard, and Hermann M. Behre, eds. 1998. *Testosterone: Action, Deficiency and Substitution.* New York: Springer.

Nolan, Edith, Kenneth Gadow, and Joyce Sprafkin. 2001. "Teacher Reports of *DSM-IV* ADHD, ODD and CD Symptoms in Schoolchildren." *Journal of the American Academy of Child and Adolescent Psychiatry* 40(2): 241–249.

Oakley, Ann. 1984. *The Captured Womb: A History of the Medical Care of Pregnant Women.* Oxford and New York: Blackwell.

Ochs, Elinor, and Carolyn Taylor. 1995. "The 'Father Knows Best' Dynamic in Dinnertime Narratives." Pp.183–216 in *Gender Articulated: Language and the Socially Constructed Self,* edited by Kira Hall and Mary Bucholtz. New York: Routledge.

Ogburn, William F. 1964. "Cultural Lag as Theory." Pp. 86–95 in *William F. Ogburn on Culture and Social Change,* Selected Papers. Chicago: University of Chicago Press.

Olfson, Mark, Marc Gameroff, Steven Marcus, and Peter Jensen. 2003. "National Trends in the Treatment of Attention Deficit Hyperactivity Disorder." *American Journal of Psychiatry* 160(6): 1071–1077.

Orfila, M. J. B. 1827. Translation of "DuSperme, condidere sous le point de vue medico-legal." *Journal de Chimie Medicale de Pharmacie et de Toxicologie* 3(10): 469–480.

Orr, Jackie. 2000. "Performing Methods: History, Hysteria, and the New Science of Psychiatry." Pp. 49–73 in *Pathology and the Postmodern: Mental Illness as Discourse and Experience,* edited by D. Fee. London: Sage Publications.

Osherson, Samuel D., and Lorna R. AmaraSingham. 1981. "The Machine Metaphor in Medicine." Pp. 218–45 in *Social Contexts of Health, Illness, and Patient Care,* edited by Elliot G. Mishler. New York: Cambridge University Press.

Oudshoorn, Nelly. (1994). *Beyond the Natural Body: An Archeology of Sex Hormones.* London and New York: Routledge.

Parker, Richard, Regina Barbosa, and Peter Aggleton. 2000. *Framing the Sexual Subject: The Politics of Gender, Sexuality, and Power.* Berkeley: University of California Press.

Parsons, Talcott. 1951. *The Social System.* New York: The Free Press.

Parsons, Talcott, and Robert F. Bales. 1964. *Family, Socialization and Interaction Process.* London: Routledge and Kegan Paul.

Pascoe, Peggy. 1999. "Miscegenation Law, Court Cases, and Ideologies of 'Race' in Twentieth-century America." Pp. 464–490 in *Sex, Love, Race*: Crossing Boundaries in North American History, edited by M. Hodes. New York: New York University Press.

Pawluch, Dorothy. 1983. "Transitions in Pediatrics: A Segmental Analysis." *Social Problems* 30(4): 449–465.

Pawluch, Dorothy. 2003. "Medicalizing Childhood." Pp. 219–225 in *Social Problems: Constructionist Readings*, edited by D. R. Loseke and J. Best. New York: Aldine de Gruyter.

Payer, Lynn. 1988. *Medicine and Culture*. Harmondsworth, UK: Penguin.

Pearson, Dale. 1994. "The Black Man: Health Issues and Implications for Clinical Practice." *Journal of Black Studies* 25(1): 81–98.

Peninsula Medical School. 2004. *Undergraduate Prospectus*. Arts and Humanities section. New Peninsula Medical School: Universities of Exeter and Plymouth.

Persaud, Trivedi V. N. 1967. *A History of Anatomy: The Post-Vesalian Era*. Springfield, IL: Charles C Thomas.

Petersen, Alan R. 1998a. *Unmasking the Masculine: 'Men' and 'Identity' in a Sceptical Age*. London: Sage Publications.

Petersen, Alan. 1998b. "Sexing the Body: Representations of Sex Differences in *Gray's Anatomy*, 1858 to the Present." *Body & Society* 4(1): 1–15.

Petersen, Alan. 2003. "Research on Men and Masculinities: Some Implications of Recent Theory for Future Work." *Men and Masculinities* 6(1): 54–69.

Pinto-Correia, Clara. 1997. *The Ovary of Eve: Egg and Sperm and Preformation*. Chicago: University of Chicago Press.

Pleck, Elizabeth H., and Joseph H. Pleck, eds. 1980. *The American Man*. Englewood Cliffs, NJ: Prentice-Hall.

Pleck, Joseph H. 1981. *The Myth of Masculinity*. Cambridge, MA: MIT Press.

Pleck, Joseph H. 1992. "Men's Power with Women, Other Men, and Society: A Men's Movement Analysis." Pp. 19–27 in *Men's Lives*, edited by M. Kimmel and M. Messner. New York: MacMillan Publishing Co.

Pleck, Joseph H., and Jack Sawyer, eds. 1974. *Men and Masculinity*. Englewood Cliffs, NJ: Prentice-Hall.

Pollner, Melvin, and Jill Stein. 2001. "Doubled Over in Laughter: Humor and the Construction of Selves in Alcoholics Anonymous." Pp. 45–65 in *Institutional Selves: Troubled Identities in a Postmodern World*, edited by Jaber F. Gubrium and James A. Holstein. New York: Oxford University Press.

Porter, Roy. 1997. *The Greatest Benefit to Mankind: A Medical History of Humanity from Antiquity to the Present*. London: Harper Collins.

Porter, Roy. 2003. *Blood and Guts: A Short History of Medicine*. London: Penguin.

Potts, Annie. 2000. " 'The Essence of the Hard On': Hegemonic Masculinity and the Cultural Construction of 'Erectile Dysfunction.'" *Men and Masculinities* 3(1): 85–103.

Preidt, Robert. July 26, 2002. "Testosterone: Shot in the Arm for Aging Males." *USA Today*.

Premkumar, Kalyani. 2003. *The Massage Connection: Anatomy and Physiology.* Philadelphia: Lippincott, Williams and Wilkins.

Pugliesi, K. 1992. "Premenstrual Syndrome: The Medicalization of Emotion Related to Conflict and Chronic Role Strain." *Humboldt Journal of Social Relations* 18(2): 131–165.

Pyke, Karen D. 1996. "Class-based Masculinities." *Gender & Society* 10(5): 527–549.

Rafalovich, Adam. 2001. "The Conceptual History of Attention Deficit Hyperactivity Disorder: Idiocy, Imbecility, Encephalitis and the Child Deviant 1877–1929." *Deviant Behavior: An Interdisciplinary Journal* 22: 93–115.

Ramos e Silva, Marcia. 2000. "Male Pattern Hair Loss: Prevention Rather Than Regrowth." *International Journal of Dermatology* 39: 728–731.

Randall, Valerie A. 2000. "The Biology of Androgenetic Alopecia." Pp. 123–133 in *Hair and Its Disorders: Biology, Pathology and Management*, edited by F. Camacho, V. Randall and V. Price. London: Martin Dunitz.

Rappley, Marsha, Joseph Gardiner, James Jetton, and Richard Houang. 1995. "The Use of Methylphenidate in Michigan." *Archives of Pediatric Adolescent Medicine* 149: 675–679.

Raymond, Janice. 1994. *The Transsexual Empire: The Making of the She-Male.* New York: Athene.

Reid, Helen M., and Gary Alan Fine. 1995. "Self-disclosure in Men's Friendships: Variations Associated with Intimate Relations." Pp. 132–152 in *Men's Friendships,* edited by Peter M. Nardi. Newbury Park, CA: Sage Publications.

Reid, Robert, John Maag, Stanley Vasa, and Gail Wright. 1994. "Who are the Children with Attention Deficit-hyperactivity Disorder? A School Based Survey." *Journal of Special Education* 28: 117–137.

Reinert, Patty. 1997. "Rebuilding a Shattered Trust." *Houston Chronicle* (accessed December 1, 1997). www.chron.com.

Reissman, Catherine Kohler. 1983. "Women and Medicalization: A New Perspective." *Social Policy* 14(1): 46–63.

Reissman, Catherine K. 2003. "Women and Medicalization: A New Perspective." Pp. 46–62 in *The Politics of Women's Bodies: Sexuality, Appearance, and Behavior,* edited by R. Weitz. New York: Oxford University Press.

Renson, Roland, and Chris Careel. 1986. "Sporticulous Consumption: An Analysis of Social Status Symbolism in Sports Ads." *International Review for the Sociology of Sport* 22(2–3): 152–171.

Richardson, Ruth. 2000. *Death, Dissection and the Destitute.* London: Penguin.

Riley, Glenda. 1986. *Inventing the American Woman: A Perspective on Women's History 1607–1877.* Arlington Heights, IL: Harlan Davidson, Inc.

Rimke, Heidi, and Alan Hunt. 2002. "From Sinners to Degenerates: The Medicalization of Morality in the 19th Century." *History of the Human Sciences* 15(1): 59–88.

Riska, Elianne. 2002. "From Type A Man to the Hardy Man: Masculinity and Health." *Sociology of Health and Illness* 24(3): 347–358.

Riska, Elianne. 2003. "Gendering the Medicalization Thesis." Pp. 59–87 in *Gender Perspectives on Health and Medicine: Key Themes. Advances in Gender Research* 7(1–9), edited by M. S. Segal and V. Demos. Oxford, UK: Elsevier Press.

Riska, Elianne. 2004. *Masculinity and Men's Health: Coronary Heart Disease in Medical and Public Discourse.* Lanham, MD: Rowman and Littlefield Publishers, Inc.

Ritzer, George. 1995. *The McDonaldization of Society: An Investigation into the Changing Character of Contemporary Social Life.* Newbury Park, CA: Pine Forge Press.

Roach, Mary. 2003. *Stiff: The Curious Lives of Human Cadavers.* Harmondsworth, UK: Penguin.

Robbins, Thomas, and Dick Anthony. 1982. "Deprogramming, Brainwashing and the Medicalization of Deviant Behavior." *Social Problems* 29(3): 283–297.

Roberts, Dorothy. 1999. *Killing the Black Body: Race, Reproduction, and the Meaning of Liberty.* New York: Vintage Books.

Robinson, Linda, David Sclar, Tracy Skaer, and Richard Galin. 1999. "National Trends in the Prevalence of Attention-Deficit/Hyperactivity Disorder and the Prescribing of Methylphenidate Among School-Age Children: 1990–1995." *Clinical Pediatrics* 38(4): 209–217.

Rose, Hilary. 1983. "Hand, Heart and Brain: Towards a Feminist Epistemology of the Natural Sciences." *Signs: A Journal of Women in Culture and Society* 9(1): 73–90.

Rosecrance, John. 1985. "Compulsive Gambling and the Medicalization of Deviance." *Social Problems* 32(3): 275–284.

Rosenfeld, Dana, and Eugene B. Gallagher. 2002. "The Life Course as an Organizing Principle and a Socializing Resource in Modern Medicine." Pp. 357–390 in *Advances in Life Course Research: New Frontiers in Socialization,* edited by R. A. Settersten, Jr., and T. Owens. London: Elsevier Press.

Rosenman, Ellen Bayuk. 2003. "Body Doubles: The Spermatorrhea Panic." *Journal of the History of Sexuality* 12(3): 365–399.

Rosse, Cornelius. 1995. "The Potential of Computerized Representations of Anatomy in the Training of Health Care Providers." *Academic Medicine* 70: 499–505.

Rothman, Sheila M., and David J. Rothman. 2003. *The Pursuit of Perfection: The Promise and Perils of Medical Enhancement.* New York: Pantheon Books.

Rowland, Andrew, Catherine Lesesne, and Ann Abramowitz. 2002. "The Epidemiology of Attention-Deficit/Hyperactivity Disorder (ADHD): A Public Health View." *Mental Retardation and Developmental Disabilities Research Reviews* 8: 162–170.

Roy, Benjamin. 1995. "The Tuskegee Syphilis Experiment: Biotechnology and the Administrative State." *National Medical Association* 87(1): 56–67.

Rudin, Norah, and Keith Inman. 2002a. *An Introduction to Forensic DNA Analysis* 2nd ed. Boca Raton, FL: CRC Press.

Rudin, Norah, and Keith Inman. 2002b. "Forensic Science Timeline." http://www.forensicdna.com (accessed September 2, 2003).

Rudy, David R. 1986. *Becoming Alcoholic: Alcoholics Anonymous and the Reality of Alcoholism.* Carbondale, IL: Southern Illinois University Press.

Sabo, Don. 1995. "Pigskin, Patriarchy and Pain." In *Men's Lives,* edited by M. Kimmel and M. Messner. Boston: Allyn and Bacon.

Sabo, Donald, and David F. Gordon, eds. 1995. *Men's Health and Illness: Gender, Power, and the Body.* Thousand Oaks, CA: Sage Publications.

Safer, Daniel, and Michael Malever. 2000. "Stimulant Treatment in Maryland Public Schools." *Pediatrics* 106(3): 533–539.

Safir, Howard, and Peter Reinharz. 2000. "DNA Testing: The Next Big Crime-Busting Breakthrough." *City Journal.* http://www.city-journal.org/html/10_1_dna_testing.html (accessed January 20, 2004).

Sagan, Leonard. 1989. *The Health of Nations.* New York: Basic Books.

Sage, George. 1998. *Power and Ideology in American Sport: A Critical Perspective.* Champaign, IL: Human Kinetics.

Saint-Aubin, Arthur F. 2002. "A Grammar of Black Masculinity: A Body of Science." *The Journal of Men's Studies* 10(3): 247–270.

Santiago-Irizarry, Vilma. 2001. *Medicalizing Ethnicity: The Construction of Latino Identity in a Psychiatric Setting.* Ithaca and London: Cornell University Press.

Sappol, Michael. 2002. *A Traffic in Dead Bodies: Anatomy and Embodied Social Identity in Nineteenth-Century America.* Princeton and Oxford: Princeton University Press.

Sattel, Jack W. 1983. "Men, Inexpressiveness, and Power." Pp. 119–124 in *Language, Gender and Society,* edited by Barrie Thorne, Cheris Kramarae, and Nancy Henley. Rowley, MA: Newbury House Publisher, Inc.

Sault, Nicole, ed. 1994. *Many Mirrors: Body Image and Social Relations.* New Brunswick, NJ: Rutgers University Press.

Savitt, Todd. 1978. *Medicine and Slavery: The Diseases and Health Care of Blacks in Antebellum Virginia.* Urbana: University of Illinois Press.

Savitt, Todd. 1982. "The Use of Blacks for Medical Experimentation and Demonstration in the Old South." *The Journal of Southern History* 48(3): 331–348.

Savitt, Todd. 1988. "Slave Health and Southern Distinctiveness." Pp. 120–153 in *Disease and Distinctiveness in the American South,* edited by T. Savitt and J. Young. Knoxville: University of Tennessee Press.

Sawicki, Jana. 1991. *Disciplining Foucault: Feminism, Power, and the Body.* New York: Routledge.

Sax, Leonard, and Kathleen Kautz. 2003. "Who First Suggests the Diagnosis of ADHD?" *Annals of Family Medicine* 1(3): 171–174.

Scheff, Thomas. 2001. "Male Emotions and Violence." *Journal of Mundane Behavior* 2(3): 409–413.

Scheper-Hughes, Nancy, and Margaret M. Lock. 1987. "The Mindful Body: A Prolegomenon to Future Work in Medical Anthropology." *Medical Anthropology Quarterly* 1: 6–41.

Schiebinger, Londa. 1986. "Skeletons in the Closet: The First Illustrations of the Female Skeleton in Eighteenth-century Anatomy." *Representations* 14 (Spring): 42–82.

Schiebinger, Londa. 1990. "The Anatomy of Difference: Race and Sex in Eighteenth Century Science." *Eighteenth Century Studies* 23(4): 387–405.

Schmidt, Matthew, and Lisa Jean Moore. 1998. "Constructing a Good Catch, Picking a Winner: The Development of Technosemen and the Deconstruction of the Monolithic Male." Pp. 17–39 in *Cyborg Babies: From Techno-Sex to Techno-Tots,* edited by Robbie Davis-Floyd and Joseph Dumit. New York: Routledge.

Schneider, Joseph W. 1978. "Deviant Drinking as a Disease: Alcoholism as a Social Accomplishment." *Social Problems* 25(4): 361–372.

Schoen, Johanna. 2001. "Between Choice and Coercion: Women and Politics of Sterilization in North Carolina, 1929–1975." *Journal of Women's History* 13: 132–156.

Schram, Sanford F. 2000. "In the Clinic: The Medicalization of Welfare." *Social Text* 18, 1(62): 81–107.

*Science News.* 1999. "Gene Therapy Tackles Hair Loss." October 30, 283.

Scott, Thomas M. 1994. "A Care-based Anatomy Course." *Medical Education* 28: 68–73.

Scott, Wilbur J. 1993. *The Politics of Readjustment: Vietnam Veterans Since the War.* New York: Aldine de Gruyter.

Scow, Dean Thomas, Robert S. Nolte, and Allen F. Shaughnessy. April 15, 1999. "Medical Treatments for Balding in Men." *American Family Physician.*

Scudson, Michael. 1990. *Advertising: The Uneasy Persuasion: Its Dubious Impact on American Society.* New York: Basic Books.

Scully, Diane, and Pauline Bart. 1973. "A Funny Thing Happened on the Way to the Orifice: Women in Gynecology Textbooks." *American Journal of Sociology* 78(4): 1045–1050.

Segal, Lynne. 1990. *Slow Motion: Changing Masculinities, Changing Men.* New Brunswick, NJ: Rutgers University Press.

Segal, Marcia T., Vasilikie Demos, and Jennie J. Kronenfeld. 2003. "Gendered Perspectives on Medicine: An Introduction." Pp. 1–19 in *Gender Perspectives on Health and Medicine: Key Themes. Advances in Gender Research* 7(1–9), edited by M. S. Segal and V. Demos. Oxford, UK: Elsevier Press.

Segrave, Kerry. 1996. *Baldness: A Social History.* Jefferson, NC: McFarland.

Shildrick, Margrit. 1997. *Leaky Bodies and Boundaries: Feminism, Postmodernism and BioEthics.* New York: Routledge.

Shildrick, Margrit, and Janet Price. 1999. "Openings on the Body: A Critical Introduction." Pp. 1–14 in *Feminist Theory and The Body: A Reader,* edited by Janet Price and Margrit Shildrick. New York: Routledge.

Shilling, Chris. 1993. *The Body and Social Theory.* London: Sage Publications.

Shorter, Edward. 1975. *The Making of the Modern Family.* London: Collins.

Showalter, Elaine. 1985. *The Female Malady: Women, Madness, and English Culture, 1830–1980.* New York: Penguin.

Sievert, Lynette L. 2003. "The Medicalization of Female Fertility: Points of Significance for the Study of Menopause." *Collegium Antropologicum* 27(1): 67–78.

Sinclair, Rodney. 1998. "Male Pattern Androgenetic Alopecia." *British Journal of Medicine* 317: 865–869.

Singh, Illina. 2003. "Boys Will Be Boys: Fathers' Perspectives on ADHD Symptoms, Diagnosis, and Drug Treatment." *Harvard Review of Psychiatry* 11(6): 308–316.

Singh, Illina. 2004. "Doing Their Jobs: Mothering with Ritalin in a Culture of Mother Blame." *Social Science and Medicine* 59: 1193–1205.

Smith-Rosenberg, Carroll. 1985. *Disorderly Conduct: Visions of Gender in Victorian America.* New York: Knopf.

Solomon, Martha. 1985. "The Rhetoric of Dehumanization: An Analysis of Medical Reports of the Tuskegee Syphilis Project." *The Western Journal of Speech Communication* 49: 233–247.

Somerville, Siobhan. 1997. "Scientific Racism and the Invention of the Homosexual Body." Pp. 37–52 in *The Gender Sexuality Reader*, edited by M. di Leonardo and R. Lancaster. New York: Routledge.

Sontag, Susan. 1978. *Illness as Metaphor.* New York: Farrar, Straus and Giroux.

Spark, Richard. 1988. *The Infertile Male: The Clinical Guide to Diagnosis and Treatment.* New York: Plenum.

Stansby, Gerard. May 2004. "Teaching Anatomy without Cadavers: No Educational Justification" Letter to Editor, *Medical Education.*

Staples, William.G. 1997. *The Culture of Surveillance.* New York: St. Martin's Press.

Star, Susan Leigh, and James Griesemer. 1989. "Institutional Ecology 'Translations' and Boundary Objects: Amateurs and Professionals in Berkeley's Museum of Vertebrate Zoology 1907–39." *Social Studies of Science* 19: 387–420.

Starr Report. 1998. Grand Jury Testimony of Monica S. Lewinsky. Washington, DC: Federal Document Clearing House, Inc.

Starr, Paul. 1982. *The Social Transformation of American Medicine: The Rise of a Sovereign Profession and the Making of a Vast Industry.* New York: Basic Books.

Stas, Sameer N., Aristotelis G. Anastasiadis, Harry Fisch, Mitchell C. Benson, and Ridwan Shabsigh. 2003. "Urologic Aspects of Andropause." *Urology* 61: 261–266.

Stearns, Peter. 1979. *Be a Man: Males in Modern Society.* New York: Holmes and Meier.

Stearns, Peter N. 1990. *Be a Man: Males in Modern Society.* 2nd ed. New York: Holmes and Meier.

Stevenson, Howard, Jr. 1994. "The Psychology of Sexual Racism and AIDS: An Ongoing Saga of Distrust and the 'Sexual Other.'" *Journal of Black Studies* 25(1): 62–80.

Stillion, Judith M. 1995. "Premature Death Among Males: Extending the Bottom Line of Men's Health." Pp. 46–67 in *Men's Health and Illness: Gender, Power, and the Body*, edited by D. Sabo and D. F. Gordon. Thousand Oaks, CA: Sage Publications.

Stillman, Paula L., Jane S. Ruggill, and Darrell L. Sabers. 1978. "The Use of Live Models in the Teaching of Gross Anatomy." *Medical Education* 12: 114–116.

Stoler, Ann L. 1997. "Carnal Knowledge and Imperial Power." Pp. 13–36 in *The Gender Sexuality Reader*, edited by M. di Leonardo and R. Lancaster. New York: Routledge.

Stough, Dow B., and Robert S. Haber, eds. 1996. *Hair Replacement: Surgical and Medical*. St. Louis, MO: Mosby.

Strauss, Anselm, and Juliet Corbin. 1994. "Grounded Theory Methodology: An Overview." Pp. 273–285 in *Handbook of Qualitative Research*, edited by N. Denzin and Y. Lincoln. London: Sage Publications:

Substance Abuse and Mental Health Services Administration. 2003. *Results from the 2002 National Survey on Drug Use and Health: National Findings* (Office of Applied Studies, NHSDA Series H-22, DHHS Publication No. SMA 03–3836). Rockville, MD.

Swanson, James, Marc Lerner, and Lillie Williams. 1995. "More Frequent Diagnosis of Attention Deficit-Hyperactivity Disorder." *New England Journal of Medicine* 333(14): 944.

Tan, Robert S., and John W. Culberson. 2003. "An Integrative Review on Current Evidence of Testosterone Replacement Therapy for the Andropause." *Maturitas* 45: 15–27.

Tannen, Deborah. 1990. *You Just Don't Understand: Women and Men in Conversation*. New York: Ballantine Books.

Taylor, Brian. 1993. "Unconsciousness and Society: The Sociology of Sleep." *International Journal of Politics, Culture, and Society* 6(3): 463–471.

Teather, David. 2003. "Glaxo and Bayer's Orange Pill Challenges Viagra." *The Guardian*, April 21. (accessed November 11, 2003. Available: LEXIS-NEXIS).

Terry, Jennifer. 1995. "The Seductive Power of Science in the Making of Deviant Subjectivity." Pp. 135–161 in *Posthuman Bodies*, edited by Judith Halberstam and Ira Livingston. Bloomington, IN: Indiana University Press.

Thomas, Stephen, and Sandra C. Quinn. 2000. "The Tuskegee Syphilis Study, 1932–1972: Implications for HIV Education and AIDS Risk Education Programs in the Black Community." Pp. 404–417 in *Tuskegee's Truths: Rethinking the Tuskegee Syphilis Study*, edited by S. Reverby. Chapel Hill: University of North Carolina Press.

Thompson, Edward H. 1994. "Older Men as Invisible Men in Contemporary Society." Pp. 1–21 in *Older Men's Lives*, edited by E. H. Thompson. Thousand Oaks, CA: Sage Publications.

Thompson, Lana. 1999. *The Wandering Womb: A Cultural History of Outrageous Beliefs about Women*. New York: Prometheus Books.

Thorne, Barrie. 1993. *Gender at Play: Girls and Boys in School*. Milton Keynes: Open University Press.

Tiefer, Leonore. 1987. "The Pursuit of the Perfect Penis: The Medicalization of Men's Sexuality." Pp. 165–186 in *Changing Men: New Directions in Research on Men and Masculinity*, edited by M. Kimmel. London: Sage Publications.

Tiefer, Leonore. 1994. "The Medicalization of Impotence: Normalizing Phallocentrism." *Gender & Society* 8(3): 363–377.

Tiefer, Leonore. 1996. "The Medicalization of Sexuality: Conceptual, Norma-
tive, and Professional Issues." *Society for the Scientific Study of Sex* 7: 252–282.
Tiefer, Leonore. 2001. "A New View of Women's Sexual Problems." *Women &*
*Therapy* 24: 63–94.
Tiefer, Leonore. 2004. *Sex is Not a Natural Act and Other Essays*, 2nd ed. Boulder,
CO: Westview Press.
Tissot, Samuel Auguste David. 1760. *L'Onanisme*. Lausanne; [Reprinted as A
Treatise on the Diseases Produced by Onanism. New York: Collins & Han-
nay; 1832, pp. 17–18].
Tolman, Deborah. 2002. *Dilemmas of Desire: Teenage Girls Talk about Sexuality*.
Cambrige MA: Harvard University Press.
Trumbach, Randolph. 1994. "London's Sapphists: From Three Sexes to Four
Genders in the Making of Modern Culture." Pp. 11–136 in *Third Sex, Third*
*Gender: Beyond Sexual Dimorphism in Culture and History*, edited by G. Herdt.
New York: Zone Books.
Tsoffar, Ruth. 2004. "The Body as Storyteller: Karaite Women's Experience of
Blood and Milk." *Journal of American Folklore* 117(463): 3–21.
Turner, Bryan. 1984. *The Body and Society*. Oxford: Basil Blackwell.
Turner, Bryan S. 1992. *Regulating Bodies: Essays in Medical Sociology*. New York:
Routledge.
Turner, Bryan. 1995. *Medical Power and Social Knowledge*. London: Sage Pub-
lications.
Turner, Bryan. 1996. *The Body and Society*. London: Sage Publications.
U.S. Department of Education, Institute of Education Sciences, National Center
for Education Statistics, National Assessment of Educational Progress. 2002
Writing Assessments.
U.S. Department of Education, National Center for Education Statistics, the
NCES Common Core of Data, "State Nonfiscal Survey of Public Elementary/
Secondary Education," 1988–89 through 2001–02, and Projections of Edu-
cation Statistics to 2013.
U.S. Drug Enforcement Administration ARCOS database, 2000.
Umberson, Debra, Kristin L. Anderson, Kristi Williams, and Meichu D. Chen.
2003. "Relationship Dynamics, Emotion State, and Domestic Violence:
A Stress and Masculinities Perspective." *Journal of Marriage and the Family*
65(1): 233–247.
Ussher, Jane. 1992. *Women's Madness: Misogyny or Mental Illness*. Amherst, MA:
University of Massachusetts Press.
Van Neste, M. D. 2002. "Assessment of Hair Loss: Clinical Relevance of Hair
Growth Evaluation Methods." *Clinical Dermatology* 27: 362–369.
Vastag, Brian. 2003. "Many Questions, Few Answers for Testosterone Replace-
ment Therapy." *Journal of the American Medical Association* 289: 971–972.
Veatch, Robert. 1987. *The Patient as Partner*. Bloomington, IN: Indiana Univer-
sity Press.
Wacquant, Loic. 1995. "Pugs at Work: Bodily Capital and Bodily Labour among
Professional Boxers." *Body & Society* 1: 65–93.

Waitzkin, Harold. 1991. *The Politics of Medical Encounters: How Patients and Doctors Deal with Social Problems.* New Haven: Yale University Press.

Waldby, Catherine. 2000. *The Visible Human Project: Informatic Bodies and Posthuman Medicine.* London and New York: Routledge.

Waldron, Ingrid. 1990. "What Do We Know about Sex Differences in Mortality? A Review of the Literature." Pp. 45–56 in *The Sociology of Health and Illness: Critical Perspectives.* 3rd ed., edited by Peter Conrad and Rochelle Kern. New York: St. Martin's Press.

Wallsgrove, Ruth. 1980. "The Masculine Face of Science." Pp. 228–240 in *Alice through the Microscope: The Power of Science over Women's Lives,* edited by Brighton Women and Science Group. London: Virago.

Warren, Lynda W. 1983. "Male Intolerance of Depression: A Review with Implications for Psychotherapy." *Clinical Psychology Review* 3: 147–156.

Watkins, Elizabeth. 1998. *On the Pill: A Social History of Oral Contraceptives, 1950–1970.* Baltimore, MD: Johns Hopkins University Press.

Watson, Jonathan. 2000. *Male Bodies: Health, Culture and Identity.* Buckingham: Open University Press.

Weber, Max. 1958. *The Protestant Ethic and the Spirit of Capitalism.* New York: Scribner's Press.

Weber, Robert P. 1990. *Basic Content Analysis.* Newbury Park, CA: Sage Publications.

Weeks, Jeffrey. 1977. *Coming Out: Homosexual Politics in Britain from the Nineteenth Century to the Present.* London: Quartet.

Weinberg, Darin. 2001. "Self-Empowerment in Two Therapeutic Communities." Pp. 84–104 in *Institutional Selves: Troubled Identities in a Postmodern World,* edited by Jaber F. Gubrium and James A. Holstein. New York: Oxford University Press.

Weinberg, Martin S., and Colin J. Williams. 1988. "Black Sexuality: A Test of Two Theories." *The Journal of Sex Research* 25(2): 197–218.

Wellman, David. 2000. "From Evil to Illness: Medicalizing Racism." *American Journal of Orthopsychiatry* 70(1): 28–32.

Wells, Pamela A., Trevor Willmouth, and Robin Russell. 1995. "Does Fortune Favor the Bald? Psychological Correlates of Hair Loss in Males." *British Journal of Psychology* 86: 337–344.

Welner, Amos, Sue Marten, Eliza Wochnick, Mary A. Davis, Roberta Fishman, and Paula J. Clayton. 1979. "Psychiatric Disorders among Professional Women." *Archives of General Psychiatry* 36: 169–173.

Werner, August A. 1939. "The Male Climacteric." *Journal of the American Medical Association* 112: 1441–1443.

Wertz, Richard, and Dorothy Wertz. 1989. *Lying In: A History of Childbirth in America,* expanded edition. New Haven, CT: Yale University Press.

Wespes, E., and C. C. Schulman. 2002. "Male Andropause: Myth, Reality, and Treatment." *International Journal of Impotence Research* 14: S93–S98.

West, Cornell. 1993. *Race Matters.* Boston: Beacon Press.

White, Phillip, and James Gillett. 1994. "Reading the Muscular Body: A Critical Decoding of Advertisements in Flex Magazine." *Sociology of Sport Journal* 11: 18–39.

Whitehead, Stephen M., and Frank J. Barrett. 2001. "The Sociology of Masculinity." Pp. 1–26 in *The Masculinities Reader,* edited by S. M. Whitehead and F. J. Barrett. Cambridge, UK: Polity Press.

Whitely, Richard. 1999. "The Institutional Structuring of Innovation Strategies and Technological Development." Ms. Prepared for the Sociology of Sciences Meeting, Uppsala, Sweden, September 1999 in H. Nowotny, P. Scott, and M. Gibbons. *Re-thinking Science: Knowledge and the Public in an Age of Uncertainty.* Cambridge: Polity Press.

Whiting, David A. 1998. "Male Pattern Hair Loss: Current Understanding." *International Journal of Dermatology* 37: 561–566.

Wiegman, Robyn. 1993. "The Anatomy of Lynching." *Journal of the History of Sexuality* 3(3): 445–467.

Wienke, Chris. 2000. "Better Loving through Chemistry: How New Impotence Treatment Technologies Promise to Change Male Sexuality." *Disclosure: A Journal of Social Theory* 9: 69–93.

Williams, David, and Chiquita Collins. 1995. "U.S. Socioeconomic and Racial Differences in Health: Patterns and Explanations." Pp. 5–43 in *Perspectives in Medical Sociology,* edited by P. Brown. New York: Waveland Press.

Williams, Kristi, and Debra Umberson. 1997. "Gender, Medicine, and Technology: The Social Construction of Expectant Fatherhood." Paper presented at American Sociological Association Annual Conference.

Williams, Rhys H. 2001. *Promise Keepers and the New Masculinity.* New York: Rowan and Littlefield.

Williams, Simon J., and Gillian Bendelow. 1998. *The Lived Body: Sociological Themes, Embodied Issues,* London: Routledge.

Willis, Paul. 1981. *Learning to Labour.* New York: Columbia University Press.

Wolf, Maria. 2002. "From Care to Responsibility: Medicalisation of the Mother-child Relationship in the 20th Century." International Sociological Association, Brisbane, Australia (ISA).

Woloch, Nancy. 1984. *Women and the American Experience.* New York: Alfred A. Knopf.

Wolraich, Mark, Jane Hannah, Anna Baumgaertel, and Irene Feuer. 1998. "Examination of *DSM-IV* Criteria for Attention Deficit/Hyperactivity Disorder in a County-Wide Sample." *Developmental and Behavioral Pediatrics* 19(3): 162–168.

Wolraich, Mark, Jane Hannah, Theodora Pinnock, Anna Baumgaertel, and Janice Brown. 1996. "Comparison of Diagnostic Criteria for Attention-Deficit Hyperactivity Disorder in a County-Wide Sample." *Journal of the American Academy of Child and Adolescent Psychiatry* 35(3): 319–324.

Worboys, Michael. 1999. "Tuberculosis and Race in Britain and its Empire, 1900–1950." Pp. 144–166 in *Race, Science and Medicine, 1700–1960,* edited by W. Ernst and B. Harris. New York: Routledge.

Worcester, Nancy, and Marianne Whatley. 1992. "The Selling of HRT: Playing on the Fear Factor." *Feminist Review* 41: 1–26.

Worth, David. 1990. "Minority Women and AIDS: Culture, Race, and Gender." Pp. 111–135 in *Culture and AIDS*, edited by D. Feldman. New York: Praeger.

Wright, Rosemary. 1996. "The Occupational Masculinity of Computing." Pp. 77–96 in *Masculinities in Organizations*, edited by Cliff Cheng. Thousand Oaks, CA: Sage Publications.

Yalom, Marilyn. 2001. *A History of the Wife*. London: Pandora.

Young, Caoimhe. 2003. "Battle of the Love Drugs: New Pill Cialis Proves it Can Rise to Occasion as Viagra Rival." *The Mirror*, February 25. (accessed September 18, 2003, Available: LEXIS-NEXIS).

Zavirsek, Darja. 2000. "A Historical Overview of Women's Hysteria in Slovenia." *European Journal of Women's Studies* 7(2): 169–188.

Zilbergeld, Bernie. 1992. *The New Male Sexuality*. New York: Bantam Books.

Zola, Irving K. 1972. "Medicine as an Institution of Social Control." *Sociological Review* 20: 487–504.

Zola, Irving K. 1975. "In the Name of Health and Illness: On Some Socio-political Consequences of Medical Influence." *Social Science and Medicine* 9: 83–87.

Zola, Irving K. 1997. "Medicine as an Institution of Social Control." Pp. 404–414 in *The Sociology of Health and Illness*, edited by P. Conrad. New York: St. Martin's Press.

Zurbrugg, Nicholas. 2000. "Marinetti, Chopin, Stelarc and the Auratic Intensities of the Postmodern Techno-Body." Pp. 93–115 in *Body Modification*, edited by M. Featherstone, London: Sage Publications.

# About the Contributors

**Peter Conrad** is the Harry Coplan Professor of Sciences and chair of the Health: Science, Society, and Policy program at Brandeis University. He is the author of many books and articles in the area of medical sociology. He is currently researching biomedical enhancement and writing a book on the medicalization of society.

**Sam Regan de Bere** is a fellow at the Peninsula Medical School (University of Exeter, UK). Her interests lie generally in the sociology of the body, embodiment, and identity, and she is presently researching and publishing in the field of medical anatomy. Current research projects include an ethnographic study of anatomy teaching, a survey of anatomy tutors' attitudes and beliefs, a media analysis of news coverage of the use of human tissues, and an analysis of cultural artifacts relating to anatomy throughout history.

**Heidi Durkin** is an award-winning graduate of the College of Staten Island. She is currently pursuing graduate work in social work, specializing in addiction studies. She has recently submitted a paper to the journal *Gender and Society* based on the research project entitled "Your Man in the Field: Sperm, Forensics and CODIS."

**Christopher A. Faircloth** is a research health scientist with the Rehabilitation Outcomes Research Center at the North Florida–South Georgia VA Medical Center as well as an assistant professor in occupational therapy at the University of Florida. Along with an interest in medicalization, his studies have developed from a long-standing focus on the everyday practice and impact of chronic illness on both the ill individual and the family and growing interest in a sociology of the body. He is the editor of *Aging Bodies: Images and Everyday Experience* and

253

has published in journals such as *Sociology of Health and Illness* and *Symbolic Interaction.*

**Noah Grand** received undergraduate degrees in sociology and political science from UCLA in spring 2004, where he won the sociology department's Leo Kuper Award for the top honors thesis. His interests include journalistic decision making and public knowledge about health and health care.

**Nicky Hart** is currently a professor of sociology at the University of California, Los Angeles. She served on the British Government Working Group that produced the "Black Report" on health inequalities (1980). Publications include *When Marriage Ends* (1976), *The Sociology of Health and Medicine* (1985), and articles on historical demography, health inequalities, and gender stratification. She is currently completing the article *Gender and the Health of Nations.*

**Ann Marie Hickey** is a doctoral student in the Department of Sociology at the University of Kansas. Her work investigates intersections between medicine and sexuality, including the Tuskegee experiment, female genital cosmetic surgery, and HIV/AIDS. She is currently doing research for her dissertation on the rise of HIV infection among aging populations.

**Meika Loe** was raised in California and received her Ph.D. at the University of California, Santa Barbara. She is currently an assistant professor of sociology and women's studies at Colgate University in New York, where she teaches courses on gender, sexuality, consumption, and medicine. She has published her research on the commodification of gender and sexuality in *Gender & Society, Sociological Inquiry,* and *Sexualities.* Loe's critical analysis of the Viagra phenomenon, entitled *The Rise of Viagra: How the Little Blue Pill Changed Sex in America,* was published in 2004.

**Lisa Jean Moore**, an associate professor at The College of Staten Island and The Graduate Center/CUNY, is a medical sociologist who specializes in qualitative, interpretive feminist studies of the human body. Her previous work explores human genital anatomy, safer sex technologies, and human sex in outer space.

**Alan Petersen** is a professor of sociology in the School of Sociology, Politics, and Law, University of Plymouth, UK. He has researched and written extensively in the sociology of health and illness, the sociology of the biosciences and biotechnologies, and gender studies. His recent books include *Engendering Emotions* (2004) and *Genetic Governance: Health, Risk and Ethics in the Biotech Era* (2005; edited with Robin Bunton).

**Kevin Riley**, MPH, M.A., is a Ph.D. student in sociology at the University of California, Los Angeles. His research interests include the sociology and politics of public health and the state. He is currently working on a dissertation examining the provision of medical care to prisoners in the United States.

**Dana Rosenfeld** is a Lecturer at the Department of Health and Social Care, Royal Holloway/University of London. While her interests include identity in historical and interactional context (her book *The Changing of the Guard: Lesbian and Gay Elders, Identity, and Social Change*, was published by Temple University Press in 2003), her main focus is the interpretation, management, and regulation of the body, particularly the body in ill health. She has published on the experience of chronic illness in *Symbolic Interaction*, has a forthcoming article on the experience of acute illnesses and injuries in *Social Theory and Health*, and is planning a study of movement and embodiment in institutional and home care settings.

**Marisa M. Smith** earned her Ph.D. in sociology at the University of California, San Diego. Currently, she is an investigator for the U.S. Department of Health and Human Services Office for Civil Rights in Seattle, Washington.

**Julia E. Szymczak** graduated summa cum laude and Phi Beta Kappa from Brandeis University in 2004. Her thesis, "Medicalizing the Aging Male Body," from which this chapter is derived, was awarded highest honors. She currently works as a research assistant for Video Intervention/Prevention Assessment (VIA), a qualitative health research program, at Children's Hospital Boston, and plans to continue on to a graduate program emphasizing medical sociology.

**Chris Wienke** is an assistant professor of sociology at Arkansas State University, where teaches marriage and family, intimate relations, and gender studies. His research focuses on the intersections of gender, family, and sexuality. He is currently working on two new projects: one, a study of the effects of sexual orientation and union status on personal well-being; the other, an examination of the differences in mate selection preferences of divorced and never-married adults.

# Index

The letters *f, n,* or *t* following a page number refer to a figure, note, or table on that page.

●